W S Q

WOMEN'S STUDIES QUARTERLY

VOLUME 44   NUMBERS 1 & 2   SPRING/SUMMER 2016

An educational project of the Feminist Press at the City University of New York and the College of Staten Island, City University of New York, with support from the Center for the Study of Women and Society at The Graduate Center, City University of New York

EDITORS
Cynthia Chris, College of Staten Island, City University of New York
Matt Brim, College of Staten Island, City University of New York

GUEST EDITORS
Taylor Black, New York University
Elena Glasberg, New York University
Frances Bartkowski, Rutgers University-Newark

FICTION/NONFICTION/PROSE EDITOR
Asali Solomon

POETRY EDITOR
Patricia Smith

EDITORIAL ASSISTANTS
Elena Cohen
Lindsey Eckenroth

EDITORS EMERITAE
Amy Herzog 2011–2014 ▪ Joe Rollins 2011–2014
Victoria Pitts-Taylor 2008–2011 ▪ Talia Schaffer 2008–2011
Cindi Katz 2004–2008 ▪ Nancy K. Miller 2004–2008
Diane Hope 2000–2004 ▪ Janet Zandy 1995–2000
Nancy Porter 1982–1992 ▪ Florence Howe 1972–1982; 1993–1994

The Feminist Press at the City University of New York

EXECUTIVE DIRECTOR
Jennifer Baumgardner

EDITOR
Lauren Rosemary Hook

ART DIRECTOR
Drew Stevens

SENIOR GRAPHIC DESIGNER
Suki Boynton

SALES & MARKETING MANAGER
Jisu Kim

WSQ: Women's Studies Quarterly, a peer-reviewed, theme-based journal, is published in the summer and winter by the Feminist Press at the City University of New York.

COVER ART
Visual Marginalia by Marina Zurkow

WEBSITE
feministpress.org/wsq

EDITORIAL CORRESPONDENCE
WSQ: Women's Studies Quarterly, The Feminist Press at the City University of New York, The Graduate Center, 365 Fifth Avenue, Suite 5406, New York, NY 10016; wsqeditorial@gmail.com.

PRINT SUBSCRIPTIONS
Subscribers in the United States: Individuals—$60 for 1 year; $150 for 3 years. Institutions—$85 for 1 year; $225 for 3 years. Subscribers outside the United States: Add $40 per year for delivery. To subscribe or change an address, contact *WSQ* Customer Service, The Feminist Press at the City University of New York, The Graduate Center, 365 Fifth Avenue, Suite 5406, New York, NY 10016; 212-817-7915; info@feministpress.org.

FORTHCOMING ISSUES
Queer Methods, Amin Ghaziani, The University of British Columbia, and Matt Brim, College of Staten Island, City University of New York
At Sea, Terri Gordon-Zolov, The New School, and Amy Sodaro, Borough of Manhattan Community College and the Graduate Center, City University of New York
Precarious Work, Alyson Cole, Queens College and the Graduate Center, City University of New York, and Victoria Hattam, The New School

RIGHTS & PERMISSIONS
Fred Courtright, The Permissions Company, 570-839-7477; permdude@eclipse.net.

SUBMISSION INFORMATION
For the most up-to-date guidelines, calls for papers, and information concerning forthcoming issues, write to wsqeditorial@gmail.com, or visit feministpress.org/wsq.

ADVERTISING
For information on display-ad sizes, rates, exchanges, and schedules, please write to *WSQ* Marketing, The Feminist Press at the City University of New York, The Graduate Center, 365 Fifth Avenue, Suite 5406, New York, NY 10016; 212-817-7918; marketing@feministpress.org.

ELECTRONIC ACCESS AND SUBSCRIPTIONS
Access to electronic databases containing backlist issues of *WSQ* may be purchased through JSTOR at www.jstor.org. Access to electronic databases containing current issues of *WSQ* may be purchased through Project MUSE at muse.jhu.edu, muse@muse.jhu.edu; and ProQuest at www.il.proquest.com, info@il.proquest.com. Individual electronic subscriptions for *WSQ* may also be purchased through Project MUSE.

ISSN: 0732-1562   ISBN: 978-1-55861-926-5 $25.00

Contents

Editors' Note

In recent decades, professional organizations representing the Earth sciences have debated adoption of the term *Anthropocene* as a new geological epoch—and when such an epoch may have commenced. Most broadly, some argue that the term should pertain to an era of intensified human impact on the environment since the development of agriculture, some twelve thousand or so years ago, thus replacing the currently used term *Holocene*. Others suggest that we need a new term to mark the intensification of that impact since the beginning of the Industrial Revolution in the eighteenth century. Still others date the Anthropocene to the nuclear bomb tests that preceded the U.S. atomic attack on Nagasaki and Hiroshima in 1945, and there are also arguments for dates including 1492, 1610, and 1964.[1]

In geological terms, this degree of unsettledness regarding the precise date of a new epoch may constitute historical hairsplitting. But one thing is certain—despite persistent political posturing and willful ignorance of established science, predominately among the American right wing—one of the outcomes of human activities including the use of fossil fuels is a cycle of global warming, rising sea levels, and extreme weather caused by the release of carbon dioxide and other so-called greenhouse gases into the atmosphere. As a result, acidifying oceans, desertification, and other stressors render many species' habitats newly hostile. Accordingly, many observers recognize that we are now in the midst of a "sixth extinction" that may rob the Earth of many currently extant species by the end of the twenty-first century (Kolbert 2014).

It is not only nonhuman animals that are at risk. Current trends raise

WSQ: Women's Studies Quarterly 44: 1 & 2 (Spring/Summer 2016) © 2016 by Cynthia Chris and Matt Brim. All rights reserved.

real questions about the foreseeable survival of not only some plant and animal species—and not only our most cognate species, the chimpanzee, gorilla, and orangutan, all of which are endangered—but also the human animal itself. Fears and fantasies of pending apocalypse play out in masculinist fantasies of heroicism and abjection found in novels, films, and TV series including *Left Behind, The Leftovers, The Road, 28 Days Later, The Day After Tomorrow, Armageddon, This Is the End, The Last Man on Earth*, and *The Walking Dead*. In short, in our fictional and dramatic culture, we appear to be obsessed with our own demise and the damage we inflict on ourselves, other species, the planet on which we live, and its atmosphere. In our daily lives, aggregating as social behavior, we appear to be alternatively oblivious, in denial, indifferent, or inured to prospects of our own inviability—and, occasionally, willing to engage in random (but important) acts of damage control, such as voluntary recycling or the "Paris Agreement" reached at the United Nations Climate Change Conference late in 2015. Though the Agreement was widely hailed as a global step forward in containing global warming, critics of the accord have voiced concern that the pledge to "[hold] the increase in the global average temperature to well below 2°C above pre-industrial levels" is too little, too late, too vague, or too unenforceable (Davenport 2015; Gillis 2015; Geden 2015; Goodman 2015).

According to a United Nations report gauging the impact of climate change on food security, biodiversity, water resources, and human health, women suffer disproportionately from diminishing resources and surging infectious diseases, such as those transmitted by mosquitoes that prosper in warming climates and expanding flood zones. Comprising the majority of the world's poor, women face rising labor required to obtain potable water, fuel, and foodstuffs when these resources become increasingly scarce or expensive (UN WomenWatch 2009). These global trends are measured by scientists and policy makers at macro levels, parsing changes occurring across millennia and globally sourced big data.

In contrast, this issue of *WSQ* approaches survival at micro levels, tracing the risky business of survival among individual bodies, resistant subjects, and intimate, sometimes audacious acts. Nevertheless, the specter of large-scale, world-historical survival is never, and never can be, entirely out of the picture. For their contributions to this volume—which are, throughout, both provocative and evocative—we thank the authors of both the essays and book reviews gathered here: Katherine Brewer Ball, Tiffany Johnson Bidler, Jih-Fei Cheng, Omer Aijazi, Elien Arckens, Amy

L. Brandzel, Golnar Nabizadeh, Rebecca A. Adelman, Wendy Kozol, Cynthia Barounis, Laura Shackelford, Abigail Simon, Breanne Fahs, Mairead Sullivan, Ahuva Cohen, Sarah Kessler, Lisa Poggiali, and Bethany Doane. We also extend our appreciation to the artist Marina Zurkow, whose work appears within this issue. And we thank the issue editors who proposed the theme and shepherded it so thoughtfully: Frances Bartkowski, Taylor Black, and, especially, *WSQ* Editorial Board Member Elena Glasberg.

We also offer our admiration and gratitude to those who contributed to additional sections of the journal that complete this issue. For *Survival*, *WSQ*'s fiction, prose, and creative nonfiction editor has selected two short prose pieces: "Hearing Voices" by Sokunthary Svay and "Where We'll Leave This for Now" by Jessica Estep. Svay's first-person narrator, whose parents were refugees from the Khmer Rouge, reveals how thoroughly haunted the second generation may be by parental trauma and by silence about their suffering. She searches for pathways to her own survival, eventually finding a kind of overcoming in voice lessons. Estep sutures the reader into her unpacking of a woman's decision regarding a pregnancy through both use of the second-person address and her sharp eye for the quotidian backdrop for life choices that she presents as forks in the road with irrevocable consequences. In these stories, intergenerational ties both threaten—and make possible—survival itself.

The rich poetry of *Survival* echoes with women's strong, conflicting, and sometimes silent voices as it contests facile representation at every turn. In "A Conversation with My Mother," Miriam Piilonen portrays a mother and daughter's phone call as a struggle to speak and, simultaneously, silence the other, the woman each loves most. In contrast to this call, the reverberations of nature on "a tall wheat eve" in Erica Tom's "my own chimera" blur the aural and the tactile, creating something hybrid. A darker hybrid, the sinister myth of woman-as-monster appears in Georgia Pearle's "Next Witness," and her "Sunset Limited" likewise depicts a woman disclaiming the deadly metaphor of the "train wreck" used to dehumanize her. Unsettling familiar religious and classical allusions, Jen DeGregorio's poem "Nuts" contemplates the meaning of an aimless, distracted divinity, while her intertextual "Cold Pastoral" reincarnates Keats's urn, turning the poet's "*unravish'd bride*" into a woman now "ravaged by *eternity*." Locating her poem, "Rana Plaza," at a site of recent historical disaster, Erin Murphy looks through the eyes of women and girl workers who one morning are compelled to walk into a factory that will soon collapse upon them, a building that "sounded like someone chewing uncooked rice." Threats to women's bodies appear, not surprisingly, in several poems in *Survival*. Christine Larusso's "Dear Alison" epistles portray women as physically yanked, surveilled, and driven. Deirdre Daly's poem, "Sex Ed," delineates the multiple lessons—frightful, dangerous, liberating—that girls learn about their bodies and desires. Amber Moore's "Anecdotes, an Aphorism from Billy Bob Thornton" extends this theme of instruction as a father teaches his children lessons about how to survive the dangers of the world by wearing seatbelts, using appropriate words, and acting with self-awareness and agency.

This issue concludes with the Alerts and Provocations section, featuring "The Queer Art of Survival" by Lana Lin and accompanying photo collages by Lin + Lam. We are thrilled to include this work, and thank Lana for her generously personal essay, which is incisively analytical in regard to what is sometimes called "the cancer industry," and, at times, wryly humorous in describing the writer's relationship to that establishment's expectations of survivors. We thank Lana and H. Lan Thao Lam for gorgeous images, which draw on Audre Lorde's memoir *The Cancer Journals* (1980). They recall, in robust defiance, Lorde's famous claim: "If I didn't define myself for myself, I would be crunched into other people's fantasies for me and eaten alive" (2007, 137).

Survival would not have been possible without the inspiring and meticulous support provided to *WSQ* by our editorial assistants Elena Cohen and Lindsey Eckenroth, and by the Feminist Press, especially Jennifer Baumgardner, executive director; Drew Stevens, art director; Jisu Kim, marketing and sales manager; Lauren Rosemary Hook, editor; Claire Horn, copyeditor; and Suki Boynton, senior graphic designer. We also gratefully acknowledge ongoing support for the journal provided by the Dean of Humanities and Social Sciences, Nan Sussman, at the College of Staten Island. Nor could we survive without the invaluable intellectual labors of the *WSQ* Editorial Board. With this issue, we welcome new board members Jack Gieseking and Anne Hays.

Cynthia Chris
Associate Professor of
    Communications
Department of Media Culture
College of Staten Island
City University of New York

Matt Brim
Associate Professor of
    Queer Studies
Department of English
College of Staten Island
City University of New York

Notes

1. See Lewis and Martin 2015; Hamilton 2015; Butzer 2015. For a glimpse of how the humanities and social sciences are grappling with the concept of the Anthropocene, see also Latour 2014; Povinelli 2014.

Works Cited

Butzer, Karl. 2015. "Anthropocene as an Evolving Paradigm." *The Holocene* 25 (10): 1529–41. doi: 10.1177/0959683615594471.

Davenport, Coral. 2015. "Nations Approve Landmark Climate Deal." *New York Times*, December 13, A1, A17.

Geden, Oliver. 2015. "Paris Climate Deal: The Trouble with Targetism." *Guardian*, December 14. http://www.theguardian.com/science/political-science/2015/dec/14/the-trouble-with-targetism.

Gillis, Justin. 2015. "Healing Step, If Not a Cure." *New York Times*, December 13, A1, A17.

Goodman, Amy. 2015. "Climate Scientist James Hansen Warns World Is on Wrong Track to Prevent Runaway Global Warming." *Democracy Now!* December 4. http://www.democracynow.org/2015/12/4/climate_scientist_james_hansen_warns_world.

Hamilton, Clive. 2015. "Getting the Anthropocene So Wrong." *The Anthropocene Review* 2 (2): 1–6. doi: 10/177/2053019615584974.

Kolbert, Elizabeth. 2014. *The Sixth Extinction: An Unnatural History*. New York: Henry Holt.

Latour, Bruno. 2014. "Agency at the Time of the Anthropocene." *New Literary History* 45: 1–18. http://www.bruno-latour.fr/sites/default/files/128-FELSKI-HOLBERG-NLH-FINAL.pdf.

Lewis, Simon L., and Mark A. Martin. 2015. "Defining the Anthropocene." *Nature* 519 (March 12): 171–80. doi:10.1038/nature14258.

Lorde, Audre. 2007. *Sister Outsider: Essays and Speeches*. Berkeley, CA: Crossing Press.

Povinelli, Elizabeth. 2014. "The Four Figures of the Anthropocene." Lecture at Anthropocene Feminism: A Center for 21st Century Studies (C21) Conference at the University of Wisconsin-Milwaukee, April 10, uploaded April 23. https://www.youtube.com/watch?v=V0gcOqWNG9M.

UN WomenWatch. 2009. "Fact Sheet: Women, Gender Equality and Climate Change." http://www.un.org/womenwatch/feature/climate_change/downloads/Women_and_Climate_Change_Factsheet.pdf.

Introduction: Survival, From the Other End of the Telescope

Taylor Black, Elena Glasberg, Frances Bartkowski

To survive is messy, elaborate, layered. The metaphysics of deferral are implied by the word's Latinate roots: *sur* (over) *vive* (life). Sur-vival, "to live beyond," implies competition among the living, some who go on and some who, perforce, are survived. Live, survive, preserve, and conserve all share the root *vivre*, which itself is preserved by its prefixal adaptability. Linguistically, life survives. Its animacy is not merely grammatical but neither is it a guarantee of human living; the root *vivre*'s uptake into multiple frames and fields suggests viral proliferation more than a predictive, grammar-like generation. To survive takes and creates risk, both philologically and materially.

If survival has just one affective mode, it might be defiance—the feat and fate of living beings after injury, trauma, war, captivity, and natural disaster. It would also be the survival of words, signals, and germinal states of being in the world that we sometimes call natural, but that also encode the cultural landscape. A topography of ruins, trash, exhaustion, and depletion remains and reminds us of that which lives on after in a state of belatedness that is survival: the afterlife of what was not supposed to remain, that which was to have died, but did not, after all. Survival defies nostalgia, envy, and accusation. Survival in the realm of resources—whether human, animal, or mineral—gives the lie to a necropolitics, forcing the living, those living, and those living on to accede to a call from the future to turn away from that fallen angel of history.

Survival is too often the given of living. It is the affordance of the political, that which cannot be not-assumed: no social program welcomes not-surviving. Especially within the contemporary awareness of environ-

WSQ: Women's Studies Quarterly 44: 1 & 2 (Spring/Summer 2016) © 2016 by Taylor Black, Elena Glasberg, Frances Bartkowski. All rights reserved.

mental crisis—survival and surviving against the calculations of doom—survival is a directive. It is only in the affirmative, against its negation. And yet, as a combination of instinct and drive, species survival is bound to outlive itself and to produce unrecognizable difference, either through extinction or evolution. Survival contains such impossible positions and awareness. It cannot be properly thought in time, by an individual, or by a species. How does survival work, then, as the never to be negated assumption of a politics? And what is the temporality of survival? It is not predictive, though it is only oriented toward the next moment, a form of future that is not really a future. Ultimately, survival is a will that always fails.

To underscore the untimeliness of feminist survival, we revisit for this issue Valerie Solanas's classic *SCUM Manifesto* (1965). Although hardly in need of rediscovery, *SCUM Manifesto* has not been understood for its hilarious invocation of a specifically biological rationale for the r/evolutionary (and environmentally salutary) extinction of the male sex. Its winking pseudoscientific language of male genetic abnormality and incompletion (XY is an incomplete XX) and its invitation to enlightened men to "relax" and enjoy the ride to their "demise" cast the war of the sexes as one in which gene expression, more than holistically gendered belongings, contends through sexual selection. In this case, women choosing women, the core of lesbian social action, promises an overthrow of sexual reproduction's social power as rooted in patriarchal heterosexuality. Solanas's version of gender essentialism to the death had once challenged even the most radical separatist lesbian-feminism. But to the extent that Solanas's "groovy woman-choosing-woman" has a contemporary (audience), we might say she has survived her times, only in a ghostly, diminished form. This special issue includes two articles that give *SCUM Manifesto* new life in the context of feminist philosopher Elizabeth Grosz's uptake of Darwinian evolution. In *Becoming Undone: Darwinian Reflections of Life, Politics, and Art* (2011), Grosz insists on the disruptive potential of female-driven sexual selection as an aesthetic, willful, irrational, noninstrumental force not necessarily coordinate with survival under industrial capitalism, species maintenance, or environmental management.

The articles collected for the *Survival* special issue think through survival by activating it. In the first section, "Survival Lenses," survival is a strategy, counternarrative, performance, failure, and temporal suspension. Next, in "Untimely Survivors," unlikely and, yes, untimely figures construct their own particular methods of being-and-becoming beyond themselves. In the last section, "The Mesh: Survival In-Between," the will to survive emerges out of tight, immobilizing systems. Survival throughout is a process, a method, and a way (out)—impossibly suspended between direct political aspiration and trajectories of becoming directed beyond rational, foreseeable ends.

Part I: Survival Lenses

Katherine Brewer Ball's "The Veering Escapology of Sharon Hayes and Patty Hearst" recasts the very familiar, and very American, story of Patty Hearst's "capture" and eventual incorporation into the Symbionese Liberation Army (SLA) as interpreted and reperformed by performance artist Sharon Hayes. To escape, Brewer Ball explains, means saving your skin and leaving a fake skin in the captor's clutches. What, then, does not survive? What of the false skin left behind? Hayes's performance piece works with nonteleological repetition, with precarity, with the notion that the performer is, like the "hostage," in need of support from her audience. Brewer Ball draws our attention to moments when Hayes's performance goes off script, when she forgets her lines and needs to be put back on track by the audience, who, as nation or media consumers, are folded back into the feedback loop of the American mediascape. Thus, Hayes-as-Hearst returns the audience to the drama of mediated survival that is not about the facticity of the captivity (or even Hearst's own afterlife as a suburban matron and self-assessing heroine in John Water's filmic world). Survival, in Brewer Ball's account, figures as this nonteleological feedback loop, "the repetition of visual and linguistic capture." The audience recalls memories of the Patty Hearst phenomenon through Hayes's performative synesthesia of sensation beyond the limits of rational body-sense, and even mediascape. As a survival technique, this strategy follows the instinct of the will to survive. The Hearst-Hayes performance is an enhanced form of memory—a new overcoming of the national body.

Hearst's historical transformation into Tanya is her superego, superman, her moment of overcoming Patty. Patty survives as Tanya, and with her, the politics of the SLA. Brewer Ball reads against the rescue narrative in the Hearst story while insinuating that some echo of Tanya has never died. As Tanya, Patty Hearst becomes more herself, fulfilling and living beyond her revolutionary potential. That moment of revolution is never done; it is always the potential that cannot be spoken or quite emerge under any present conditions.

Tiffany Johnson Bidler's article, "Suicide and Survival in the Work of

Kara Walker," continues Brewer Ball's feminist overcoming of victimhood. Johnson Bidler reveals survival strategies within Walker's visual odes to suicidal ideation to suggest that against a backdrop of insane, historically rooted white supremacy, black suicide can be a reasonable and resilient reproach; not pathology, but methodology. Johnson Bidler rescues Walker from pedestrian concerns about the effect of her stark and dangerous imagery and instead assigns to it an affective will to power. There is, it is important to point out, no attempting but only committing suicide in these images. Against the deadening effects of white power, these moments constitute in and of themselves a significant moral argument or even a defense of morals. The set of capacities Johnson Bidler assigns to Walker's black-and-white silhouette tableaux of suicidal agency renders them more powerful than a simple response to oppression; here, in the suspended space between the sky and the ground lies a will to live, a strategy. In the moment of suicide there is no social; in the suspense of a suicidal leap into midair, there is no failure, no return to the social, only the artistic completeness of suicidal ideation. Suicide fills up the entire life frame with the act. In this artistically replete space, suicidal ideation is given a new power as a lens of survival.

One of the most notorious statements to come out of the NYC-based AIDS crisis of the 1980s and 1990s came from British gay icon Quentin Crisp, in his eighties at the time, who pronounced, "AIDS is a fad." Crisp's dismissal of the growing urgency of AIDS activism exposed a generational tension—he had lived through WWII and was enjoying a second fame and an extended celibacy in the U.S. We read Jih-Fei Cheng's "How to Survive: AIDS and Its Afterlives in Popular Media" through the lens of Crisp's historicizing. Cheng's discussion of AIDS filmic memorialization lends credence to Crisp's admittedly impolitic (re)temporalization of crisis. We wonder, as we read Cheng's article, how AIDS organizations outlive their patients/subjects. AIDS as a disease marking a historical moment has created a queer nostalgia in its afterlife, as the HIV infection of the eighties has shifted from an inevitable death sentence to a time of extended living on. Even as survivors of the AIDS generation like Larry Kramer are nearing death and live on with the burden of survivor's guilt, how does queer collectivity change over time—how does it survive?—when death's finality had been its galvanizing force?

The politics of the editing of life and death are central to Cheng's critique of the AIDS activism documentary *United in Anger* (2012). Cheng focuses on performer and activist Ray Navarro, using him as a kind of lens into concerns over whose death and whose survival is made to matter in the film. Unlike the documentary's white activists, for Navarro there is no eulogy depicted, no funeral, nor mention of his medically assisted end-of-life choice. There is a palpable tension in Cheng's reading within queer resistance in which the deaths of "queers of color" are marked as "indelible" and "excessive absence." In Cheng's reading, Navarro's final filmed moments, as they are shown in the documentary, are "images of absence" that "return to touch." In this scene, a hand (we don't know for sure whose) is placed over the lens, touching and holding the moment of death, and leaving it available to filmic temporalities and editing—speeding up, covering over, deferring, even leaving it out. This not-to-be-seen filmic moment suggests a living on in absence and in fantasy, a painful fantasy that nevertheless allows for the reassembling of time and memory for a political purpose that remains to be seen. Despite, and even through the appropriation of his life and work into a white mediascape, Navarro lives on.

Part II: Untimely Survivors

Omer Aijazi's "Who Is Chandni bibi?" calls our attention to the problematic economies of international humanitarian aid. In work based on his interviews with earthquake survivor Chandni bibi, we get a figure who is unknowable and who resists saving within the logic of humanitarianism; as such, she is the most unlikely survivor. Chandni bibi's existence is defined by a "limited embeddedness"; blinded (perhaps) by the 2005 earthquake, Chandni bibi remains, persists, cannot be fixed, resists, and thwarts the international aid economy and the ways it seeks to make her a legible, repairable subject. She insists on an autonomous experience of her trauma, and within that worldview resists outside repair, possibly any kind of repair, since she is also dependent on her family and society. She experiences trauma endlessly, before and beyond the intervention of aid or of the putative effects of the earthquake. Making and keeping a home is central to her, and she has made a home in disaster time, where she has no identity but as a survivor. And yet through her appeals to prayer and with her passive insistence that she cannot see, she overcomes her circumstances. Chandni bibi combines a sense of lack of vision with lack of mobility. These disabilities, stitched together, become her home: the point from which she resists aid, sentimental attachment, as well as abilifying narratives. She does not draw in the gaze or the sympathies. If she is heroic in any way, it is because she is not a sympathetic figure. She is sui generis, becoming herself as a survivor, leaving others and the mechanisms of her rescue behind.

If Chandni bibi is an unlikely survivor, Marianne Moore is an unlikeable one. Elien Arckens's "'In This Told-Backward Biography'" presents Moore, the Pulitzer winner and a devout celibate (another nonreproductive survivor), as an always deferred and postponed figure. Arckens argues: "Celibacy follows a retroactive temporality that magnifies the 'repetitive compulsion' inherent in archive fever, as the intermingling of past and present lead to a cyclical time in which the repetitions can no longer be separated from each other." This celibacy postpones survival through intertexuality and reversely transferential progress. Arckens finds evidence of this "celibacy tie" in Moore's collection *Tell Me, Tell Me*, which, Arckens points out, "begins with endings and ends with beginnings." Moore, the person and the poet, sees all time as reversed, deferred, repeated—untimely. A celibate by rote and by intention, Moore's way of being in the world treats unlikeability/untimeliness as the substance of style. Unlike Chandni bibi, she does not resist temporality or oppose it. Rather, she lives strangely in time without reproducing its logic. Celibates, like asexuals, have something estranging about them. In Moore's world the outmoded is the "real." Like all untimely figures, Moore lives in explicit obscurity.

In her article, "The Subjects of Survival: The Anti-Intersectional Routes of Breast Cancer," Amy L. Brandzel asks, "Why me?" As a breast cancer survivor thinking against the weight of the question itself as well as against the privileges that attach to its manner of being asked, Brandzel is skeptical of sympathy and resists the constant references to new prosthetic forms of being (she does not think she looks better with hair). The bald female head—the public, gendered revelation of cancer—becomes for Brandzel an opportunity for "genderqueerness and coalitional subjectivity" and a way to counter contemporary breast cancer discourses that refuse to recognize alliances and affinities with disability as mourning. Instead, we get deep and rich thinking about her evolution as a person living in and through time with cancer. Brandzel takes up Sarah Lochlann-Jain's concept of "prognosis time" into a becoming breast cancer narrative that might survive the more well-known figure of the breast cancer survivor, in whose narrative "survival is sanitized and constricted to a particularly distinct, anti-intersectional, unitary subject position." Brandzel's understanding of "prognosis time" sees the survival strategies embedded in the experience of breast cancer as invested in temporality, in the calculation of life in the midst of deadly prognosis. Through a genealogy of feminist writing on breast cancer and those who have lived and have perished, Brandzel builds a home, precarious and irrationally founded as it is, writing her survival through the machinery of academic production and advancement. For her, the point is neither to reassure others of her social-aesthetic viability nor to fool herself into a prosthetics of okay-ness, but rather to access the power of thinking of what cancer can be: a nonpredictive proscription/prescription.

Golnar Nabizadeh's "Vision and Precarity in Marjane Satrapi's *Persepolis*" helps us to understand how the drawings in Satrapi's celebrated graphic novel bear witness to the unseeable of Iranian history and to ask, what is lost in modernization? And, more precisely, what gets lost in war and revolution? Through Nabizadeh's reading of *Persepolis*, we get a sense of modernity which is understood through the lens of double trauma: of living through and living on after war. The graphic novel form traces autobiography, merging low and high cultural forms. Nabizadeh is interested in the ways that *Persepolis* camps mourning, how "the comedic element is frequently produced through the divergent messages delivered by the written text on one hand and the image on the other." The story of survival this article offers falls between the modern and postmodern, the high and low, trauma and its aftermath, the cartoon and the graphic letter, amounting to what Nabizadeh refers to as "the heterodoxy of mourning." This mode, then, "speaks of a strategy of making difficult things bearable," telling the story of grief beneath genre, ritual, performance (and the veil?). These messy and elaborate forms of survival are to be understood in concert with one another and are "irreducible and creative, embedded as they are in historical, political, and cultural specificities." The sensation or the untimely vision of survival that we get occurs between these registers but also as a result of them.

What unites this text with the others in this section is the problem of autobiography as storytelling. Autobiography is nothing if not the narrative form of an author's survival; the wartime memoir, to an even greater extent, fully invests in the promises of survival in its attempts at reconceiving its own experiences of trauma. Through Nabizadeh's presentation of this graphic novel as a survival story, we are able to sense the colorful, multilayered history of Satrapi's past in black and white. The format requires its author to reduce in order to suggest what is absent, paring down in order to amplify its affective resonance: subverting to survive.

Part III: The Mesh: Survival In-Between

Each of the articles in this section approaches bodies of work that are historical but do not add up to anything, that do not contribute to some securely historical sense of the past. Rather, these articles focus on the survival strategies that occur creatively in the space between and outside of teleology. Rebecca A. Adelman and Wendy Kozol situate feminist survival practices in the context of ongoing crisis. Their article brings our attention to Esther Krinitz's needlework projects, which she began working on in 1970 at the age of fifty as an artistic response to her memories of Poland during the Holocaust. These pieces, they argue, function as an ongoing memoir-art project that works through her memories of the Holocaust. Her needlepoint, they explain, displays a material focus on the art of surviving warzones, militarization, and conflict without end for which the "ongoing task of surviving war lasts as long, or longer, than the conflict itself." Adelman and Kozol are interested in duration as a reparative practice "that work[s] to ameliorate the traumatic impacts of structural violence." Like many of the authors in this collection, Adelman and Kozol emphasize the significance of repetition in Krinitz's artistic life, in the "temporal extendedness and experiential repetitiousness, which makes the work of survival exhausting and often inimical to visual representation." The aesthetics they propose emphasize the nonspectacular, the banal, and the commonplace wartime experience. "Unlike the indexical imprint of a photo," they say, "Krinitz's needlepoint sketches survival ironically, giving it material shape, weight, texture, fiber, and presence in time." The "haptic intensity and ornamentality," "profound liveliness," and even "near cartoonishness" of Krinitz's work, as they describe it, invite reflection on conditions of survival amid the horrors of war, even as it resists an uncritical acceptance of the real of history. They understand Krinitz's work to be uncomfortably close to apolitical, much like the unsung work of the survival of the least fit, like Krinitz. Krinitz is thus a queer and untimely survivor in that her work is not sui generis, is not phantasmagorical, is not elevated, but rather is materially and ethically inventive. Krinitz's stitch work connects life in the mesh through its ordinariness, placing her as a survivor both outside and inside history.

In her contribution, Cynthia Barounis introduces Nadya Vessey, an Australian double amputee who became famous for her "perverse" mermaid tail lower-limb prosthesis, which gave her a new mobility in the water. Within a genealogy of the mermaid fantasy in twentieth-century culture that includes Bette Midler's cabaret performance, Dolores Del Lago (as a mermaid in a wheelchair performing Gloria Gaynor's "I Will Survive"), and going back to P. T. Barnum's mermaid, a half-ape half-fish hybrid, Barounis catches Vessey in her net and names her a "'throwback' who has failed to adapt, and therefore, failed to survive." Barounis describes Vessey's performance of "temporal drag" as irreverence and ambivalence in the face of her accidental embodiment of a little girl's mermaid/princess fantasy. Vessey's "posthuman disinterest" in this common fantasy allows for Barounis to locate in her performance a "uniquely crip variation on the queer dandy's aesthetic boredom and his related proficiency in resurrecting and repurposing discarded objects." This campy performance of mermaidness, this embodiment of the (literally) trashy fantasy allows for Vessey to "[exceed] both the 'human' and the mainstream media's necropolitical 'interest' in disability." Vessey's prosthetic performance is for Barounis a kind of untimely occupation not only of disability and adulthood but also of the present and the future.

Laura Shackelford's "Surviving Codespace" takes as its object Teri Rueb's site-specific installation *Drift*, asking whether the "very topographies of survival have not already shifted," as the shoreline of Rueb's interactive and globally positioned locative narrative-sound installation "explores how prior dimensions of lived space and material space-making practices 'survive' the transformations introduced by computational processes, infrastructures, and their late capitalist political economies." Through *Drift*, Shackelford reconceptualizes survival as life enmeshed in "computationally legible and manipulable terms." Her understanding of survival is not "a spatial or temporal 'living beyond' the technical transformations and introversions of codespace. Instead, it comes to be premised on, and understood as, the tactical engagement and apprehension of . . . codespace." Shackelford picks up Elizabeth Grosz's understanding of the untimely in order to "reconsider the dynamic temporal force of material and biological life of many kinds as an ontological impetus to variation, unpredictability, and change." Untimeliness in both their work suggests that the material processes of becoming are the cause and effect of survival; to become aware of drift/ing is to be caught up in the mix of an environment shaped by humanity, or to be surprised by what one already knows or feels, walking along the shore. *Drift* is, of course, nonteleological. Shackelford's essay contributes to new materialist concerns with the limits of Cartesian, static coordinates of mattering and mapping, and instead understands "spatial practice" as an "ongoing, unfolding, unpredictable, emergent untimely activity to which multiple human, nonhuman, and technological agents co-contribute." Is codespace yet another scale of surveillance? Or is it a nonhuman interstitial space of survival? The constant need to cross-reference and update one's coordinates in flow is perhaps a hindrance to living, thus the nostalgia for the absolute space of the shore (as opposed to the sand between one's toes). Surviving, Shackelford argues, is the sensation and reality of all these realities combined. Surviving codespace is to endure within the ongoing project and paradox of what can and cannot be digitally captured.

Abigail Simon's "The Story of Oil" closes with the word "and." "Anxiety," she writes, "is eternal and immortal. Anxiety and." With this, we are stuck in the sentence and in the anxiety of Simon's words. Anxiety is, of course, merely "a dark force in the universe of material things . . . the unseen coefficient of Time." This anxiety is a mesh, and we are mired in between "Now (the eternal pleasant)" and "Then (the atoms of everything from the atoms of everything else)." This anxiety is also a force, isolating this now from this then. We are stuck, just as Simon finds herself stuck, in the sludge of evolution. "Our symbolic orders," she writes, "are unreliable, and have a tendency to shift, leaving us stranded and floating." The story of evolution, and of time itself, is on shaky, sticky ground. Simon's piece immortalizes all those noble creatures that the natural order has done away with. All that's left is mud and oil. The bottom is the top. The continents drift, sure, and the ice caps too, with their pitiful polar bear mahouts along for the ride. Trapped in this eternal drift and stuck in the mire, Simon's "The Story of Oil" fixes us all in the mesh of the cruelty of the natural order. "All beings live, starve, suffer, and die," she writes. "We are not a disruption but simply a flavor." The taste that's left in Simon's mouth is the bitter taste of time, which has both a shitty flavor and a gritty, oily texture: "Immortality means there is always time for another roll of the dice—perhaps there are many ways to be consumed by the inevitable, and being stuck in a lake of tar is only one." We survive as immortal trash.

In "*Visual Marginalia*: Marina Zurkow's Immortal Trash" we fantasize about letting go of editorial power. There's been enough "ecological management": seeding, planting, curating, propitiating. Our devolutionary inspiration in exploring what she calls "near-impossible nature culture intersection" is media artist Marina Zurkow, whose increasingly large-scale installations include *Slurb* (2000), *Necrocracy* (2012–15), and *Mesocosm* (*Times Square, New York*) (2015). Here we collect the leftovers and interstices of Zurkow's system-works, the "marginal" doodles, digital trash, and forms of waste that did not survive her process. And yet they live in the special issue to give ephemeral form to Zurkow's career-long fascination with system interruptions, incommensurate scales of time, size, and duration; with paradoxes such as pixel screen depth or digital death; and with the threatening interdisciplinarities of invasive species, methods, and ideas. Perhaps these visual ear worms are the other side of invasion: a directionless, motiveless piling up of parts that, like the deathless plastics loosed by industrialism into the oceans and then macerated by the water's ceaseless motion, form plastic-ocean gyres, notorious and illegitimate ecosystems of their own. These parts of Zurkow's process are accidental survivals already becoming strange: becoming new systems and modes of living on.

Part IV: Classics Revisited: Valerie Solanas's *SCUM Manifesto*

Solanas is Nietzschean. In his autobiography, *Ecce Homo*, Nietzsche explained "Why I Am So Clever"; before penning *SCUM Manifesto* Solanas mock-heroicized her aspirations with "A Young Girl's Primer, Or How to Attain the Leisure Class." Solanas is aware and not aware of her own untimeliness, and of her predicament. But it is only the untimely who can truly critique as they surpass and overcome their own times. This is what makes them, and indeed Solanas, so clever. Like Nietzsche, Solanas was and is easy to mock and she herself employs mockery, writing her manifesto from the edges of a literary world and even selling out—strategically—to men's magazines. Through Nietzsche, we understand that mockery is the first step to imitation, which, through time, sticks to us in such a way that it comes to define us: thus it is that we come to identify, almost unwillingly, with the thing we once rejected. Solanas is so scummy that there is no point outside, no escaping her predicament, which is why she is so perfectly untimely, and why her critique remains so important. This is also why she is so dangerous, and like Nietzsche, strategically courts being misread—to having her tone be misunderstood by people not in on the joke. Solanas's *SCUM Manifesto* is an overcoming of what she terms "the shit you have to go through just to survive."

Solanas performs a transvaluation of values in *SCUM Manifesto*. Etymologically, she turns virtue against itself, replacing moralism with scum ethics. The male is so low, so vile that he objectifies women and ultimately, in her eyes, becomes his own idea of a woman: lowly and depraved. Also like Nietzsche, Solanas employs a tense humor, a bombastic ranting that then always offers up an aphorism. Her aphorisms are little bombs, waiting to go off, covering us in the slime of scum. The untimeliness is the engine of *SCUM Manifesto*'s persistent appeal through time as well as its reliable ability to repel. *SCUM* outlives its times and even its vernacular; certainly it has outlived its author. Because of its transvaluation, its elements of repulsion and incitement, if there is any part of you that clings to the status quo, to being justified or triumphant, *SCUM* will offend and embarrass you into rejecting it. *SCUM* retains a power to shock. In spite of its camp appeal, what makes *SCUM* so powerful is its insistent sincerity. *SCUM* means it, and Solanas is not joking.

Avital Ronell, in her 2004 introduction to *SCUM Manifesto*, gets into the spirit of *SCUM* and properly recognizes Solanas as a "mutant Nietzschean" (18). However, groovy as her reading of *SCUM* may be, Ronell does not avoid falling into Solanas's trap by returning to an earnest, pre-*SCUM*, feminist response. Solanas's method is dangerous and powerful; there are twists and turns awaiting each of us, trap doors that will always drag us back down into the tar pits of civilized society. Solanas's pejorative references to mindless daddy's girls, Ronell accuses, "scapegoats and minoritizes women" (29). Ronell thinks this creation of difference within the category of XX-woman as pitting girl-against-girl, but she misses the potential for this seemingly minoritizing distinction to amplify the singularity of woman and to break away from sex-gender binarism. Solanas offers *SCUM* as the category beyond: it is neither women nor men. It surpasses, transvalues sex and gender, sex from gender; one cannot read it with an earnest political drive. If anything, former and renewed resistance to *SCUM Manifesto* is always a way of covering over one's own inadequacies or fears (or worse, covering the tracks of one's exploits/exploitations), which are translated into patient political pragmatics. Solanas is, after all, feminism's tar baby: the abject trickster whose triumph is in sticking with debasement and sticking it to those who think they can safely separate from the morass. No matter how much you think you are with *SCUM*, down in its groove, some part of it will alienate; no matter how clean you try to make your escape, some part of it will stick to you, leaving you, like Dr. Seuss's Grinch, "STINK, STANK, STUNK."

Breanne Fahs, Valerie Solanas's biographer, brings us back to the pre-history of *SCUM Manifesto* through digging out Solanas's earlier work, "A Young Girl's Primer, or How to Attain the Leisure Class," from a 1966 edition of *Cavalier* magazine, a *Playboy*-like men's publication. The article, Fahs argues, "sprouts an alternative, fictionalized self—audacious, pan-handling for fun rather than necessity, taking advantage of men as dupes, and chiding middle-class women as fools—in order to survive the conditions of her actual self." In "A Young Girl's Primer" we see the beginnings of Solanas's philosophy of the gutter, "where knowledge, revolution, and selfhood are produced within conditions of trash, waste, and excess." In her broader body of work, Solanas produces a vision of feminist scumminess as a response to and attack against all the shit it takes for her to survive. The sense that we get reading the "Primer" of Solanas's actual life is that she has long dealt with paranoid schizophrenia, homelessness, and abject anger. All of these debilities are in Solanas's work rerouted through scumminess, a will to survive by reveling and wallowing in filth and spewing it so democratically that friends and enemies alike cannot be cleansed of the lingering, sticky scum. No longer the feminist as victim, Solanas goes on the attack and no one she meets is getting away clean. Solanas aims her jokes and jabs at the earnest among us: socialists, nonviolent protesters, and well-meaning women. "The self Solanas constructs in the Primer amuses herself above all else," Fahs writes, "cracking herself up while pulling a fast one on passersby." The title *SCUM Manifesto* is not, Fahs informs us, an acronym of "society to cut up men" as many now believe. SCUM is a philosophy. This is a distinction that allows us to see *SCUM Manifesto* as "at once, a manifesto, a state of mind, a sort of performance art, and a revolutionary underworld force." The misreading of the acronym is but another way we have all failed Solanas, another way in which we have failed to live up to the ethos of scum. We still can't wash it off.

Solanas lives in the groove, the cunt groove, so deep down in the groove, that we, any and all readers, can never be there with her. The joke is on us. *SCUM Manifesto* is of the gutter: it comes from everything we don't want, we objectify, and we discard (about ourselves). Those people born with a "scum state of mind" are, writes Fahs (quoting Solanas), "whores, dykes, criminals, homicidal maniacs." These survival selves necessarily come from the gutter; they live there and remain there. You can't wash it off. "A Young Girl's Primer," Fahs argues, "*stands in* for the actual self, *becomes* the real self while the real self becomes the primer persona; she *is* the survival self." Solanas's written work both blurs and overcomes the line between fiction and reality. She has, Fahs tells us, created a new lens, a scummy lens, for seeing and believing the world. This self is Solanas's best self, and her aim in writing the "Young Girl's Primer" and *SCUM Manifesto* is that some of her scum may stick to her readers, who in an ideal world, could get and stay down in the groove with her.

We still can't scrub off the scum. Nor can Mairead Sullivan, whose article, "Kill Daddy: Reproduction, Futurity, and the Survival of the Radical Feminist," details the afterlife of *SCUM Manifesto*. She begins in her women's studies classroom, commiserating with her students, who idealize feminism but cannot abide actual feminists. The clinging stereotype of the radical feminist just won't wash off of feminism. And the problem extends beyond undergraduates. Sullivan asks, "How has the radical feminists' survival as a malevolent extremist enacted her effacement as a critical figure in contemporary queer and feminist theory?" With Solanas as her guide, Sullivan follows her nose, tracing *SCUM* in lesbian separatism, the "C.L.I.T. Papers," and the sinthomosexual from Lee Edelman's *No Future*. Sullivan insists on the feminist as always already lesbian, angry, nonreproductive, and noncompliant. "Like the feminist's lesbian," she argues, "Edelman's sinthomosexual names [the] cultural fantasy of queerness as simultaneously abject, other, and [a] defining border of the normative political subject." Through Solanas, Sullivan updates the project of sinthomosexuality against heterosexual reproduction with *SCUM Manifesto*'s desire to kill off the machineries of reproduction, to "kill daddy." *SCUM* is a stain on not only futurity but also on the heterosexual present-pastness. *SCUM* adds verve to Edelman's social negativity, giving it both a cause and a way of being. Without *SCUM*, the negativity attached to queerness is only a mistake; with *SCUM*, it is an opportunity.

Both the sinthomosexual and the lesbian separatist contain a seed of social and reproductive negativity. The male homosexual is oriented towards sexual desire, the lesbian towards isolation. Between pleasure and abstemiousness, we understand the two twentieth-century categories of gay man and lesbian to be simultaneously trading, and thus trapped, in economies of sexual narcissism and nihilism. In response to this, Sullivan reminds us of Solanas in her afterlife in order to present her as the lesbian-feminist Overman. Solanas completes the equation: *SCUM Manifesto*,

Sullivan says, "takes radicalism as destruction to its limit." The central philosophy of *SCUM* is *homo-cidal* ideology. The groovy *SCUM* feminist not only says no to her reproductive capabilities, she also says no to yours. This overcoming heterosexual reproduction is not, Sullivan argues, something to be taken lightly: "It calls for a homicidal revolt whose ultimate goal is not equality, assimilation, or recognition but the wholesale destruction of the male sex and with it any vestiges of biology, culture, and capital that would tie women to reproduction." Sullivan makes the most of Edelman's suicidal *jouissance* in order to add Solanas to the equation as an honorary homo-cidal sinthomosexual. *SCUM* offers us a way of surviving by murdering as a not-dying, an outward spray. There's a pleasure in this for us, if not for you.

Solanas has no sympathy for your future, only an escape plan that reroutes us all through the gutter. The lesbian feminist is the vanguard of this movement. Her lesbianism is a structural position against the family, the future, the child, and most of all, daddy. Why did we not understand this? Why be a suicide when being a murderer has so much more of a future to it? *SCUM* asks us not only to resist the seduction of the child but also to give in to the pleasure of killing daddy—and all the shit he brings with him—over and over again.

Taylor Black received his PhD in American studies from Rutgers University in 2015 and currently teaches in the Expository Writing Program at New York University. His academic work has been published in WSQ, American Quarterly, Discourse, and the Journal of Popular Music Studies. Black is the cocreator, with Elena Glasberg, of the popular music blog Junebug vs. Hurricane. His first book project is Time Out of Mind: Style and the Art of Becoming.

Elena Glasberg writes about U.S. culture in transit and has taught at American University in Beirut, Princeton University, Duke University, and California State University, Los Angeles. Author of Antarctica as Cultural Critique: The Gendered Politics of Scientific Exploration and Climate Change, Glasberg currently teaches in the Expository Writing Program at New York University.

Frances Bartkowski is chair of the Department of English at Rutgers University-Newark. Her most recent books are *Kissing Cousins: A New Kinship Bestiary* and a forthcoming novel, *An Afterlife*. She directs a public art project, Cherry Blossoms in Winter, and the Collaboratory, an interdisciplinary community of scholars and citizens at Rutgers University-Newark.

Works Cited

Edelman, Lee. 2004. *No Future: Queer Theory and the Death Drive.* Durham, NC: Duke University Press.

Grosz, Elizabeth. 2011. *Becoming Undone: Darwinian Reflections of Life, Politics, and Art.* Durham, NC: Duke University Press.

Nietzsche, Friedrich. 2009. *Ecce Homo: How One Becomes What One Is.* Oxford, UK: Oxford University Press.

Ronell, Avital. 2004. "The Deviant Payback: The Aims of Valerie Solanas." In *SCUM Manifesto.* New York: Verso.

PART I. **SURVIVAL LENSES**

The Veering Escapology of Sharon Hayes and Patty Hearst

Katherine Brewer Ball

Symbionese Liberation Army (SLA) Screeds #13, 16, 20 & 29 (2003) by Sharon Hayes begins with the title card, "Patricia Hearst's First Tape." An androgynous white woman with short hair that eagerly curls out around the ears begins speaking in a monotone voice. She gives very little away. On screen, Sharon Hayes takes the place of Patty Hearst, reading out the audio-screed ransom notes initially broadcast on Berkeley's KPFA radio station in 1974. Only, Hayes is not reading them—she is more nearly reciting them. The frame fits neatly around her face as she stares out to the deferred audience beyond the lens. Emotionless, she speaks directly into the camera, "Mom, Dad, I'm okay. I had a few scrapes . . . and stuff . . . but they washed them up and they're getting okay?" On the word "okay," her intonation trails up at the end, so that it sounds more like a question than a statement. Around fifteen seconds into *Screed #13*, the first of the four Patty Hearst ransom tapes that Hayes respeaks, she misses her line and you hear that Hayes is not alone. There is a live studio audience for this recorded performance, a room full of people whom we cannot see, but who are present for the recording of the video.

An audience member positioned behind the camera, somewhere in Hayes's line of sight, corrects her, feeding her the line that she should be performing instead of the one that she has incorrectly uttered. Hayes nods ever so subtly, and easily picks up with the correct line that comes next, "I am not being starved, or beaten, or unnecessarily frightened." She stumbles through the words, not stuttering, but not delivering the lines with their attendant bodily or emotional meanings. She maintains steady eye contact with the camera, performing specifically for the video. It quickly

WSQ: Women's Studies Quarterly 44: 1 & 2 (Spring/Summer 2016) © 2016 by Katherine Brewer Ball.

FIG.1. *Symbionese Liberation Army (SLA) Screeds #13, 16, 20 & 29,* installation shot, 2003, courtesy of the artist.

becomes clear, however, that the invisible live audience in the time of the video recording is in possession of Hearst's transcript. They have been instructed to correct Hayes when she deflects from the script and to feed her Hearst's exact lines, however inarticulate or awkward they may be. Hayes concentrates to remember the proper words, fluttering her eyes and momentarily closing them, or scrunching her nose and squinting as though she is straining to see something in the distance as she reaches inside to find the words in their correct order.

From respeaking public documents, such as the Guantánamo Bay prison tribunals (the collaborative *Combatant Status Review Tribunals, pp. 002954–003064: A Public Reading*) and Ronald Reagan's official "Address to the Nation" speeches (*My Fellow Americans: 1981–1988*), to her performance of political protest slogans on the streets of Manhattan (*In the Near Future*), Hayes's performances, installations, and videos explore the manner in which words, politics, and histories tend to "find a home in the body" (Interview by the author, February 20, 2012). Her work is performance based—expanding across video, painting, lithography, and sound installation—and often has an initially "public" moment on the street featuring unknowable open audiences, or a "live" crowd in the moment of address. Afterward, the performance script, audio recording, or video documentation of that action is reframed and presented in the space of the gallery. Hayes's work, like the various audiences and moments created in her choreography of media, engages questions of public address to explore the power of recitation in the body and on the tongue. Coming of age and coming into art in the New York City of the early nineties, Hayes is deeply attached to the specificity of space and context, to the performance situation in which art comes to be, and comes to be seen. She explains emerging into a political, queer, dance, theater, and performance scene in 1991 in NYC—from ACT UP to Queer Nation to the Lesbian Avengers—saying, "We became political, we became artists in deep relation to precise historical conditions and these singularities, these precisions linger with us; they're carried along with us in our bodies" (Hayes 2009). Reminding us of the political subject-formation that created her historical stuttering repetitions—what I will call her echoed *stutterances*—Hayes shows us how our stories, our narratives of self, are never strictly autobiographical, but are instead reflective of a time and a space in which we were mutually constituted by what she calls the "singularity" of experience (2009). Moving away from the dominance of the individual, Hayes likewise turns from the reign of the visual, and returns us to the scene of speech and voice, to the textured plane of utterance.[1]

This version of the story begins in 1974 when self-proclaimed "soldiers" of the Symbionese Liberation Army kidnapped nineteen-year-old white Californian media heiress Patty Hearst. Having grown up with the 1950s era promise of innocence, insularity, and safety, America's white college youth were confronted by the inadequacy of their middle-class ideals and felt disappointed by the level of change brought about by the civil rights movement and the publicly televised, and often personal, trauma of the Vietnam War. The majority-white radicals of the SLA seemed to realize that the world was dramatically unfree, and the only way they saw to respond to the violence of imperialism, poverty, incarceration, and racism was through terms that would garner public attention, fear, and—they hoped—respect. Adopting the rhetoric, mannerisms, and vocal inflections of radicals such as the Black Panthers and the Soledad Brothers, the SLA sought to align themselves with Black and Latino radicals, and were thus seen—in the dominant public eye—as racialized voices of radicalism.[2] Held hostage and kept in a closet for two months, Patty Hearst eventually came to identify with her captors, going so far as to change her name to Tania in solidarity with the SLA. At the time of the kidnapping, the FBI and Hearst's parents vigorously pursued rescue efforts, and the American public rallied behind the Hearst family, identifying with the pain and frustration they must have felt at losing their daughter to a racialized militant "terrorist" organization. Yet public opinion quickly changed as Hearst began to record "audio communiqués"—publically broadcast on the radio—allying herself with the political aims of the SLA. Hearst's radio missives ranged from radical ideas, confusedly spoken as through the mouth of a ventriloquist dummy, to the rehearsed words of a revolutionary committed to the cause. The content of the audiotapes followed the rhetoric and style of previous SLA documents, as Hearst demanded free food for California's poor and proclaimed, "Death to the fascist insect that preys upon the life of the people" (Pearsall 1974, 117). Advertising this confused alignment of rhetoric and the racial makeup of the organization was certainly one of the ways that the media sought to discredit the SLA and undermine radical politics more generally. No longer a "victim" captured against her will, Hearst became a criminal coconspirator, an "urban guerilla" (Hearst 1982, 39, 100).

Hearst's story altered the genre script that captivity narratives—from Mary Rowlandson's 1682 narrative on—move teleologically from free, to hostage, to free, ending in a glorious, if slightly wounded, return home. Note that I do not phrase it "the story of Hearst," as her audio performances will carry us into the troubling but generative sounds of her voice, a flickering potential for radicality amidst heavy framing and capture. But in Hearst's publically perceived failure to escape from the SLA—an escape that should be performed but is instead refused—she allied herself with the kidnappers who had emotionally and physically abused her under the guise of revolution and "free sex" (Hearst 1982, 97). Perhaps her alleged refusal to escape was a psychological defense mechanism, intelligently worked out as the most viable option, or perhaps Hearst realized the ways of the tyrannical bourgeois pigs of America and decided she would rather stay and fight in the "people's army" than return to her home culture" (Pearsall 1974, 106). Notably, Hearst was tasked to escape back into the wealthy white culture of her birth, to return to the "us" of the popular media viewership that felt a need to reclaim the stolen property that was Hearst and her allegorical relevance. In the end, she was legally faulted and found guilty for choosing wrongly, for failing to reject the potentially radical and violent ideologies of the SLA, and she was sentenced to serve seven years in jail for her participation in the Hibernia Bank robbery, her image forever captured on security camera footage.[3]

While I am not primarily interested in Patty Hearst as a radical subject, I do perversely care about her tongue, her linguistic fidelity, or infidelity, to certain narratives. Hearst's audio communiqués are messy and confusing documents, scenes in which self and voice are hard to unify. Hayes's tactics of repetition and reverberation demonstrate a virtuosic stuttering break— to think with Fred Moten (2003)—in the asymmetry between voice and body, between Hearst and her proliferating media representation, between escape and freedom. This is a break from the fantasy that freedom is a place where one can live, or that escape will get you there.

In Sharon Hayes's restaging of Hearst, we can trace what I call the *optic of escape* to refer to the expanded audiovisual field of the escape story. The word escape comes from the Latin *excappare*, meaning to get out of one's cape, to leave the pursuer with just one's cape. At its etymological root, escape contains the theatrical flare of a nineteenth-century escapologist. With the twirl of a cloak, her body is gone, disappeared like magic into thin air. The escapee saves her own skin, saves it from capture by way of the cape that got between her and the fingers trailing behind to grasp her. No longer protected by the cloak, which at first let her blend into the wrinkles, the folds, the skin of the night, she becomes visible, but lost. The term escape contains within it a mountainous landscape, valleys in shadow, holding and hiding spots.[4] As opposed to branding a new term such as *critical escapism*, which might make a case for the recuperation of escapism toward the political, I instead wish to retain the term *escape*. I argue that escape contains all of these contradictions within its articulation—its meanings run wild and undress themselves like hedonists, wanderers, and fugitives. The veering optic of escape is thus articulated to name both the hypervisibility of the singular escaping hero, as well as the opacity of the movements that cannot be seen.

Cloaked in her position as media heiress, Hearst and her capture were highly visible. The SLA knew that through her image their words would be broadcast and repeated; Hearst would become their microphone, a graspable object that would garner public attention. Thinking in line with Black philosophies of the freedom drive that break from white logics of reason and transparency (Moten 2003; Kelley 2002; Weheliye 2014; Brooks 2006), and queer and brown theories of temporality which move against linear straight time (Love 2007; Freeman 2010; Muñoz 2009), I contend that Hayes's sonic performance brings the viewer's attention to a minoritarian strategy of resistance beyond the binary of freedom and captivity. The Brechtian act of alienation performed by Hayes through the repetition of visual and linguistic capture demonstrates Hearst's odd sort of narrative survival into the present. This is not simply Hearst's narrative that neatly ends in Darien, Connecticut, with Hearst married to her bodyguard, nor is it the camp survival of Hearst in five of John Waters's films.[5] Instead, I am configuring an optic of escape that, through the specificity of Hayes's own queer and feminist political body of work, agitates the stagnant narrative that fixes Hearst in just one pose. A veering optic of escape is not predicated on the empty promise of freedom as an end point but allows us to imagine a movement and politics that cannot fully be seen, that does not take us on the teleological path, but instead is a practice, a performance, and a stage.

Escape turns from the straight and narrow path of narrative to veer into a story of the complicated radicality of sonic textures. Spatializing escape creates room for escape to illustrate another movement, another way to tell the story of getting away from capture or constraint. In Hayes's work, the optic comes through by way of the sonic. In other words, escape is *seen* in the space opened up in the stutterance. Invoking Eve Kosofsky Sedgwick's idea of texture as involving more senses than just touch, so that "we hear the brush-brush of corduroy trousers or the crunch of extra-crispy chicken," the sound of Hayes's performance shows us different strategies for texturing the story of escape (2003, 19).

The SLA's first eleven communiqués were written documents sent to major newspapers for print. Emerging at the end of the new left movement and influenced by the writings of Soledad Brother, George Jackson, as well as Che Guevara and the Tupamaros of Uruguay, the SLA aspired to continue the radical reform that had begun a decade earlier through violent guerilla tactics and media manipulation. *Communiqué #12* was the first audio message the SLA taped and sent to the radio station for public broadcast. The tape introduced the SLA to the public, taking full advantage of the media frenzy around the kidnapping of Hearst.[6] It was not until *Communiqué #13*, received by KPFA on February 12, 1973, over a week after Hearst's disappearance, that the public first heard her voice. Throughout Hearst's first tape there are many stops and starts, the stop button pushed to arrest the flow and buy the speaker time. Starting with the recording of the first audiotape, Hearst was portrayed by the media and the public as a voice without a voice of her own, as "the SLA's amanuensis" (Isenberg 2000, 649). The sound was right and the phrasing was right; the actual fingerprint of Hearst's voice was identifiable. But the interior identity reflected on the tape was not her. It was not representative of what the public already wanted to hear of and as Hearst. The recording was widely believed to be the words of the SLA, projected through Hearst as though she were merely an amplification device, a loud speaker through which to send out their message. The tape continues, "I'm kept blindfolded usually so that I can't identify anyone. My hands are often tied, but generally they're not. I'm not gagged or anything, and I'm comfortable. And I think you can tell that I'm not really terrified or anything and that I'm okay" (Pearsall 1974, 59). After her violent abduction and inevitably traumatic captivity, it is impossible to tell which parts of the recorded message contain "the truth," contain the "real" feelings of Hearst, and genuinely reflect her well-being.

Troubling this confluence of voice and truth, Mladen Dolar—by way of Derrida and Saussure—reminds us that the voice is separated from other "noise" because the voice is a sound that is imagined to have "meaning." It is endowed "with the will to 'say something,' with an inner intentionality" (Dolar 2006, 14). Although the voice seems to flow from nowhere in particular, vaguely originating somewhere in the throat or the mouth, it is imagined to be indelibly attached to the core of the body and mind, and even to bridge the two. The voice reflects the subject at the center of the body, the inner being; it is "the hidden bodily treasure beyond the visible envelope" (71). When this already intimate and revealing voice is removed from the body—as in the case of Hearst's audiotapes—it further adds to the sense of the meaning behind the voice. Such recordings contribute an air of omnipotence to the voice that, no longer bound by the body, can travel anywhere and do anything, haunting us like the acousmatic voice of God himself. The timbre, the character, the intonation of the voice also contain information as we see in the inevitable state interpretations of Hearst's voice as "tired" or "drugged." Yet the quality of the voice—unlike its linguistic signifiers—possesses a meaning that is open to interpretation. The color of the voice does not add to signification, but is instead the nonlinguistic element of the voice, its material "ancillary" (17). These extra-linguistic elements of the voice—"the accent, the intonation, the timbre"—tell us something else that cannot quite be measured (20). Interestingly, it is this character of Hearst's voice that the FBI and media paid attention to. Yet instead of this attention to the quality of her voice opening up the potential to listen to her words for a variety of meanings, for their veering trajectories, the analysts of Hearst's audio read the sound of her voice through the legitimating lenses of medical and psychoanalytic diagnostics. What the "tape experts" do not notice, or rather, cannot hear, is the potential for contradictory or ambivalent meanings that are carried through the timbre and accent of Hearst's voice.[7] To read Hearst's voice in this first tape as reflecting a drugged and traumatized young girl is only part of the story. The language used to describe the voice relies on the language of interiority and intention which makes it difficult to explain precisely Hearst's voice without falling back on diagnostic words like "dissociative," "meek," or "lost." The simple act of describing the material of Hearst's voice in these tapes captures the speaker in a double bind because of the ways in which voice originates in Western theology as a mediation of the true word.

Veering from this approximation of voice as true word, Sharon Hayes's four-channel respeaking starts with *Screed #13*, Hearst's first communication with the public. The video begins with a tight headshot of Hayes staring directly into and through the camera lens as though she were speaking to both the large glassy eye of the camera as well as to the audience beyond. The background of the studio space is white and Hayes is well lit, drawing our attention away from formal and aesthetic elements of the shot to Hayes herself, her face and voice. Hayes's blank stare reveals little about who she is or what she feels. She begins speaking to us, "Mom, Dad, I'm okay." Hayes remembers this line without faltering; her affect is nervous and her voice sounds a little bit shaky, but perhaps this reflects Hayes's own vocal intonation, her own specific texture that gets read in this instance as the viewer's projected feeling of Hearst's abduction and detainment. On one level, Hayes does know her lines, as she speaks for twenty to thirty minutes in each video without forgetting whole paragraphs or pages; she only ever requires a prompt when she has lost her footing or is seeking reassurance from the audience that she is speaking the dated dialect in its proper order. On another level, however, Hayes is not actually performing the SLA communiqués in any theatrical or convincing sense, so her words sound like lies or, rather, words with which she has no personal connection.

As she utters the now famous phrase, "Mom, Dad, I'm okay," Hayes performs what J. L. Austin calls a "misfire" (1975, 16). The performative utterance does not carry the weight of either convention or ritual. The external vocalization does not appear to have any relationship to the inward performance of feeling or information that the words are meant to convey. As Shoshana Felman suggests, the performative has a tendency to fail; it is defined in part by its very openness to failure. So when a speech act has misfired, it is "not because something is missing, but because something else is done" (Felman 2002, 57). A misfire is not simply a failed performative, or a failure to act the part in a convincing manner, but a moment of potential, a moment of insight. As José Muñoz elaborates, "The misfire, this failure, is intrinsic to how the performative illustrates the ways different courses are traveled in contrast to what heteronormativity [or "straight time"] demands" (Muñoz 2009, 154). In other words, the misfire produces generative meanings that are not already mapped by dominant organizing temporal or spatial structures. Hayes's misfires are reminiscent of Hearst's perceived infelicity, as her captured voice—its rhetorical whiteness and potential approximate blackness—does something else. Watching Hayes, I am more aware of the relationship between memory, the body, and her public than I am of the information or content of her words. Hearing the audience correct Hayes and watching her recall the lines as she asks her live audience, "I'm sorry, the whole line?" brings my attention to the citation process itself—from theatrical lines, to the gendered and racialized presentations we are expected to recite perfectly in order to survive.

It isn't until about four minutes into *SLA Screed #13* that the audience begins to feel comfortable chiming in and correcting Hayes. Initially, solitary voices correct her sparingly, but as the performance goes on, the audience gets braver. At first there is a lone female voice feeding Hayes the lines, but as the audience becomes more confident in their role as narrative corrections officers, they speak out in cacophonous chorus, and through the monitor of the playback screen it becomes hard to hear precisely what they are saying. Hayes's eyes move to different faces, not grazing the audience's, but departing from the eye of the camera to look directly at different voices. She searches for her cue, trying to visually register the words that she has gotten wrong and understand which were the right words. She asks the audience, "Cuz? Cuz?" before understanding what they are saying and then correcting herself, stating "*be*cause." Hayes's stutterances are both definitive statements coming from a woman under duress and a series of scripted ransom notes. Her performance is one of liminality, vulnerability, and contradiction. Hearst has been called "a cipher" and an exemplary postmodern legal subject for being unremarkable beyond the words that the SLA projected through her (Isenberg 2000, 641). Hayes, however, takes a different performative approach, mining the tapes for sounds that were foreclosed in the original performance. Thinking with Gayatri Spivak, I would ask, how might we be able to listen to voices that are not immediately legitimized through legal and ideological traditions?

Originally produced as an unlimited edition, Hayes's four screeds appeared in VHS format, stacked against the wall of the gallery (fig. 2). Hayes meant for the tapes to be taken by the viewers and watched at home with the viewer stopping and starting the tape at will. Mirroring the original distribution of the SLA communiqués—which the SLA would drop off at remote locations, only to later anonymously inform the press of the tape's whereabouts—Hayes's video screeds are messages sent into the darkness. The *SLA Screeds* move with a performative dependence on both previous and forthcoming media—on both Hearst's audio utterances broadcast over the public radio airwaves, and on the viewership and circulation of her performance that takes place not in the live moment but in the work's circulation and repetition to come. The intended public is the mediated one reached through the technological repetition of voice and image.

While Hearst's first audio recording was made from within the enclosed space of the SLA safe house closet in which she was kept, Hayes chooses to focus on the optical for a re-sounding of what was once only auditory. The sound of Hearst is now dominated by the visual of Hayes's face. Instead of listening into the darkness, over the radio waves, Hayes-as-Hearst turns into a deer in headlights, the whiteness of her face reflects the racialized fear and desire of the SLA. I read the staggering whiteness of this image as key to Hearst as a narrative anomaly, as a white heiress who chose to think with philosophies that sounded Black.[8] The public imagined Hearst's captors as Black in part due to the "third world" radical black and brown ideology the SLA mimed in their language and vocal intonations. Consequently, to look upon Hayes is to hear the narrative framing mechanisms of Hearst's story, depicting her as a failed radical, silly, rich girl, and ventriloquist dummy. We see Hayes's face in order to visualize the game being played out between her and the invisible audience, to understand the stops and starts on the audiotape as narrative interruptions that lead to neither capture nor survival. Whereas Hearst was rendered as a voice, a wounded victim taken from her own body by imagined Black captors, Hayes's face becomes a sonic texture that has everything to do with the color and shape of these audio communiqués.[9] In her transition away from

FIG. 2. *Symbionese Liberation Army (SLA) Screeds #13, 16, 20 & 29*,
installation shot, 2003, courtesy of the artist.

the framing of her wealthy white home of origin, Hearst is tainted by her captors; she is infiltrated by a blackness-as-radical polemic and becomes a proponent of rhetorical miscegenation.

In *Communiqué #28*—day fifty-nine of the kidnapping—Patty Hearst came out to the public as Tania.[10] In this tape Hearst's voice is calm and evenly paced. She explains, "I have been given the choice of (one) being released in a safe area, or (two), joining the forces of the Symbionese Liberation Army and fighting for my freedom and the freedom of all oppressed people. I have chosen to stay and fight" (Pearsall 1974, 116). The SLA saw "freedom" as an opposition to the state's protection of the middle and upper classes, while the Hearst family and the FBI saw "freedom" as a return to the warm embrace of the state and its protection for those benefiting from its social policies. Hearst, presumably having learned that her tapes were being discredited in the media as false, prefaces this last communiqué with an authenticating statement. Emphasizing her intent, free will, and individual authorship of the words, she explains, "It's what I feel. I have never been forced to say anything on tape. Nor have I been brainwashed, drugged, tortured, hypnotized or in any way confused"

(116). Hearst's final transformation from good girl to bad comes in her now famous statement and sound bite: "I have been given the name Tania after a comrade who fought alongside Che [Guevara] in Bolivia for the people of Bolivia. I embrace the name with the determination to continue fighting with her spirit. There is no victory in half-assed attempts at revolution" (117). She promises to continue to fight with "total dedication" in "the oppressed American people's revolution" (116). It is this hyperbolic attachment to revolution that John Waters picks up as camp sensibility in his subsequent films featuring Hearst as the clueless normative mother, or the juror who must be killed because she breaks the rules and wears white shoes after Labor Day. Any coherent sense of self is discredited in Hearst's transition; her life and affiliations become a joke because they cannot be accounted for.[11]

I am drawn to Hearst's story and its comedic rhyme precisely because it provides a complicated space in the traditional history of radical politics. Revisiting Hearst as a space of generative contemplation, as "an arresting image" to which both Sharon Hayes and the nation have cathected, Hayes explains, "Through these relationships we accumulate a field of events to which we are witnesses, not passive observers of a thing that has past, but watchers with collective and individual spectatorial responsibility in the present moment" (2011, 90). Hearst's trial in 1976, and how her voice was heard within it, has everything to do with the singularity of the historical moment and Hearst's location; it has everything to do with the public that was reading Hearst.[12] We might ask, had she been tried in 2003—post-9/11, in the George W. Bush era, during massive Iraq War protests, at the birth of the legalization of gay marriage—what might have been different? Do Hearst and the SLA's misguided action and serious political aspiration merely get read as camp today, as in Kristen Wiig's recent Comedy Central *Drunk History* (2013) reenactment of Hearst's kidnapping? I suggest that the radio and television circulation, and the continued circulation in the public imagination of Hearst's story—to return to Muñoz and Felman— *does something else*. This is not just a story of the theatricality of failed 1970s radical political projects of captivity, trauma, and survival, but this *style* of political theater resurfaces in Hayes's queer aesthetics of political demonstrations, videos, and performances.

Part of what keeps Patty Hearst alive in the public imagination is that her story veers from the prescribed course of escape. She made the peculiar move toward identifying with her racialized white captors. Hearst becomes a joke due to the naïveté of the SLA's political demands and the public's inability to believe Hearst chose to be a radical. And this joke is funny precisely because—to follow Paolo Virno in his discussion of the logic of the joke (2008)—it alters the rules of the game. Hearst-turned-Tania radically rejects the national captivity narrative placed upon her, but by the time the FBI figures this out, Hearst is already a media sensation that needs to be managed. In *SLA Screeds* Hayes plays on the mass media's demand that Hearst be visible and legible—that her story be comprehensible through the logics of capital, femininity, and whiteness. She restages the hyper-visible erasure of Hearst, which is always an erasure of her play into the racially mixed and "sexually liberated" SLA. Hayes's recitation in the gallery setting as installation, as "relational aesthetics," illustrates the catch of visibility and re-sounds escape not as the movement toward survival but as sidestepping the regulation of narrative. Reading Hayes, it becomes clear that Hearst's escape was not *from* the SLA *back* to the warm embrace of the FBI and the Hearsts, but more nearly, it was an escape from a representational demand that would fix Hearst's body and political affiliation through allegory and narrative gender conventions. The escape strategy that Hayes demonstrates has everything to do with a failure and infelicity in the time and space of the utterance, an escape manifest in the interval of circulating VHS headshots, a stutterance that illustrates a different kind of narrative survival.

In viewing the *SLA Screeds*, we are not looking for clarity, for a truth in what happened to Patty Hearst—instead we are listening for the veering allure of escape that moves in and out of the visible and legible. I want to take this moment to pause on escape, how it is used and what it does. The word is everywhere, but rarely theorized. Escape takes you on a turn that is not bound by narrative or genre. It is a scene of contradictions, as it signals both passive acquiescence and a radical rejection of a closed system. It is also a racialized term stemming from eighteenth- and nineteenth-century slave narratives, and rises with theoretical articulations of fugitivity in the Black radical imagination. Instead of claiming that escape is either a political movement against the state or a cathartic move away from the real, I contend that the realist and the escapist hang out, which is to say, these are not cleaved realms of thought. Consequently, the polemic that sets up escape as the movement between capture and freedom—where escape marks either the impossibility of freedom or the route toward freedom—is already inadequate. Escape is a stage, a vast terrain on which the friction between passivity and action, movement and confinement plays out. The optic of escape contains these contradictions, as it is a veering move that does not get you where you thought you were going. While traditional captivity narratives begin and end in "freedom," escape keeps going; it repeats and is never finished. Escape is not a gesture of clarity that lends itself to the visible, legible, or reasonable. Instead, escape exists in gradations, and it is in these gradations—these plays between negativity and utopianism—where worlds are being worked out, worlds in which queer, Black, and Latino artists imagine a life neither free nor unfree but built into the daily negotiations of escape, into scenes of cloaking revelations.

We walk into an LA gallery in 2003 and collect a VHS tape of Hayes's *SLA Screeds* to watch at home. The tape will fall apart and degrade; it will leave a fuzzy trace across its middle; it will move like bootleg videos. Or in 2012, with VHS long dead, we walk into a black box in the open floor space of the Whitney to gaze upon Hayes's head projected large in the dark. She is anxiously captured again in white, reciting the lines. The gallery floor is filled with Hayes's other speech acts, some on protest signs in a mock front yard that covers the left side of the gallery, some spoken from speakers facing each other in a square, and some woven into a large banner the length of the gallery wall. The way out is found in the microforms of "survivance" that such repetitions suggest—against conceptions of captivity and freedom, against the demand to survive, when *to survive* is to be swallowed in narrative, and produced by the linearity of a fixed narrative genre.[13] Thinking with Gerald Vizenor, "survivance" is a way to mark a desire for a narrative or representational presence while at the same time, refusing dominant forms of survival that are predicated on dominance, normativity, and erasure. Instead of a grand trajectory of escape that ends in liberation and freedom, the veering strategies of escape offered by Hayes are made through nonpragmatic movements of repetition, infelicity, and constant audiovisual capture. Escape does not represent a scene of rescue, but it does provide a narrative flicker of another kind of relationship with radical aesthetics. Hayes recites the joke of Hearst, the joke of Hearst's failed performances as either a victim or a revolutionary, the joke that there is no self in Hearst's audiovisual projections. Yet, as we know, subject formation isn't that simple, and Hearst's story has been straightened out in our retrospective popular retellings of what counts as radical politics that are worth repeating. The joke is on us for not listening to the movement of black thought as it is resounded in a backward political moment. In the stutterance that is the *SLA Screeds*, I hear radical thought that cannot be contained by discrete narratives. Hayes's narrative rhyme-in-white flickers with a different trajectory of radical thought, staged for us by way of its messy inability to be heard just once, just right.

Katherine Brewer Ball is Visiting Assistant Professor of performance studies at Wesleyan University, where she previously held the Andrew W. Mellon Postdoctoral Fellowship. Her current book project, *The Only Way Out Is In: The Queer & Minoritarian Performance of Escape*, traces contemporary Black, Latina/o and queer performances that break from the language of freedom to theorize escape.

Notes

1. Speaking in an interview about another project, Hayes asks, "What if queer studies didn't steer itself so intensely toward visibility but instead steered itself toward questions of speech? What if, following Gayatri Chakravorty Spivak, we were focused as much on hearing and speaking as on seeing?" (Bryan-Wilson 2009, 90).

2. Pearsall writes that SLA members would adopt markedly black vocal inflections and language which he claims were indicative of the SLA's "play-school tactic of 'let's pretend'" (Pearsall 1974, 123). Elsewhere he calls these vocal performances by members such as Teko and Gelina "conscious projection[s] of emotional tones [through] counterfeited Black accents" (94).

3. That Hearst was the only one prosecuted for the bank robbery and that she was tried before her kidnappers, Bill and Emily Harris, were tried for their witness-verified crime of abduction, indicated the priorities of the U.S. government in prosecuting Hearst not just for the bank robbery—which the Harrises participated in as well—but more nearly for everything Hearst's abduction and defection to the SLA meant for the nation. In a 1997 interview with *Dateline*, Hearst said, "It's really shocking the way the case was presented. I mean no other people were prosecuted for that bank robbery except me, none of my kidnappers were charged or prosecuted. That is another thing that America has just accepted, like that's normal" (Mankewicz 2009).

4. Here, I am specifically thinking of Moten's idea of "choreography-in-confinement" a term he coins in "Taste Dissonance Flavor Escape" (2007), a concept of the "cramped and capacious" which returns in his writing with Stefano Harney on "the hold" of the slave ship in *The Undercommons* (2013).

5. After serving twenty-two months in prison, Hearst was released and eventually married her bodyguard and settled in the affluent suburbs of Connecticut. She has since appeared in five John Waters films: *Crybaby* (1990), *Serial Mom* (1994), *Pecker* (1998), *Cecil B. DeMented* (2000), and *A Dirty Shame* (2004). As Christopher Castiglia notes, "Waters chose Hearst to appear in

his films, she reports, because he knew she could play a role without being any trouble. In treating Hearst like an obedient participant in any script he put before her, Waters used Hearst as much as the SLA or the FBI did, even while his deployment of the figure of Patty Hearst continues the subversive work of her autobiography" (1996, 105).

6. Donald DeFreeze's, aka Cinque's, voice explained, "The Symbionese Liberation Army is a federated union of military/political elements of many different liberation struggles, and of many different races. Our unified purpose is to liberate the oppressed people around the world in their struggle against fascist imperialism and the robbery of their freedom and homeland" (Pearsall 1974, 55).

7. Pearsall writes, "Her voice was thin and strained, and it was immediately conjectured that she spoke under the influence of medical sedation or street drugs. Her discourse was also chopped into short sections by starting and stopping of the tape recorder" (1974, 58). In his effort to contextualize Hearst's message, we can see the confusion that he imagines she must have felt, the projection of chemical interference in Hearst's person that he finds evidenced in the sound of her voice. This interpretation of her voice brings our attention to the need to project the role of victim onto Hearst. Pearsall's interpretation marks her as both unable to fight back (through the infliction of force, drugs, etc.) and as unable to access her true self—a self that should automatically and intrinsically try to resist the captors and escape. For more on the various tape experts employed by the FBI see Associated Press 1974 and U.S. Congress, House of Representatives, Committee on Internal Security 1974.

8. One of the ways in which Hearst's theater of abduction activated the social and national imaginary was through the specter of race. The kidnapping was racialized from the beginning, Hearst's body and her image had been stolen from their rightful owners—her father and white America—and now were in the possession of "the poor, the black, the sexually 'liberated'" (Castiglia 1996, 88). Hearst's alleged affairs with both Donald DeFreeze (Cinque) and William Wolfe (Cujo) added to the public feeling and perception that Hearst had not only allied herself with black thought but had also let her physical body be overtaken by it.

9. Cinque was by most accounts the only Black member of the SLA. At one point, the SLA did have help from fellow ex-prisoner and Black radical Thero Wheeler, but there are conflicting stories about when exactly Wheeler left the organization, and by most accounts he had gone before the shooting of Oakland Superintendent Marcus Foster (Cumming and Sayles 2011, 7).

10. What Hayes refers to as Screed 29, Pearsall numbers Screed 28.

11. The primary argument used by the defense in Hearst's trial for the Hibernia

Bank Robbery was that she was brainwashed, or what the defense labeled "coercive persuasion" (Graebner 2008, 7). As reflected in her audio communiqués, Hearst and the SLA were aware that her words were being dismissed as false. Her failure to surface both after the shoot-out and fire at the Los Angeles SLA "safe house" on May 17, 1974 (which killed all other SLA members except Hearst and the Harrises), and during what is referred to as "the missing year" in which Bill and Emily Harris took her into hiding, only furthered public opinion that she had lost control of her own will and mind. The brainwashing explanation was the only way the public could rationally understand the duration of Hearst's absence and her perceived wealth of escape opportunities.

12. As William Graebner speculates, "Had Patty been tried in 1965, she would surely have been acquitted, judged to be nothing more, nothing less than the unfortunate victim of kidnapping, rape and physical and mental torture. Had she been tried in 1985, she would surely have been convicted, steamrolled by the Reagan revolution, judged to be just another person who had failed to take personal responsibility for her acts. The moment of her conviction, in March 1976, was somewhere between, participating at once in a culture of the victim, grounded in experience and deeply felt, and an incipient culture of personal responsibility" (2008, 8).

13. Here, I am thinking about "survivance," a term articulated by Gerald Vizenor to mark both the survival and resistance of Native American narrative presence that happens against native genocide and settler colonialism and continues to mark the representational erasure of Native American lives (1994, 15).

Works Cited

Associated Press. 1974. "FBI Statement on Recording by Kidnapped Hearst." *AP Archive*. February 16. http://www.aparchive.com/metadata/youtube/d1e8de38090d709c75ece72afdff5372.

Austin, J. L. 1975. *How to Do Things with Words*. Cambridge, MA: Harvard University Press.

Brooks, Daphne. 2006. *Bodies in Dissent: Spectacular Performances of Race and Freedom*. Durham, NC: Duke University Press.

Bryan-Wilson, Julia. 2009. "We Have a Future: An Interview with Sharon Hayes." *Grey Room* 37 (Fall): 78–93.

Castiglia, Christopher. 1996. *Bound and Determined: Captivity, Culture-Crossing, and White Womanhood from Mary Rowlandson to Patty Hearst*. Chicago: The University of Chicago Press.

Cumming, Gregory, and Stephen Sayles. 2011. "The Symbionese Liberation
    Army: Coming Together, 1973." *History Compass* 9 (6): 485–97.
Dolar, Mladen. 2006. *A Voice and Nothing More*. Cambridge, MA: MIT Press.
Felman, Shoshana. 2002. *The Scandal of the Speaking Body: Don Juan with J. L.
    Austin, or Seduction in Two Languages*. Stanford, CA: Stanford University
    Press.
Freeman, Elizabeth. 2010. *Time Binds: Queer Temporalities, Queer Histories*.
    Durham, NC: Duke University Press.
Graebner, William. 2008. *Patty's Got a Gun: Patricia Hearst in 1970s America*.
    Chicago: University of Chicago Press.
Harney, Stefano, and Fred Moten. 2013. *The Undercommons: Fugitive Planning &
    Black Study*. Oakland, CA: AK Press.
Hayes, Sharon. 2009. "Morning Session Keynote Address." The Creative Time
    Summit: Revolutions in Public Practice. New York City, October 9.
    http://creativetime.org/summit/2009/10/24/sharon-hayes/.
———. 2011."Certain Resemblances: Notes on Performance, Event, and Political
    Images." In *On Horizons: A Critical Reader in Contemporary Art*, edited by
    Maria Hlavajova, Simon Sheikh, and Jill Winder. Utrecht, Netherlands:
    BAK, basis voor actuele kunst.
Hearst, Patricia Campbell, and Alvin Moscow. 1982. *Every Secret Thing*. New
    York: Pinnacle Books.
Isenberg, Nancy. 2000. "Not 'Anyone's Daughter': Patty Hearst and the
    Postmodern Legal Subject." *American Quarterly* 52 (4): 639–81.
Kelley, Robin D. G. 2002. *Freedom Dreams: The Black Radical Imagination*.
    Boston: Beacon Press.
Love, Heather. 2007. *Feeling Backward: Loss and Politics of Queer History*.
    Cambridge, MA: Harvard University Press.
Mankewicz, Josh. 2009. "Interview with Patricia Hearst." *Dateline*, July
    25. http://www.msnbc.msn.com/id/32089504/ns/dateline_nbc-
    newsmakers/t/kidnapped-heiress-patty-hearst-story/#.T8dXR5lYv68.
Moten, Fred. 2003. *In the Break: The Aesthetics of the Black Radical Tradition*.
    Minneapolis, MN: University of Minnesota Press.
———. 2007. "Taste Dissonance Flavor Escape: Preface for a Solo by Miles
    Davis." *Women & Performance: A Journal of Feminist Theory* 17 (2): 217–46.
Muñoz, José Esteban. 2009. *Cruising Utopia: The Then and There of Queer Futurity
    (Sexual Cultures)*. New York: NYU Press.
Pearsall, Robert Brainard. 1974. *The Symbionese Liberation Army: Documents
    and Communications*, 55. Edition from NYU's Tamiment Library with
    corrections made to this copy by individuals claiming to be SLA members.
    The cover page reads "annos by Joe Romero & Russ Little." Amsterdam:
    Rodopi.

Rowlandson, Mary. 2013. *Narrative of the Captivity and Restoration of Mrs. Mary Rowlandson*. Reprint of the 1682 edition, Project Gutenberg. June 1.

Sedgwick, Eve Kosofsky. 2003. *Touching Feeling: Affect, Pedagogy, Performativity*. Durham, NC: Duke University Press.

U.S. Congress, House of Representatives, Committee on Internal Security. 1974. *The Symbionese Liberation Army: A Study Prepared for the Use of the Committee on Internal Security*, 93rd Cong, 2nd sess., February 18.

Vizenor, Gerald. 1994. *Manifest Manners: Postindian Warriors of Survivance*. Hanover, NH: Wesleyan University Press.

Virno, Paolo. 2008. *Multitude: Between Innovation and Negation*. Los Angeles: Semiotext(e).

Weheliye, Alexander. 2014. *Habeas Viscus: Racializing Assemblages, Biopolitics, and Black Feminist Theories of the Human*. Durham, NC: Duke University Press.

Suicide and Survival in the Work of Kara Walker

Tiffany Johnson Bidler

Young, black and Artist

gifted, dead at sixteen overwhelmed

by

an overdose of sentimentality,

admiration and awe.

> —Kara Walker: The Renaissance Society
> at the University of Chicago

Kara Walker's visual essay, "Chronology of Black Suffering: Images and Notes, 1992–2007," was assembled from items in Walker's personal picture files and included in the catalog for her retrospective exhibition *Kara Walker: My Complement, My Enemy, My Oppressor, My Love*. Within the essay, Walker includes an altered promotional still from the obscure film *Professional Sweetheart* (1933) written by Maurine Watkins, best known for her play *Chicago* (1926). The original still captures the character Vera, a maid played by the actress Theresa Harris, appealing to a group of white male characters. Vera is holding her arms out before her, with her wrists turned upward, as if she were pulling a string taut. Walker has altered the still in a number of ways, most notably by adding splashes of red paint that transform the still into a pulpy image of suicide (fig. 1). Although the iconography of suicide in Walker's body of work has not been comprehensively studied, it is extensive. Walker's images of suicide refer to representations of the suicides of slave women and mothers in nineteenth-century

WSQ: Women's Studies Quarterly 44: 1 & 2 (Spring/Summer 2016) © 2016 by Tiffany Johnson Bidler.

FIG. 1. Kara Walker, "Chronology of Black Suffering: Images and Notes, 1992–2007." Detail. In Philippe Vergne, *Kara Walker: My Complement, My Enemy, My Oppressor, My Love* (Minneapolis: Walker Art Center, 2007). © Kara Walker

abolitionist narratives, where these deaths functioned rhetorically to engender sympathy and condemn slavery's injustices. "Narrative," Walker explains, "is very important to my work. I appropriate from many sources . . . frontispieces for slave narratives, authentic documents, as well as a novel or a great sort of artistic spectacle" (quoted in Golden 2002, 47). Walker's life-size silhouette *Cut* (1998) (fig. 2) draws from the frontispiece of William Wells Brown's *Clotel* (1853), which depicts Clotel's tragic leap into the Potomac, and from an illustration in Jesse Torrey's *A Portraiture of Domestic Slavery* (1817), which shows a woman named Anna leaping from a window after learning she would be returned to slavery without her children.

In her sensitive account of Anna's leap, historian Terri L. Snyder argues that the act of slave suicide contained within it the contradictions of slavery itself:

> Suicide, an anguished assertion of personhood, undermined the human commodification . . . fundamental to enslavement. Once dead, a slave ceased to be an object of property, an entity to be traded, or a subject from which to extract labor. In this sense, self-destruction by enslaved people was often viewed as an act of power, a visceral rejection of enslavement as well as a visible statement of personhood. Yet there was a

FIG. 2. Kara Walker, *Cut*, 1998. Cut paper on wall. 88 x 54 inches. © Kara Walker.

fatal cost in asserting the power to die, of course. Death by suicide was not always, consistently, or even typically, an unequivocal, unambiguous, or intentional act. (Snyder 2015, 4)

The suicide rate of slaves is likewise equivocal and difficult to ascertain, as suicidal deaths were misperceived or went unrecorded (Lester 1998, 9). Nevertheless, narrative accounts of slave suicide survive in abolitionist literature, in oral accounts passed down intergenerationally, and in Works Progress Administration (WPA) interviews of ex-slaves (Snyder 2015, 14). Walker's images of suicide are half fictions that assume and transform the contradictions Snyder outlines while attending to the ways in which history is apocryphal, romanticized, and ever-present. To the image of Clotel's suicide included in "Chronology of Black Suffering," for example, Walker added a red superhero cape (fig. 3). Clotel plays the "tragic mulatta" in Brown's narrative, and by recasting Clotel's suicide as a scene of heroic self-sacrifice, Walker alludes to the "superwoman" stereotype, a contemporary controlling image rooted in the myth that black women are "unshakable" and thus not susceptible to depression or suicidal tendencies (Jones and Shorter-Gooden 2003, 21).

The image of Anna's leap from *A Portraiture of Domestic Slavery* is reproduced in the exhibition catalog Walker created for the Renaissance Society at the University of Chicago (fig. 4). Anna's image is in conversation with Andy Warhol's *Suicide* (1964) from his pulpy *Death and Disaster* series (fig. 5). Warhol reproduced and displaced a grainy newspaper image of a man leaping from a building. The man is silhouetted against a gray sky and the image is fractured. Anna's image is likewise fractured. Opposite Anna's image, Walker inserted layered vellum pages impressed with narrative text running vertically and horizontally. Anna's image is displaced from its original context in abolitionist literature and resituated within a contemporary "historical romance." The horizontal narrative, written by Walker, is that of a violent love triangle between a light-skinned slave woman, a dark-skinned slave man, and the white plantation master's son. The master's son has taken advantage of the slave woman's sexual availability. When he catches her having sex with the black man *she* desires, the son flies into a jealous rage and orders the slave castrated, tortured, and killed. Walker's narrative is cast as one of suffering and survival—"Women know how this happens, and women hafta learn to accept it if they wanna survive"—overlaid with knowing capitulation—"She understands her value.

. . . She sold herself. She sells herself." The text running vertically behind the horizontal text is a narrative about a black woman and a white man. The vertical text echoes the domestic architecture of the original image and reiterates the action of Anna's fall. Two themes run through this narrative. The first is, as Walker puts it, "soft-core race relations." The white man embodies everything the black woman hates and fears and she desires him for this reason. The second is self-destruction, the internalization of the white man's "(culturally induced) will-to-death" (Walker 1997a). These motifs of survival, selling oneself, and self-destruction circle around the heroines and antiheroines that populate Walker's work.

The promotional still appropriated from the film *Professional Sweetheart* stands out as an exception to Walker's other images of suicide because it points to a nonliterary twentieth-century source in which no suicide takes place. Walker's work is intertextual, though, and the method of suicide depicted in the promotional still turns viewers back to *Cut*. In this way, the source imagery to which *Cut* refers is folded into the image of Vera. Taken together, Walker's suicide images serve as a compendium of gendered cultural scripts of suicidal acts caught in suspension—leaping, drowning, hanging, and cutting. Walker harnesses and refigures historical imagery of suicides that attempted to make "black suffering" visible. In doing so, she highlights the notion of "black suffering" itself as a trope open to critique. Walker's images of suicide employ black humor to explore the psycholog-

FIG. 3. Kara Walker, "Chronology of Black Suffering: Images and Notes, 1992–2007." Detail. In Philippe Vergne, *Kara Walker: My Complement, My Enemy, My Oppressor, My Love* (Minneapolis: Walker Art Center, 2007). © Kara Walker.

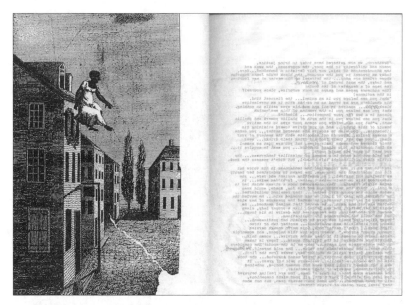

FIG. 4. Anna's leap. Detail. Kara Walker, *Kara Walker: The Renaissance Society at the University of Chicago, January 12–February 23, 1997*. (Chicago: The Renaissance Society at the University of Chicago, 1997). © Kara Walker.

ical pitfalls of performing the role of the suffering black woman artist who engages in heroic acts of self-sacrifice to ensure survival and success.

In addition to providing a reading of Walker's altered still of Vera in relation to *Cut* and to the film *Professional Sweetheart*, this essay is a preliminary exploration of what I identify as an ideational imaginary in Walker's work. Suicidal ideation is a compelling lens through which to view Walker's images of suicide, because it is an imaginary mode that is intrinsically pictorial. "Ideation," a term coined in 1829 by the philosopher James Mill, is the process of forming ideas or mental images of things that are not experienced through sensation at the time (42). Today, the term is more often encountered in the realm of discourse on suicidal tendencies in psychology. Suicidal ideation involves the formation of ideas or mental images of one's self-inflicted death. These ideas or mental images may or may not include a formulated plan (Harris and White 2013, 445). Suicidal ideation, then, is the imagining of the scene or tableau of self-killing. The tableau, like a photograph, is a frozen moment that belongs to an intimate narrative of suffering and despair. It is an imagining that takes into account questions of presentation and interpretation. How will the tableau appear

FIG. 5. Andy Warhol, *Suicide*, 1964. © 2015 The Andy Warhol Foundation for the Visual Arts, Inc. / Artists Rights Society (ARS), New York.

to those who come across the scene of one's suicide? The imagined staging is sometimes intended to produce a traumatizing affective response in the imagined viewer, to sear the scene onto private or public memory.

The imagined method also bears a relation to the form of one's suffering and one's cultural context. In "Women and Suicidal Behavior: A Cultural Analysis," psychologist Silvia Sara Canetto explains that suicidal behavior is socially scripted and regulated:

> There are cultural scripts of suicidal behavior, that is, collective, implicit beliefs about the meaning and permissibility of suicidal behavior. These scripts likely influence individual suicidal behavior, including when suicidal behavior becomes a possibility as well as the forms it takes. Individuals draw on these cultural scripts in determining their course of action and in giving their suicidal act public significance and legitimacy. Cultural scripts also guide communities' interpretations and responses to suicidal behavior. (2008, 264)

A given method of suicide is a culturally recognizable sign that makes visible suffering that is experienced in the realm of sensation. The imagining of the performance of the "script" is a form of expression borne of desperation and linked to a strong desire that suffering—invisible and felt internally—be manifested externally—on the body and in the visible realm. The expression, among other things, is a form of relief that, I maintain, has an aesthetic dimension. Motivated by compulsion, the dissonance between internal and external states is harmonized. Suicidal ideation follows a representational logic that involves the scripting and staging of a mish-mash of borrowed and self-generated imagery in the realm of suffering and desire. The paradoxes Walker calls up in her suicide imagery lie at the heart of suicidal ideation—in the face of unbearable suffering, imagined self-harm can *feel* like a form of self-care. Walker's iconography of suicide points to an ideational imaginary, but this imaginary is also evident in Walker's tableaux that do not represent suicide. The content of these tableaux—violent fantasies that depict scenes of degradation and destruction—participates in this imaginary. However, Walker's practice of borrowing, scripting, and staging is equally significant.

Art historians have confronted suicide in Walker's work in analyses of *Cut*. Constructed from black paper and adhered to a white gallery wall, this life-size silhouette depicts a leaping (or falling) woman who has slit her wrists with a straight razor. Pinned in midair, Walker indefinitely postpones the figure's fall and death. The woman is a still life, forever occupying a threshold. She is portrayed holding a posture that connotes pain and joy, capitulation and agency, self-destruction and self-care. Her arms are flung far above her head as she clicks the heels of her daintily clad feet together. The outstretched arms partly obscure the woman's loosely defined profile. The arching of her back pushes out her bust, drawing our attention to her corseted waist. Two short braids of hair have slipped loose and hang beneath the figure's right arm. The braids visually echo the reach of her arms above her head and the click of her heels beneath her skirt. Her left hand holds the straight razor. The fountains of blood that pour from the figure's wrists are rendered as graceful arabesques. Beneath the figure's outstretched arms, blood pools. *Cut*'s suicide is a fantasy, a figment of the imagination. The figure's hands are attached to the wrists by the narrowest of paper bands. How could this woman cut the wrist of one hand so irredeemably and retain the ability to cut the other? How could she slit her wrists while leaping? We are watching two suicidal acts—the jump, the cut—collapsed into one. Is Walker referencing the filmic jump cut, which is known for disrupting the narrative continuity Walker eschews?

Curator Yasmil Raymond asserts that "maladies of power" are Walker's central concerns in *Cut* and other images of suicide. Walker depicts the plantation master and the slave as equally capable of inflicting corporal violence on the other (Raymond 2007, 353). In this master-slave scenario—alluded to in large-scale tableaux such as *Presenting Negro Scenes* (Walker 1997b)—suicide is the ultimate revenge. "A slave committing suicide was viewed as an assault on the master's property," Raymond writes, "and those who attempted it but did not succeed were severely punished" (2007, 354). Raymond offers readings that move beyond revenge, characterizing Walker's suicides as "fables of martyrdom," and describing *Cut* as "a woman's shameless gesture of bliss and defiance, which suggests that her suicide stands as an act of transgression and empowerment" (354). However, an ambiguous suicide by hanging/murder by lynching from *Presenting Negro Scenes*—which goes unmentioned by Raymond and exemplifies the complexity of Walker's suicide images—lacks the tenor of revenge, martyrdom, transgression, or empowerment that often characterizes accounts of slave suicide. A young girl is suspended by a billowing cotton sack/parachute/noose, out of which fall bolls of cotton (fig. 6). The cotton sack takes the form of a lifesaving device, but ironically, it has caused her demise. The silhouette embodies the paradoxes of suicidal ideation.

FIG. 6. Kara Walker, *Presenting Negro Scenes Drawn Upon My Passage Through the South and Reconfigured for the Benefit of Enlightened Audiences Wherever Such May Be Found, By Myself, Missus K.E.B. Walker, Colored*, 1997. Detail. Cut paper on wall. 144 x 1860 inches. Installation view: The Renaissance Society at The University of Chicago, 1997. Photo: Tom van Eynde. © Kara Walker

Cut has been the focus of debate between art historians Gwendolyn DuBois Shaw and Darby English, centered on the question of Walker's artistic agency. Shaw interprets *Cut* as a self-portrait of the artist sacrificing her artistic body for professional success. "One can almost hear the command, 'Jump! When I say 'jump!'" She responds willingly, with an eager to please grin on her face" (Shaw 2000, 131). For Shaw, *Cut* illustrates the ways in which Walker fails to free herself from the mainstream art world and fails to control the mode of her own artistic production and interpretation. The "legacy of the past," which Shaw characterizes as both the racist historical imagery that Walker appropriates and the history of unequal power relationships between black artists and the predominately white art world, is "too much for the artist of the present to overcome" (131). Walker's attempts to employ representation as a means to confront and overcome the legacy of the past are doomed to fail. There is "no possibility of transcendence through visuality," Shaw laments, "the pain of invention

will all too soon outweigh the pleasure of self-expression" (131). This latter statement from Shaw points to the imaginary of suicidal ideation, in
that the "pleasure" of the expression of intense suffering is ultimately out-
weighed by the steep price one pays to express it.

Darby English does not support Shaw's view that *Cut* is, in his rephras-
ing, "a self-portrait expressing Walker's sense of her professional identity
and fate" (2007, 143). He argues that Shaw's conclusions are the outgrowth
of a confusion of the work's identity statements with the artist's identity:

> The picture would seem to be a self-conscious send-up of the perfor-
> mances of self demanded by those who have simply caricatured Walk-
> er's (*caricatural*) work, as a way of annulling or rendering invisible her
> refusal to be disciplined. *Cut* is, in effect, a performance of the very per-
> formance that Walker never consents to give. In its place we are given
> a satire at once chilling and cheery of the obligation put upon her—to
> own up to a "self-destructive" tendency. (144)

Cut, then, is a defiant tongue-in-cheek rendering of Walker's self-destruction—a fantasy held by African American viewers who oppose Walker's
use of negative imagery and wish to censor it. These viewers believe that
her appropriation and reworking of racist imagery contribute to antiblack
racism and act as a manifestation of betrayal, self-hatred, and complicity
with white supremacy in the art world (Reid-Pharr 2002, 38). English's
interpretation, too, points to the logic of ideation. Ideation involves imagining how the staged tableau of self-destruction will read to others, and
sometimes to others who intensely disapprove of aspects of one's self.

In this essay, however, I want to shift the framework of analysis of Walker's work from one that focuses on whether her appropriation of racist stereotypes contributes to or combats antiblack racism to one that focuses
on her manipulation of controlling images. Controlling images, such as
the "tragic mulatta," Jezebel, Strong Black Woman, and Superwoman, are
discursive formations that construct racialized gender identities. Feminist
scholar Patricia Hill Collins writes:

> As part of a generalized ideology of domination, these controlling im-
> ages of Black womanhood take on special meaning because the author-
> ity to define these symbols is a major instrument of power. In order to
> exercise power, elite white men and their representatives must be in a
> position to manipulate appropriate symbols concerning Black women.

They may do so by exploiting already existing symbols, or they may create new ones relevant to their needs. (2000, 67–68)

Is it significant that Walker places herself in a position to manipulate controlling images of black women? Is this a usurpation of a major instrument of power? Walker explains that she was drawn to the ephemerality of her paper installations because it allowed her to "make these kind of archetypes, these stereotypes, and put them up there in this format that's easily destroyed . . . " (quoted in Golden 2002, 48). In the manipulated still from *Professional Sweetheart*, we literally see "elite white men and their representatives . . . in a position to manipulate appropriate symbols concerning Black women."

Black feminist literary scholarship has examined controlling images and provides insight into the literary themes and tropes that pervade Walker's work. Alice Walker and Mary Helen Washington have addressed black women's internalization of controlling images and black women authors' deconstruction of controlling images. Walker and Washington also have identified a number of figures in literature that harbored a tragic susceptibility to self-destruction: the divided self, or woman split in two, the suspended woman, and the Saint. Regarding the suspended woman, they explain, "the pressures against [the suspended woman] are so great they cannot move anywhere. Suspended in time and place, they are women whose life choices are so severely limited that they either kill themselves, retreat into insanity, or are simply defeated one way or another by the external circumstances of their lives" (Washington 1982, 212). With the exception of the figure of Vera, all of Kara Walker's figures engaged in acts of suicide are suspended women. The Saint is a controlling image similar to the Strong Black Woman. As with the suspended woman, suicide hovers at the contours of her image. "Instead of being perceived as whole persons, their bodies became shrines: what was thought to be their minds became temples suitable for worship. These crazy Saints stared out at the world wildly, like lunatics—or quietly, like suicides" (Walker 1973, 401). Ultimately, Alice Walker refigures Saints as suppressed Artists, "driven to a numb and bleeding madness by the springs of creativity in them for which there was no release" (402). *Cut* echoes Alice Walker's imagery. Thus, Kara Walker's work furthers a line of investigation and deconstruction of controlling images begun by black feminists.

Cut has been characterized as a depiction of martyrdom, transgression, empowerment, failure, capitulation, and defiance. This confusing array of readings is rooted in the intertextuality, ambiguity, and affective power of Walker's imagery. In critiquing Shaw's analysis, one of the points with which English takes issue is the implication that Walker is "like a prostitute" in that she sacrifices her body for professional success as an artist and functions as a kind of black professional sweetheart for the white art world (2007, 145). For Shaw, the black woman artist cannot function as a figure of survival because her survival is always already tainted by capitulation. Walker has no choice but to represent the black women artist as self-destroying, because it is—paradoxically—only by way of performing self-destruction that one can survive as a black woman artist in a white art world. Significantly, the film *Professional Sweetheart*, from which Walker's image of Vera is taken, is about the types of gendered and raced performances required of both black and white women for success and survival as professional artists.

In *Professional Sweetheart*, Vera is the maid of Glory Eden (Ginger Rogers), a New York radio pitchwoman known as the "Purity Girl of the Air" for the Ippsie-Wippsie Radio Hour sponsored by Sam Ipswich, the washcloth king. As the Purity Girl, Glory is sold as sweetness incarnate, but truthfully Glory is a flirt who wants nothing more than to dance and dally in smoke-hazed and jazz-filled Harlem black and tans. Ipswich and his publicity team believe that if they catch a sweetheart for Glory it will "tame" her. The team recruits a "professional sweetheart" in the form of unsuspecting Kentuckian Jim Davey (Norman Foster) who had been writing fan letters to Glory. Jim is chosen because he is naive, but also because he embodies a normative conception of rural white American masculinity that compliments Glory's Purity Girl image. Soon after he is brought to New York, Jim realizes he has been duped. Enraged, he kidnaps Glory and holds her captive in his Kentucky cabin. There, the two argue about Jim's deception and he physically assaults Glory, leaving her unconscious. She awakes "tamed," a sincere embodiment of the image of domestic sweetness the radio pitchmen sought to manufacture. A cabin-bound and apron-clad Glory contentedly serves up pancakes and refuses to return to her life in the big city. The publicity team, however, wants Glory back. Their strategy is to instill jealousy in Glory by allowing Vera to sing as the Purity Girl. While gathered around the radio in the Kentucky cabin, Jim and Glory listen to Vera sing. After witnessing the arousal Vera's "Jezebel" voice elicits in Jim, Glory's jealousy provokes her to reclaim the role of the Purity Girl.

In *Professional Sweetheart*'s narrative, white femininity is constituted vis-à-vis the media's maintenance of a false appearance of white purity and by a manufactured rivalry between white and black women in the realm of voice and desire.

Professional Sweetheart's narrative speaks to the precarious labor of black actresses and black maid characters in the early twentieth century. The black maid is marginally positioned—figuratively and literally—in relation to the central white female lead. Vera frequently occupies thresholds in the diegetic space of the film, which is appropriate given that she is imagined in dual terms: as an instrument for the maintenance of white femininity, with its assigned patriarchal attributes of purity and docile domesticity, and as a duplicitous enabler of white women's rebellious desires to escape the confines of purity and domesticity by flirting with sexual taboos and black culture. In one shot, in the same sequence from which Walker's still is taken, Vera stands at the threshold between Glory's bedroom and the public reception room in which she meets reporters. Vera is almost always shown shifting between these two spaces—one private, one public—and she must present a different persona in each space. In Glory's room, she functions as a confidant, mentor, and enabler, teaching Glory a new dance step from Harlem and sneaking in lacy black pajamas. In the reception room, Glory's publicity team imagines Vera as an instrument of Glory's maintenance and control.

Remarkably, *Professional Sweetheart* gives voice to Vera's dreams and ambitions. In contrast to Glory's ambitions, which are presented as superficial, immature, inconsistent, and shaped entirely by others, Vera's ambitions are presented as authentic and unchanging. The promotional still Walker manipulates is from a scene in which Vera attempts to convince Ipswich's publicity men to allow her to sing in Glory's place. Vera stands before Ipswich and declares, "Don't you worry Mr. Ipswich. What, if she don't come back I know her songs. I can sing 'em." He replies, "If you tell it to me once more . . . " Ipswich's response implies that Vera has been persistent with her request. Vera interrupts Ipswich's protests and raises her hands in a pleading gesture, "But I can sing 'em." She snaps her fingers and swings her hips provocatively as she sings the opening bars to "My Imaginary Sweetheart." The dance she performs is the same dance she taught Glory. Vera confidently and opportunistically voices her ambition and demonstrates her professionalism. However, the scene ends with the press agent promoting a story that Glory has been kidnapped and taken to

Harlem. Vera exits the scene quietly through the doorway. She is pushed off to the side of this film whenever she is no longer needed.

Vera disappears entirely from the film the moment Glory reclaims the role of the Purity Girl. Our final encounter with Vera is with her disembodied voice transmitted over diegetic radio waves. We never learn how Vera responds to her lost opportunity. She is cut from the film, and her sudden absence feels violent. Black actresses and black maid characters, as well as the real and fictional labor they performed, were subject to multiple instances of marginalization and erasure; they were erased from film credits, film history, and filmic narratives. Theresa Harris's character is central to the plot of *Professional Sweetheart*, and yet she received no screen credit. (Maurine Watkins knew something of this too; she was often unaccredited for the screenplays she wrote.) Vera's narrative mirrors the narrative of Harris's career, as described in the 1952 *Jet* interview "Maid of Hollywood." Opening with a condemnation of racist typecasting of black actresses, the article praises the ways in which Harris was innovative in her film roles, despite the tedium of playing "one maid role after the other" (*Jet* 1952, 64). Harris laments that due to typecasting she "has not been properly exploited" (65). Nevertheless, the author ends on a high note: "In spite of Hollywood's rebuffs to her ambitions, Miss Harris is not one to give up. 'All I can do,' [Harris] says, 'is keep on plugging and hoping'" (65). Harris's statement articulates a blunt strategy of artistic survival in the face of Hollywood's longstanding practice of typecasting black actresses, and is reminiscent of Vera's "plugging and hoping" in *Professional Sweetheart*.

Studies such as Charisse Jones and Kumea Shorter-Gooden's *Shifting: The Double Lives of Black Women in America* (2003) show how this figure of survival Harris embodied and bequeathed functions as a controlling image. Jones and Shorter-Gooden contend that black women's survival is tied to their ability to endure the stress of shifting between black and white worlds. (Vera performs this shifting in *Professional Sweetheart*.) In a section titled "Shifting as Survival, Shifting as Self-Destruction," the authors explain the negative effects of shifting on black women in a contemporary context:

> Pressured to bounce between divergent identities—one "Black," one "White"—experiencing what we call the yo-yo paradox, she may start to feel that she is constantly treading on shaky ground; confused, self-conscious, and conflicted. She may become psychologically or even physically ill from the stress of being all things to all people and nothing to

herself. She's adrift spiritually, and the process of shifting, initially a life preserver in stormy seas, has morphed into a weighty anchor, and she's drowning. (Jones and Shorter-Gooden 2003, 64)

By referencing this study, my aim is not to speculate on whether the above reflects Harris's or Walker's personal experiences. I wish to maintain, rather, that this account of the contemporary experience of black women is significant to understanding the larger cultural context of Walker's work, and can elucidate one of the many ways in which the image of Vera/Harris may resonate with viewers. The phenomenon of shifting voiced by black women informs our understanding of the *reception* of Walker's images. Its affective vocabulary resonates with interpreters of Walker's images who find themselves drowning in or confused by the interpretive possibilities of images that are layered, doubled, morphing, shifting, and suspended.

Curator Thelma Golden postulates that Walker takes on various personas in order "to speak for them, from them, and such speaking comes out in many ways" (2002, 49). Voice is evoked in Walker's altered still by the painted dots and X-Acto-knife–pricked piercings floating as a band across the photograph's emulsion. "There's a sweet violence in the act of cutting, of accepting and rejecting cultural stereotypes," Walker admits (Chambers 2008). This polka-dot band reads as Vera's singing, while it falls across Vera's face like a screen or veil. This layering of voice/veil/screen alludes to the filmic voice's potential for self-expression and deception, while attending to instances of silencing and erasure. Fred Moten describes black vocal performance as suffuse with paradox: "an erotics of the cut, submerged in the broken, breaking space-time of an improvisation. Blurred, dying life; liberatory, improvisatory, damaged love; freedom drive" (2003, 26). The relationship between black and white dots, absence and presence, reflects the dynamic of Vera standing in for Glory when she is absent and Vera's subsequent disappearance upon Glory's reappearance. It reflects the practice of black women's voices "doubling" as white actresses' voices (McCann 2010, 242). Vera's seductive and arousing voice is productive of Glory's innocent and pure voice. In an interview with art critic Jerry Saltz, Walker explained that she used scatological imagery in her work as a metaphor for a displaced voice that comes out impure or dirty. "It's about finding one's voice in the wrong end, searching for one's voice and having it come out the wrong way" (1996, 84). Walker's statement leaves open the possibility that the floating dots and cuts are a malodorous scent.

Doubleness pervades the film *Professional Sweetheart* and Walker's al-

FIG. 7. Kara Walker, "Chronology of Black Suffering: Images and Notes, 1992–2007." Detail. In Philippe Vergne, *Kara Walker: My Complement, My Enemy, My Oppressor, My Love* (Minneapolis: Walker Art Center, 2007). © Kara Walker

tered still of Vera. It reflects the experiences of contemporary black women described in *Shifting* and the concept of double consciousness—the phenomenon of ever feeling one's "two-ness"—coined by W. E. B. Du Bois (1994, 2). Vera and Glory serve as each other's doubles and shadows. The promotional still of Vera is an image of doubleness—as a historical document it is an image of both Vera and Harris. The image addresses, on the level of character and actor, how under a system of white supremacy black women perform labor that produces, secures, and draws the boundaries of specular white femininity. Walker's dots and knife piercings show Vera caught in a net of black and white relations. The use of white paint against the black and white photograph recalls the formal dynamic between black paper and white walls in Walker's silhouettes, and the racial dynamic between black and white characters in *Professional Sweetheart*. Walker's remarks about her silhouettes could be made about both white femininity and Vera's character: "It's a blank space, but it's not at all a blank space, it's both there and not there" (Saltz 1996, 82).

On the page opposite Vera's image in "Chronology of Black Suffering,"

Walker inserted an ink drawing on vellum of a black woman in bondage (fig. 7). The white band that covers her mouth, binds her arms to her side, binds her wrists together, and immobilizes her legs, is produced using the negative space of the inky figure. The band across the woman's mouth that renders her unable to speak echoes the band across Vera's mouth. The bands that hold the woman's wrists together echo the white cuffs of Vera's uniform. The bands immobilizing the woman's legs fall at the same length as Vera's apron. Her Afro and white areolas punctuated by black nipples echo the dots and cuts scattered across the altered still. The vellum veils another image in the bottom right corner of a woman wearing a black-and-white floral-print dress holding a white cloth over her mouth. Her hand gesture echoes Vera's. (It is perhaps a vintage toilet paper advertisement, alluding then to discourses of purity, strength, and cleanliness while referencing the scatological and "finding one's voice in the wrong end.") The juxtaposition of these images suggests that the image of Vera is also an image of bondage and silencing. They conjure up a mix of sincerity and satire. Their dark humor critiques the idealization, romanticization, and eroticization of the black woman artist as a figure of suffering and survival insofar as this figure functions as a controlling and confining image.

Unlike *Cut*, Vera's imaginary suicide lacks a subtext of transgression and empowerment; its subtext is one of self-sacrifice. However, the image of Vera addresses questions of agency, and, as English has noted, "Indeed, if Walker's work is about anything, it is about agency, its possibilities and limitations whenever representation is at issue, and the depths into which some of us must go to find it" (2007, 145). Vera's agency and its limitations are on display in *Professional Sweetheart*: she offers up what Walker calls sidelong glances ("little look[s] . . . full of suspicion, potential ill-will, or desire"), she articulates her desires persistently, and she successfully performs the song she claims she can sing (Saltz 1996, 82). The lyrics to "My Imaginary Sweetheart" obliquely allude to Vera's imagined self-conception as a successful performer: "My imaginary sweetheart/I imagine that you're real/You're everything I want you to be/You're my ideal." Vera nevertheless remains disposable. She is treated as a placeholder, a dark figure against which the outlines of lighter figures are made visible, a constructed rival used to manipulate Glory's emotions such that Glory performs according to white men's expectations (and reaps the benefits). Although Vera's agency as an artist is on display in *Professional Sweetheart*, we cannot ignore Shaw's probable observation that Vera's attempt to play the role of the Purity Girl was doomed to fail. Still, there is no way to know if for Vera "the pain of invention . . . [outweighed] the pleasure of self-expression" (Shaw 2000, 131).

Walker's images of suicide are not self-portraits or confessions. They are not diaristic transcriptions of Walker's ideations. Rather, they are images suspended in the realm of an ideational imaginary. Suicidal ideation is a mode of imagining engaged with questions of power and agency, with the limitations of representation, with the depths to which people feel they must go. Walker's suicides reference a pictorial mode in which the suicidal act—as imagined—does feel adequate as a reflection of an internal psychological state. Suicidal ideation is an imaginary realm in which the visual does not seem to fail, where inherited age-old tropes of self-harm are expressions that feel intensely personal, authentic, and hyper-contemporary. Where, perhaps, suicide is a sweetheart. Suicidal ideation's adequacy as personal representation is of immense significance within the context of suffering because it restores some sense of agency in the face of emotional and situational quagmires that feel out of one's control. Suicidal ideation can be an alluring picture of a way to survive.

Tiffany Johnson Bidler is an assistant professor of art history at Saint Mary's College in Notre Dame, Indiana. She is a specialist in contemporary art and critical theory, and American art and material culture.

Works Cited

Brown, William Wells. 1853. *Clotel; or, The President's Daughter: A Narrative of Slave Life in the United States.* London: Partridge & Oakey.

Canetto, Silvia Sara. 2008. "Women and Suicidal Behavior: A Cultural Analysis." *American Journal of Orthopsychiatry* 78 (2): 259–66.

Chambers, Veronica. 2008. "Kara Walker: The Artist." *Glamour,* October 29. http://www.glamour.com/inspired/women-of-the-year/2008/kara-walker.

Du Bois, W. E. B. 1994. *The Souls of Black Folk.* New York: Dover Publications, Inc.

English, Darby. 2007. "This Is Not About the Past: Silhouettes in the Work of Kara Walker." In *Kara Walker: Narratives of a Negress,* edited by I. Berry, D. English, V. Patterson, M. Reinhardt, 141–67. New York: Rizzoli Press.

Golden, Thelma. 2002. "Kara Walker: A Dialogue." In *Kara Walker: Pictures from Another Time,* edited by Annette Dixon, 43–49. New York: Distributed Art Publishers.

Harris, John, and Vicky White. 2013. "Suicidal Ideation." In *A Dictionary of Social Work and Social Care*. Oxford: Oxford University Press.

Hill Collins, Patricia. 2000. *Black Feminist Thought: Knowledge, Consciousness, and the Politics of Empowerment*. New York: Routledge.

Jet. 1952. "Maid of Hollywood." September 11, 62–65.

Jones, Charisse, and Kumea Shorter-Gooden. 2003. *Shifting: The Double Lives of Black Women in America*. New York: HarperCollins.

Lester, David. 1998. "Suicidal Behavior in African-American Slaves." *OMEGA: Journal of Death and Dying* 37 (1): 1–13.

McCann, Bob. 2010. *Encyclopedia of African American Actresses in Film and Television*. Jefferson, NC: McFarland & Company, Inc.

Mill, James. 1829. *Analysis of the Phenomena of The Human Mind*. London: Baldwin and Cradock.

Moten, Fred. 2003. *In the Break: The Aesthetics of the Black Radical Tradition*. Minneapolis, MN: University of Minnesota Press.

Professional Sweetheart. 1933. Directed by William A. Seiter. Los Angeles: RKO Pictures.

Raymond, Yasmil. 2007. "Maladies of Power: A Kara Walker Lexicon." In *Kara Walker: My Complement, My Enemy, My Oppressor, My Love*, edited by Philippe Vergne, 347–69. Minneapolis, MN: Walker Art Center.

Reid-Pharr, Robert F. 2002. "Black Girl Lost." In *Kara Walker: Pictures from Another Time*, edited by Annette Dixon, 27–41. New York: Distributed Art Publishers.

Saltz, Jerry. 1996. "Kara Walker: Ill-Will and Desire," *Flash Art* 29 (191): 82–86.

Shaw, Gwendolyn Dubois. 2000. "Final Cut." *Parkett* 59: 129–37.

Snyder, Terri L. 2015. *The Power to Die: Slavery and Suicide in British North America*. Chicago: University of Chicago Press.

Torrey, Jesse. 1817. *A Portraiture of Domestic Slavery in the United States*. Philadelphia: Jesse Torrey.

Vergne, Philippe, ed. 2007. *Kara Walker: My Complement, My Enemy, My Oppressor, My Love*, Minneapolis, MN: Walker Art Center.

Walker, Alice. 1973. *In Search of Our Mother's Gardens: Womanist Prose*. San Diego, California: Harcourt Brace Jovanovich.

Walker, Kara Elizabeth. 1997a. *Kara Walker: The Renaissance Society at the University of Chicago, January 12–February 23, 1997*. Chicago: The Renaissance Society at the University of Chicago.

———. 1997b. *Presenting Negro Scenes Drawn Upon My Passage Through the South and Reconfigured for the Benefit of Enlightened Audiences Wherever Such May Be Found, By Myself, Missus K. E. B. Walker, Colored*. Cut paper on wall.

———. 1998. *Cut*. Cut paper on wall.

Warhol, Andy. 1964. *Suicide*. Silkscreen on canvas.

Washington, Mary Helen. 1982. "Teaching Black-Eyed Susans: An Approach to the Study of Black Women Writers." In *All the Women Are White, All the Blacks Are Men, but Some of Us Are Brave: Black Women's Studies*, edited by Gloria Hull, Patricia Bell-Scott, and Barbara Smith. Old Westbury, NY: The Feminist Press.

How to Survive: AIDS and Its Afterlives in Popular Media

Jih-Fei Cheng

A recent trend in documentary and "true story" films revisiting the early years of the AIDS crisis and its activism has gained a foothold in popular media. These include *We Were Here* (2011), *Vito* (2011), *United in Anger* (2012), *How to Survive a Plague* (2012), *Dallas Buyers Club* (2013), and the film adaptation of activist Larry Kramer's 1985 autobiographical play *The Normal Heart* (2014), to name a few. These films adapt the video footage and stories about activism generated during the early years of the crisis. With the exception of *United in Anger*, each film depicts AIDS activism through the lens of white male heroes. This is not new. What differs is that, unlike popular AIDS films of the 1990s—including *And the Band Played On* (1993) and *Philadelphia* (1993)—today's films narrate white men's struggle for survival as initially tragic, yet ultimately successful in prolonging their lives against the odds.[1] Women and queers of color are marginal in these films, and appear only in order to go missing by the narrative's end.

Given the extensive documentation that recalls the central role women and queers of color have played in AIDS activism since the onset of the crisis, these misrepresentations of the past are egregious. Nonetheless, they continue to receive popular endorsement. *How to Survive* gained an Oscar nomination for best documentary feature. *Dallas Buyers Club* garnered a bevy of industry nominations and awards for its script and cast. Though the film's lead protagonists pass, they are survived by the accolades that, presumably, could only be heaped upon white, male, and cisgender actors Matthew McConaughey and Jared Leto. *The Normal Heart* was nominated for and won a number of Golden Globe, television, and online film awards for the movie and its cast. What does this popular revision of the AIDS past say about our present?

WSQ: Women's Studies Quarterly **44**: 1 & 2 (Spring/Summer 2016) © 2016 by Jih-Fei Cheng. All rights reserved.

Focusing on *How to Survive*, this article argues that the renewed interest in AIDS crisis activism has much to do with a historical impasse we have reached in the valuation of the living over the dead. The AIDS crisis emerged concurrently with late twentieth-century Reaganomics, including the arms buildup, dismantling of the welfare state, and criminalization of precarity.[2] During this time, AIDS activism became the first U.S. social movement to integrate handheld camcorder technology into direct action to record the lives laid bare to state violence and vehement social neglect (Juhasz 1995). Since then, the further removal of social safety nets, recent economic downturn, the exacerbation of class disparities, increased policing, retrenchment of freedoms, and continued global U.S. military occupations have made the experience of crisis ordinary (Berlant 2011, 11). AIDS crisis videos portray the modes of survival and livelihood that activists fought for which were alternative to what Lauren Berlant calls "cruel optimism"—the unrequited fantasy for "the good life" that is sustained by a thin thread of hope, in spite of evidence that opportunities to thrive have severely diminished (1). Archival AIDS activist documentary footage, then, is a living testament to collective will against the perpetuation of state oppression and colonial terror.

The advance and proliferation of handheld audiovisual technologies, such as the smartphone, begs the question of what it means to record death as a mundane activity—and for the video to survive, "go viral," and galvanize social movements. Yet, according to *How to Survive*, the value or quality of one's life is measured and represented principally by an individual's biological endurance. The film trains attention on certain white men within the Treatment and Data Committee of the AIDS Coalition to Unleash Power (ACT UP). Mixing archival and present-day video footage, it focuses exclusively on their efforts to seek a medical panacea. The advance of this endeavor is attributed largely, if not entirely, to the white men. That Treatment and Data helped to forge life-extending medications, and that *some* of these white men survived the crisis, become the film's evidence that biomedical interventions can and should work for everyone. This interpretation of events drastically reduces the revolutionary politics of ACT UP, and ignores the important work that activists performed to improvise other strategies for survival using the medium of video to collectively sustain the living and the dead.

If white men who physically survived the crisis constitute the core agents of AIDS politics, then the narrative arc of AIDS history bends toward a very narrow notion of justice. *How to Survive* prompts audiences to assume that images of women and queers of color are missing because these individuals failed to survive. The film suggests that the lives of these groups are always already less valuable, less qualified, and less representable. However, as I underscore in this article, archival video footage of the crisis as it is adapted in *How to Survive* inevitably conjures the alternative strategies that AIDS activists employed to confront the historical impasse of valuing the living over the dead. Turning to the scholarship and cultural productions of artist-activists Ray Navarro, Alexandra Juhasz, Sarah Schulman, and others, I trace an incipient archive of feminist AIDS video activism. Faced with the massive loss of people—especially women and queers of color—AIDS activists invented new political imaginations and representations of life.

Afterlives and the Archive

How to Survive a Plague's production relied on approximately seven hundred hours of compiled footage significantly derived from footage shot or collected by artist-activist James Wentzy, and over one thousand hours of footage collected from other video activists and preserved by artist-activist Jim Hubbard. Both Wentzy and Hubbard made this footage available to others for free (Sullivan 2012; Schulman, pers. comm.). The co-optation of archival AIDS videos does not merely extend the duration and feeling of AIDS activism. Rather, I contend that archival AIDS video activist images—especially those generated by and for women and people of color video collectives—surface in the mainstream precisely because they show how and why certain images survive in the face of biological duress and eventual technological failure.

Like the bodies of those who became sick during the early crisis years, the material medium of analog video recordings breaks down. Video makers' preservation of potential affective, corporeal, and material absences is what makes the production and distribution of AIDS images so inimitable. It is important to consider the correlation between corporeal and imagistic existences that are sustained by the physical and affective labor of video making. AIDS video artist-activists cared for the bodies and the images of those who were most vulnerable to the crisis not simply to prolong life— they anticipated that these videos and images would return as the afterlives of those who might come to pass (Juhasz 2006, 319–28).

In tracing the feminist video activist practices invested in the production of and care for queer of color AIDS images, I propose such images as "afterlives," and as a method for exceeding the limits of social and political recognition. That is, queer of color AIDS afterlives serve as a method for representational and materialist critiques against AIDS commodification and the fetishizing of biological longevity as the end goal to all politics. This method draws together past and present AIDS representations, prompting us to revisit feminist AIDS video activism to reconsider the possible scholarly and activist meanings, aesthetic practices, and political valences for queerness and survival in the political imagination.

From 1995 to 2000, James Wentzy assembled the "AIDS Activist Videotape Collection," which he made available at the New York Public Library (Jim Hubbard, pers. comm.). The collection contains Wentzy's own works and "the work of thirty to forty individuals and several collectives" (Jim Hubbard, pers. comm.). In 2001, artist-activists Jim Hubbard and Sarah Schulman began to conduct and video record new interviews with activists to create a database that would document the history of AIDS, in order to prevent what they perceived as the activist past being forgotten and misappropriated (Schulman 2012, 2–4). Wentzy operated as their cameraman (Sarah Schulman, pers. comm.). Between 2001 and 2011, Schulman "took clips of interviews to universities and community centers around the world." She "met with professors and students trying to get people to use the database. Finally, in 2011, Helen Molesworth, then curator for the Harvard Art Museums, contacted [Schulman and Hubbard] about exhibiting the interviews. This was the first institution to feature the material" (Sarah Schulman, pers. comm.).

Hubbard and Schulman's painstaking efforts also culminated in the feature-length independent documentary film *United in Anger*, as well as the ongoing, massive undertaking of the online free and open-access ACT UP Oral History Project. Both projects chronicle the multiracial, multigendered, and coalitional stakes of historical AIDS activism. According to Schulman, the efforts she and Hubbard made catalyzed a "paradigm shift," and regenerated interest in the public memory of AIDS (Sarah Schulman, pers. comm.). What Hubbard and Schulman did not anticipate was that the process of publicly archiving ACT UP history would inaugurate the interest of others, such as journalist David France, who would use the material to tell a contradictory story. France "was never a member of ACT UP," but had "a long history of mainstreaming gay subject matter" once its significance began to move "beyond subcultural recognition" (Sarah Schulman, pers. comm.). This provides critical insight into why issues of race and gender, as they relate to the unending AIDS pandemic, remain unresolved in France's rendition.

United in Anger and How to Survive are contrary in that United in Anger confronts commercialism by historicizing AIDS activists' efforts to expose and combat the corporate greed of pharmaceutical companies (Brim 2013, 176–7). ACT UP staged at least three demonstrations on Wall Street (Jim Hubbard, pers. comm.).[3] The presence of video activists was crucial to the staging and documentation of these direct actions. For instance, United in Anger and How to Survive both use significant footage from their predecessor, Voices from the Front (1992), which is produced by the Testing the Limits video collective, and heavily emphasizes the multiracial, multigender, and anticapitalist politics of AIDS activism. United in Anger uses stretches of Voices footage to show the 1989 ACT UP protest that forced the New York Stock Exchange to halt its operations for the first time in history, long before Occupy Wall Street attempted to do the same. These momentous direct actions waged against the market exploitation of AIDS led to several decreases in the price of Azidothymidine (AZT), the first U.S. government–approved drug used to treat HIV, and the most profitable drug in history. How to Survive forecloses the historical significance of these demonstrations from its narrative. During a March 2013 panel at the New School, organized by Visual AIDS and members of the New School staff and faculty, Hubbard and France debated their differing depictions. It became clear that France's representation is drawn from his belief that the effective outcome of historical AIDS protest is the eventual manufacture of a pill that will provide a global solution to AIDS (The New School 2013; Theodore Kerr, pers. comm.).

As an abundant number of archival AIDS videos show, AIDS has never been only a medical problem. Rather, the way we medicalize and value life presents a significant problem for changing the course of the pandemic. HIV/AIDS is the longest-running contemporary pandemic without a remedy. Today, the drug presumed most effective for stymying the pandemic is the Pre-Exposure Prophylaxis (PrEP), a once-a-day pill that is meant to prevent the onset of HIV-infection (but not cure those already diagnosed as HIV-positive). Yet, PrEP remains largely unknown and inaccessible worldwide (Ayala et al. 2013; O'Neal 2015). For women of color, trans people of color, and queer men of color, the lack of knowledge and access to PrEP is correlated to their conditions of precarity, which entails downward socioeconomic mobility, unstable housing, inadequate health-care, exposure to violence, preexisting HIV-positive status, HIV stigma and criminalization, the dearth of research on PrEP's impact among these communities, and more (Ayala et al. 2013; O'Neal 2015). These structural issues, which facilitated the AIDS crisis, continue unabated. As during the early crisis years, women and queers of color *continue* to be deprived of basic health needs, such as condoms, research, and care, in a privatized sys-tem where their experiences with medical neglect and mistreatment and vulnerability to HIV/AIDS persist (Ayala et al. 2013; O'Neal 2015). In short, the increased focus on biomedical solutions, such as PrEP, and the simultaneous decrease of socioeconomic safety nets and medical access, *normalizes* HIV risk for those most vulnerable.

Recently, Gregg Gonsalves, who is featured in *How to Survive* as a key AIDS activist, has been challenging corporate pharmaceutical lobbyists to prevent the exploitation of ACT UP's historical success in expediting FDA drug trials (Associated Press 2014). Notably, *How to Survive* does not in-clude recent interview footage of Gonsalves among its other present-day survivors. Meanwhile, *Voices* and *United* carefully portray how AIDS activ-ists have countered capitalism, racism, sexism, and transphobia as barriers to universal healthcare. By ignoring the longstanding history of racialized and gendered precarity, *How to Survive* distorts the past and deceives the public into equating biomedical interventions with progress.

The Queer of Color Image in AIDS Video Activism

A few white women are interviewed briefly in *How to Survive*. Only one queer person of color is named and permitted to speak, while the rest re-main in obscurity. Chicano AIDS activist Ray Navarro is introduced first as a hypervisual sign of AIDS activist vitality. Later, rendered incongruent to the narrative of success, his image disappears before the film's end. To describe the absence of women and people of color in *How to Survive* as being "stark" is not to proclaim that they are merely invisible and/or de-ceased. Rather, their absence is marked indelibly and excessively.

Navarro appears in the film as tangential to the story of AIDS activism, a passing—if compelling—figure in the AIDS movement. According to Juhasz, Navarro was cherished, adored, and considered pivotal by fellow artist-activists (Alexandra Juhasz, pers. comm.). As Hubbard states, "He was the sort of person who, five minutes after you met him, you felt you had known him your entire life" (Jim Hubbard pers. comm.). Navarro's art and activism were foundational to conceiving the radicalism of AIDS cultural productions. He appears in *How to Survive* precisely because his art, media, performance, and scholarly works helped inaugurate AIDS visual politics.

Navarro, importantly, infused AIDS video activism with the revolutionary spirit of a decolonizing racial and gender critique. His work drew from critical theory and was informed by longer histories of antistatist political movements. Navarro, Juhasz, and other video activists like Gregg Bordowitz, Catherine Gund (Saalfield), and Ellen Spiro were acquainted through their participation in the Whitney Museum of Art Independent Study Program, where critical theory and aesthetic practice were combined (Hallas 2009, 278). Confronted with the AIDS crisis, they formed collectives that responded to misrepresentations with innovations in video that were informed by radical and postmodern theories (Juhasz 1997, 24).

Navarro was cofounder of Damned Interfering Video Activist Television (DIVA TV), which was an ACT UP "affinity group" that "organized to . . . document, provide protection and countersurveillance, and participate" (Juhasz 1995, 62). Affinity groups, according to artist-activist Debra Levine, were derived from "Spanish anarchists in the 1930s" (Levine 2005, 5). Affinity groups were designed to catalyze revolution through "micro-sites of resistance: politically inspired alternative-lifestyle formations existing within dominant culture." ACT UP adapted this model so that affinity groups "doubled as the site of both political action and active caregiving where the able bodies understood themselves as a prosthesis for the disabled body" (Levine 2005, 3). DIVA TV involved "guerrilla video" that was formed through a radical politics of caregiving for those racialized and gendered bodies that were most peripheral to the state and to their white male counterparts (Saalfield and Navarro 1991, 363).

DIVA TV's video style was "alternative" because it simultaneously worked alongside and intervened into other AIDS videos that omitted representations of women and people of color. Juhasz names and describes "alternative AIDS videos" as "indebted to a long tradition of cultural theory and production" and the "struggle for representation: from the Third Cinema and the New American Cinema in the fifties and sixties, to the large shifts in documentary and ethnographic film production and the development of minority cinemas (like the feminist and black film movements) in the seventies, into the production of indigenous media and camcorder activism of the eighties and nineties" (Juhasz 1995, 33). Hence, DIVA TV's documentary practice did not merely *record* political action—it *was* and *is* ongoing revolutionary political action through the legacy of antiracist, feminist, and decolonizing filmmaking, where the methods for creating "images as a form of collective direct action" install "counter-memories" (Saalfield and Navarro 1991, 347) about historically repressed subjects in U.S. media.

In their 1991 essay, Saalfield and Navarro offer an early feminist and queer of color theorization of "queer temporality" that challenges racism, patriarchy, and colonial conceptions of space-time. They argue that "counter-memory activism . . . establishes itself between the pages of official record" (347). AIDS counter-memories are an "internal critique of racism and sexism within ACT UP" and function through "the culture of pleasure and the politics of desire [which] are always threatening to explode the 'official' history or the police record" (Saalfield and Navarro 1991, 347). Navarro's art and activism consistently drew attention to the "stratification of resources along the lines of race and gender not only in dominant culture but in ACT UP itself" (Levine 2005, 10). His cultural productions reveal and intervene into "the price minority subjects pay by joining a predominantly white gay male movement" (Levine 2005, 10).

DIVA TV inserted antiracist, feminist, and anticolonial interruptions into the white male-dominated video archive of ACT UP. The adaptation of Navarro's archival footage rouses counter-memories. Between the folds of scientific and white male heroic progress narratives there emerges a recursive politics involving the circulation of the images of women and queer people of color, in spite of their representational and historical erasure. The footage of Navarro in *How to Survive* is derived primarily from the twenty-nine minute alternative AIDS video *Like a Prayer* (1990), where he appears in what Roger Hallas calls "Jesus Christ Drag." According to Hallas, Navarro's performance as Christ invokes seemingly familiar religious images and discourses, but renders through camp, parody, and black humor uncontainable meaning about the historical traumas that converge upon his body (2009, 9). The images of Navarro fold together and critique the violence of state and religious institutions and their colonial legacies.

Excerpts from *Like a Prayer* form two short sections that serve as transitions in *How to Survive*. Almost forty-five minutes into *How to Survive*, Navarro appears for the first time reporting for the "Fire and Brimstone

FIG. 1. Ray Navarro in "Jesus Christ Drag" during the 1989 "Stop the Church" protest before New York City's St. Patrick's Cathedral. Original footage: *Like a Prayer* (DIVA TV, 1991). Footage re-mediated: Navarro appears for the first time as the image of Christ in *How to Survive a Plague* (2012).

Network." He moves alongside protestors outside a church, swathed in a white robe, and adorned with a crown of thorns. The film places him outside the "die-in" taking place inside New York City's St. Patrick's Cathedral as part of the momentous 1989 "Stop the Church" protest. Navarro's exhilarating and humorous reportage establishes the context for the action as a response to Cardinal John O'Connor's denouncement of condom use. The editing of *How to Survive* conceals that this footage of Navarro resulted from carefully crafted collaborations among video activists. His performance in Jesus drag, however, summons the coalitional labor poured into alternative AIDS videos (fig. 1).

The "Stop the Church" protest was organized through the cooperative action between ACT UP and Women's Health Action and Mobilization (WHAM!). Wrenched from this context and forced into *How to Survive*'s narrative, Navarro's image is ventriloquized to suggest that ACT UP acted alone. His appearance through video, however, reflects joint organizing efforts. *Like a Prayer* was the outcome of DIVA TV's work with ACT UP and WHAM! and was intended to document the action while also educating on safer sex practices. The video addressed the history of the Catholic Church, and deconstructed the mainstream press's inaccurate portrayal of the demonstration. DIVA TV cofounder, Saalfield, explains that Navarro's playful performance of Christ and media reportage decodes mainstream news and exposes its distortion (1993, 344–5). Activists are shown discussing how the mainstream press missed significant coverage of the event and asked them for footage. Once provided, the news media skewed facts about the event. The video points this out while also covering the actions of Operation Ridiculous, which sent clowns to intervene in the "pro-life" organizing events of Operation Rescue (Juhasz 1995, 16).

Anticolonial, feminist, and queer of color critiques are fused together in *Like a Prayer* to intervene into popular media. AIDS and abortion rights are entwined and are irreducible to the "AIDS-ravaged" gay male body or the "hysterical" female body. Jesus-as-drag-as-reporter evokes multiple racial, gender, religious, and sexual significations. Navarro's performance and video production not only affected AIDS visibility but also altered the language of representation—both its articulation and reading practices—to suture seemingly disparate marginal communities. These include but are not limited to women, Latinas/os, and other racial/ethnic groups who are significantly Catholic-identified and those who may generally find a critique of the Church and its colonial history resonant. His image is situated within a broader network of multi-issue, coalitional organizing. Instead of invoking realism by representing the "here and now" of late 1980s and early 1990s crisis activism, Navarro's performance establishes a fantastical mode that reassembles time and memory, time and time again (Gómez-Barris 2008, 112). Through Navarro's queer of color representation, the exceptionalization of the AIDS crisis is placed within the frame of ongoing Western colonial and heteropatriarchal impositions.

A second clip of Navarro, still in Jesus drag and demonstrating condom usage, is taken from *Like a Prayer* and inserted into *How to Survive* to bring the latter film to its narrative climax (fig. 2). According to *How to Survive*, in 1991 and ten years into the pandemic, ACT UP experienced a deep rift resulting from mistrust and the onset of activist fatigue as people continued to die. The hope initially performed by Navarro becomes the marker for the film's moral crisis: What do we do with the images of those we have lost? Navarro's remainders are insistent reminders.[4]

AIDS Video Activism and the Touch of Absence

Analyzing the AIDS documentary film *Silverlake Life: The View from*

Here (1993), Peggy Phelan shows how AIDS media specifically prods us to rethink our attachments to Christian-inflected expectations regarding life and death (1995). Phelan points to the queer temporality of AIDS media wherein the recorded bodies of those who have passed collect in multiple places and times. AIDS media production and audience reception perform a collective practice of care. We hold dear the deaths of others—as we experience our own viscerally imagined vulnerability to death. Even in the attempt by *How to Survive* to abbreviate or edit out the stories of those who have passed, the use of archival AIDS video activist footage inevitably touches and is touched by death. The queer touch of AIDS video activism arouses audience awareness about wrinkles in time and space. AIDS videos invite what Carolyn Dinshaw describes as the "queer historical impulse" (1999, 1), which is the summoning of queer desire in the present to establish "affective relations" with the past that cut across linear time so that "entities past and present touch" (12). Elizabeth Freeman elaborates upon this desire for the past by describing how time folds when "our sexually impoverished present suddenly meets up with a richer past, or as the materials of a failed and forgotten project of the past find their uses now, in a future unimaginable in their time" (2007, 163).

How to Survive stages its last appearance for Navarro in a hospital using footage rarely—if ever—seen by the public. We are reintroduced through a close shot of Navarro seated upright. A dark-blue pattern is stitched across the top of his hospital gown. He is fragile and sickly, yet his hair is swept away from a clean and still-bearded face, his locks tied neatly to the side. His eyes are less focused. The thin fabric outlines his gaunt body (fig. 3). Navarro's mother, Patricia Navarro, introduced to the viewer through a title, cues him to speak to the camera:

> **UNIDENTIFIED VOICE:** Yeah, I just turned it on. OK, rolling. Tell him we're rolling.
>
> **PATRICIA NAVARRO:** The machine is rolling. You can start talking now, honey.
>
> **RAY:** Oh, I didn't know she meant now. What I was gonna say was I just love, I love so much to go up to the tenth floor because no one had ever explained to me that there was going to be light again in the world and that the whole world wasn't going to be dark. Some great challenges face us as young people. We're in our twenties, and . . . and this is the chal-

FIG. 2. Original footage: Navarro appearing in "Jesus Christ Drag" conducting a condom demonstration in *Like a Prayer* (DIVA TV, 1991). Footage re-mediated: Navarro performing the "second coming" of Christ in *How to Survive a Plague* (2012).

> lenge that's been placed in front of me. And, who knows, Little Camera. Lots of other blind, deaf men have lived happy lives.

Navarro's narration is spliced with a scene of him and his mother sitting near a window, presumably on the hospital's tenth floor, looking together at what seems like a greeting card. He continues:

> There are, there are many years to come … let's hope. So … what the hell … life is worth living … isn't it?

Navarro's direct address to the "Little Camera" as an embodied subject indicates a desire to arouse thinking and feeling beyond the subject position and corporeal existence of a human body anchored in a specific time and place. It is an attempt to communicate beyond the dyad of a conversation between the video subject and an ideal viewer (Hallas 2009, 21–26). Navarro appeals with bitter irony to the failed promises of Christ and Western medicine to enact miracles and heal the blind and deaf. He longs for the light, the space and time in which the image of himself might bask eternally before the screen, but he is restrained by the notion that his image

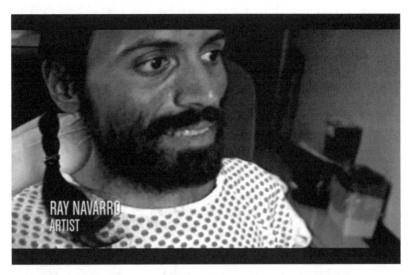

RAY NAVARRO
ARTIST

FIG. 3. Original footage: Navarro is filmed and interviewed in the hospital by Ellen Spiro shortly before his passing. Footage re-mediated: Navarro embodies Jesus Christ as the image of sacrifice in *How to Survive a Plague* (2012).

might give way to a fleeting existence. Navarro concedes to the paradox and possibilities for queer of color visibility.

The year is 1990 and *How to Survive* suggests that Navarro passes from AIDS-related illness. Unlike the deaths of white gay male activists, Navarro's funeral is not portrayed and he is not eulogized. Also not depicted is the fact that Navarro opted to end his life with medical assistance, his mother by his side (*Leap into the Void* 2014). His representation is cut from the broader context of his artistry, the fabric of his organizing labor, and the fold of activist networks. Navarro's excerpted image patches together *How to Survive*'s makeshift narrative where the queer of color image marks a breach in the fabricated tale of AIDS activist progress.

However, even as Navarro's image fades to black, hands that held and cared for his body still hold and care for his image. His mother. The person holding the camera. These hands hold the attention of the audience in this time. *How to Survive* suggests that Patricia Navarro operates the camera. However, at the top of the scene, she is addressed by a third person in the hospital, offscreen, untitled in the film: "Tell him we're rolling." The "Little Camera" is this person's embodiment. As the camera goes dark at the scene's end, we are reminded of the video artist's hands. She chooses what to record, where to direct our attention, and how to hold it. With AIDS, touch is critical.[5] Artist-activists John Greyson, Gregg Bordowitz, Jean Carlomusto, and Catherine Saalfield also created a memorial tape for Navarro to "conceptualiz[e] a reservoir for our friend, which turned out to be a reservoir for collective action" (Saalfield 1993, 33). As they scoured video footage looking for images of Navarro—"even the back of his head or his elbow"—Saalfield writes, they were "longing for an image to last forever, or better, to come back to life." The AIDS video activist archive forms a source for the redistribution of afterlives and the touch of care that reminds us that AIDS is still critical.

How to Survive would not exist as a film if video activists had not cared for the images. Without Navarro and other video activists, aggressive police behavior would not be so well monitored so that direct action could be protected and enabled. Moreover, there would be little to no source archive from which How to Survive could draw its visuals. The explicit intention of alternative AIDS videos to document disenfranchised subjects means the queer of color image must make an appearance in today's mainstream feature-length AIDS activist documentary, even if briefly. How to Survive's AIDS activist narrative begins in 1986 because the moment was critical, but also because that is when the cameras were turned on. These video activists continued the practice of care through hands that critically touch, archive, and distribute the images and care of women and queer of color absence. Viewers are returned to the feminist and queer strategies for documenting AIDS marginality. Images of absence return to touch.

Feminism, Labor, and Queer Love

> There is a force within society that cannot be contained. Call it Queer Theory. Clearly no one could have predicted the visual representation of this theory. —Ray Navarro (Levine 2005)

After our first meeting, Alexandra Juhasz gifted me Video Remains (2005). She said it held answers to questions evoked by Navarro's image. Video Remains looks back at the life of her friend, performing artist Jim Lamb, who died of AIDS-related illness in 1993. The affective and material labor vested in AIDS video activism is feminist and queer because its modes of affiliation challenge individualism, and cross racial, gender, and sexual identitarian boundaries (Hilderbrand 2006, 303–4). Juhasz's "love" for her white, gay, male friend Lamb motivated her to use video activism as "feminist history making: a practice that helps align the poetry, evidence, passion, and politics of AIDS" (2005). She overlays Lamb's footage with more recently recorded interviews with Black and Brown youth negotiating HIV risk, and conversations with lesbian video activists Alisa Lebow, Juanita Mohammed, Sarah Schulman, and Ellen Spiro. These women, one black and three white, "had all loved and supported gay men as they participated in AIDS activism in the late 1980s and early 1990s" (Juhasz 2006, 320).

These lasting queer kinships in the present are linked back to Navarro, who returns at the end of *Video Remains* as a visually formless discourse on queer radical potential. A phone call between Juhasz and Spiro transpires and is partially reproduced here:

> **SPIRO**: There's some footage of Ray Navarro that I only watched once and then I gave it to his mother. I never let it be used in anybody's documentaries or anything, although that would be up to his mother and I don't think that she told anybody. It was just this amazing sit-down with him in the hospital room . . . when he had lost most of his sight to meningitis . . . Ray . . . had become this . . . guru in the hospital. People, everybody was coming to see him and he would just spout amazing things . . . And, one day I was there and I had the camera and I asked him if I could turn it on. He said, "Yes." It was just this strange feeling like I was speaking to someone half on earth and half gone. It was as if . . . he had prepared himself to go. He was never ready to go but suddenly all these [*sic*] amazing poetry came out of his mouth. (Juhasz 2005)

Spiro cared for Navarro and cared about who touched and used his footage. Hubbard surmises that the footage was included in the NYPL's "AIDS Activist Videotape Collection 1985–2000," and subsequently incorporated by France into *How to Survive* (Jim Hubbard, pers. comm.). Regardless, *Video Remains* shows that videos are not discrete end products. Nor can video footage and its usage be controlled. Footage engages in intercourse—images moving in, through, and across each other as remnants. In 2005, even before *How to Survive* made it to mass market, *Video Remains* anticipated that Navarro's image would return through documentary filmmaking. Spiro's recorded voice provides an auditory touch for visually unrepresentable queerness. That touch indexes Navarro's image as it fails technologies of surveillance and narration.

Conclusion: Queerness and "Going Viral"

AIDS scholar-activist Cathy Cohen suggests that queerness has the potential to respond to the growing conservatism of AIDS activism and gay and lesbian identity politics aimed at white gender normative representations in popular culture (Cohen 1997, 439, 445). Simply, queerness performs through the failure to narrate. Borrowing from J. Jack Halberstam, "queer failure" stalls developmentalism and assimilation, offering instead "modes of unbeing and unbecoming [that] propose a different relation to knowledge" (2011, 23). To be clear, the queer of color image does not narrate failure; it fails narration.

The failures of queer of color images invite opportunities to recognize others who fail AIDS specifically, and narratives of biological survival generally; they forge a "politics in the image of exile, of refusal, even of failure" (Love 2007, 71). Cohen and Roderick A. Ferguson argue that we must understand queerness as the historical production of race, wherein Black women, Black families, and Blackness itself are constituted as failures of normative life and historical progress (Cohen 1997; Ferguson 2004). We only need to look to the overwhelming criminalization of Black and Brown people in cases involving HIV transmission, in conjunction with their simultaneous overrepresentation in the pandemic and the U.S. prison system (Stephens 2014; AIDS.gov 2014), to witness how the queer of color image fails the popular narration of AIDS progress. The queer political imagination embraces the failures of normative kinships, national incorporation, and biological survival. It takes an antiracist, feminist, anticapitalist stand against ongoing Euro-American colonial violence. As such, it considers the multiple points of difference that connect various marginal subjects rendered vulnerable to HIV infection and/or state abuse.

While the platforms for video archiving and distribution have changed, the political and visual strategies adopted by activists for social movements against state and colonial terror remain. AIDS afterlives transgress linear history to make possible future feminist and queer practices for videos that "go viral."[6] Situated in the folds of official narratives, queer of color AIDS afterlives make powerful representational and materialist critiques against the invisibilization of feminist labor, as mainstream media commodifies AIDS. These afterlives demonstrate how the means of media production can be perverted so that "viral" videos circulate through the multiplying networks of handheld digital devices to spread alternate stories, generate new social attachments, and spur social movements across peoples, places, and times.

Acknowledgments

My deep appreciation goes out to J. Jack Halberstam, Alexandra Juhasz, Macarena Gómez-Barris, Kara Keeling, Dorinne Kondo, Sarah Schulman, Jim Hubbard, Theodore (Ted) Kerr, Ernesto Moreno, Ho'esta Mo'e'hahne, Crystal Baik, Nishant Shahani, Anjali Nath, R. Benedito Ferrão, Lucas Hilderbrand, Akhila L. Ananth, Feng-Mei Heberer, Nic John Ramos, Mimi Thi Nguyen, and Ramzi Fawaz for incisive and insightful discussions and feedback. I thank all the editors, especially Taylor Black, Matt Brim, Elena Cohen, Claire Horn, and Lauren Hook, and the anonymous readers for their generous care. And, Ray Navarro, whose words, performances, images, and politics have guided me since my early adult years.

Jih-Fei Cheng is assistant professor of feminist, gender, and sexuality studies at Scripps College. He has worked in AIDS and queer of color organizations. His book project is titled *AIDS and Its Afterlives: Race, Gender, and the Queer Radical Imagination*.

Notes

1. To be clear, my critique is not directed at the "real life" politics of individual white men, but rather the oversimplification of their politics and AIDS history in the process of mainstreaming their stories. For instance, the original play *The Normal Heart* is set in the earliest years of the U.S. crisis when public health had not yet taken stock of the emergent epidemic among women and communities of color. Revisiting this past today warrants critical attention to how "Gay-Related Immune Deficiency" (GRID) was renamed "AIDS" once Haitian immigrants who were infected early on were taken into consideration. However, contemporary popular AIDS films continuously jettison this racial history by solely reproducing the narrative of white male protagonists.
2. I draw from Judith Butler's definition of "precarity" as the "politically induced condition in which certain populations suffer from failing social and economic networks of support and become differentially exposed to injury,

violence, and death . . . of maximized vulnerability and exposure . . . to arbitrary state violence and to other forms of aggression that are not enacted by states and against which states do not offer adequate protection" (2009, ii).

3. According to Jim Hubbard, "ACT UP's first demonstration on March 24, 1987, referred to often simply as 'Wall Street,' resulted in a 10% drop in price of AZT. 'Wall Street II' took place on March 24, 1988. 'Sell Wellcome,' the demo[nstration] where the ACT UP demonstrators [got] inside the [New York Stock Exchange and] delayed the opening, took place [on] September 14, 1989 and resulted in a further 10% drop in the price" (Jim Hubbard, pers. comm.).

4. Navarro's image functions much like Kara Keeling's "image of common sense" where "common sense is a shared set of memory-images and . . . commonly habituated sensory-motor movements [that] enable alternative perceptions and . . . alternative knowledges" (2007, 20).

5. Laura U. Marks's notion of "touch" refers to symbolization and hapticism in media, whereas I am interested in how materiality and symbolization intersect to mark the embodied labor of AIDS subjects in the performance and production of their representations (Marks 2002, xi–xiii).

6. Tony Sampson argues, "Virality is no metaphor," and calls for a "nonrepresentational approach" (2012, 4). By dismissing representation, Sampson also dismisses how bodies of color are central and yet disappeared from viral discourse generally and AIDS discourse specifically.

Works Cited

AIDS.gov. 2014. "U.S. Statistics." Accessed June 23. http://aids.gov/
hiv-aids-basics/hiv-aids-101/statistics/.

Associated Press. 2014. "Former Act Up Activist Defends FDA Bureaucracy He Once Railed Against." *FoxBusiness*, August 11. http://www.foxbusiness.com/markets/2014/08/11/former-act-up-activist-defends-fda-bureaucracy-once-railed-against/?utm_source=feedburner&utm_medium=feed&utm_campaign=Feed%3A+foxbusiness%2Flatest+%28Internal+-+Latest+News+-+Text%29.

Ayala, George, Keletso Makofane, Glenn-Milo Santos, Jack Beck, Tri D. Do, Pato Hebert, Patrick A. Wilson, Thomas Pyun, and Sonya Arreola. 2013. "Access to Basic HIV-Related Services and PrEP Acceptability Among Men Who Have Sex with Men Worldwide: Barriers, Facilitators, and Implications for Combination Prevention." *Journal of Sexually Transmitted Diseases* 2013: 1–11. doi: 10.1155/2013/953123.

Berlant, Lauren. 2011. *Cruel Optimism*. Durham, NC: Duke University Press.

Brim, Matt. 2013. "Queer Pedagogical Desire." *WSQ* 41 (3/4): 173–189.

Butler, Judith. 2009. "Performativity, Precarity and Sexual Politics." *Revista de Antropología Iberoamericana* 4 (3): i–xiii.

Cohen, Cathy. 1997. "Punks, Bulldaggers, and Welfare Queens: The Radical Potential of Queer Politics?" *GLQ: A Journal of Lesbian and Gay Studies* 3 (4): 437–65.

Dinshaw, Carolyn. 1999. *Getting Medieval: Sexualities and Communities, Pre- and Postmodern.* Durham, NC: Duke University Press.

Ferguson, Roderick A. 2004. *Aberrations in Black: Toward a Queer of Color Critique.* Minneapolis, MN: University of Minnesota Press.

Freeman, Elizabeth. 2007. Introduction to *GLQ: A Journal of Gay and Lesbian Studies.* 13 (2/3): 153–76.

Gómez-Barris, Macarena. 2008. *Where Memory Dwells: Culture and State Violence in Chile.* Berkeley, CA: University of California Press.

Halberstam, J. Jack. 2011. *The Queer Art of Failure.* Durham, NC: Duke University Press.

Hallas, Roger. 2009. *Reframing Bodies: AIDS, Bearing Witness, and the Queer Moving Image.* Durham, NC: Duke University Press.

Hilderbrand, Lucas. 2006. "Retroactivism." *GLQ: A Journal of Gay and Lesbian Studies* 12 (2): 301–15.

"How to Survive a Plague." 2014. YouTube video, 2:18. http://surviveaplague.com/trailer.

Juhasz, Alexandra. 1995. *AIDS TV: Identity, Community, and Alternative Video.* Durham, NC: Duke University Press.

———. 1997. "Making AIDS Video as Radical Pedagogy." *The Radical Teacher* 50: 23–29.

———. 2005. "Feminist History Making and Video Remains (in exchange with Antoinette Burton)." *JUMP CUT: A Contemporary Review of Media.* http://ejumpcut.org/archive/jc48.2006/AIDsJuhasz/index.html.

———. 2006. "Video Remains: Nostalgia, Technology, and Queer Archive Activism." *GLQ: A Journal of Gay and Lesbian Studies* 12 (2): 319–28.

Keeling, Kara. 2007. *The Witch's Flight: The Cinematic, the Black Femme, and the Image of Common Sense.* Durham, NC: Duke University Press.

Leap into the Void (blog). 2014. "A Day Without Art." Accessed March 3. http://imoralist.blogspot.com/2008/12/day-without-artist-ray-navarro.html.

Levine, Debra. 2005. "Another Kind of Love: A Performance of Prosthetic Politics." *e-misférica: Sexuality* and *Politics in the Americas* 2 (2): 1–20. http://hemisphericinstitute.org/journal/2_2/pdf/levine.pdf.

Love, Heather. 2007. *Feeling Backward: Loss and the Politics of Queer History.* Cambridge, MA: Harvard University Press.

Marks, Laura U. 2002. *Touch: Sensuous Theory and Multisensory Media.* Minneapolis, MN: University of Minnesota Press.

The New School. 2014. "Revisiting the AIDS Crisis: A Conversation with David France and Jim Hubbard." YouTube video, 1:29:21. March 11. https://www. youtube.com/watch?v=1jJ1nOsT4uQ.

O'Neal, Reilly. 2015. "Women and PrEP: A Q&A with Dr. Judy Auerbach." BETA, March 10. http://betablog.org/women-and-prep-qa-judy-auerbach/.

Phelan, Peggy. 1995. "Dying Man with a Movie Camera: Silverlake Life: The View from Here." *GLQ: A Journal of Gay and Lesbian Studies* 2: 379–98.

Saalfield, Catherine, and Ray Navarro. 1991. "Shocking Pink Praxis: Race and Gender on the ACT UP Frontlines." In *Inside/Out: Lesbian and Gay Theories*, edited by Diana Fuss, 341–72. New York: Routledge.

Saalfield, Catherine. 1993. "On the Make: Activist Video Collectives." In *Queer Looks: Perspectives on Lesbian and Gay Film and Video*, edited by Martha Gever, John Greyson, and Pratibha Parmar, 21–37. New York: Routledge.

Sampson, Tony. 2012. *Virality: Contagion Theory in the Age of Networks*. Minneapolis, MN: University of Minnesota Press.

Schulman, Sarah. 2012. *The Gentrification of the Mind: Witness to a Lost Imagination*. Berkeley, CA: University of California Press.

Stephens, Charles. 2014. "Black Gay Male Criminalization and the Case of Michael Johnson." *RH Reality Check*, August 28. http://rhrealitycheck.org/article/2014/08/28/black-gay-male-criminalization-case-michael-johnson/.

Sullivan, James. 2012. "'How to Survive a Plague' a Triumph of Activism." *Boston Globe*, September 29. http://www.bostonglobe.com/arts/movies/2012/09/29/how-survive-plague-triumph-activism/gPTGBJ7MsM1BeSkhbtukFP/story.html.

PART II. **UNTIMELY SURVIVORS**

Who Is Chandni bibi?: Survival as Embodiment in Disaster Disrupted Northern Pakistan

Omer Aijazi

In our academic contemplations, we mistakenly take for granted the qualities that make us human.[1] These include the very ability to form meaningful relationships, negotiate care, and experience a moral life despite adversity (Finnström 2008; Kleinman 2006). We are, however, inclined to describe the human experience in adversity far more precisely, clinically, and intellectually, allowing our scientific impulses to separate, categorize, and label. This includes the modalities of testimony, evidence, and reparation, which establish trauma as a valid moral category pushing for the political and cultural recognition of its victims and survivors (Fassin and Rechtman 2009). While it is somewhat useful to set apart our protagonists in calculated ways—to highlight the extraordinariness of their lived experiences—we may be unknowingly contributing to their dehumanization as somebody entirely else (McGown 2003; Swartz 2006). These faulty new personas we create are at risk of being noncomplex, quite ready for co-option by problematic machineries of humanitarianism, development, and social policy (Kleinman et al. 1996; Malkki 1996).

Admittedly we have come full circle, first by investing thought in establishing the very vocabularies of victim and survivor (Agamben 1998; Bouris 2007) and then allowing their absorption back into everyday sensibilities, fearing that we may have overlooked the ordinariness of the spaces where much of the work of survival is enacted (Baines and Gauvin 2014; Das 2007). Curiously, as academics we are engaged in an inherently fraught intellectual project that disembowels and defragments humans and then painstakingly pieces them back together.

To elaborate these concerns, I explore the life of Chandni bibi,[2] a resi-

WSQ: Women's Studies Quarterly 44: 1 & 2 (Spring/Summer 2016) © 2016 by Omer Aijazi. All rights reserved.

dent of the remote Siran Valley in Northern Pakistan, and her navigation of the 2005 Kashmir and Northern Areas Earthquake. The earthquake killed 73,000, severely injured over 128,304, and affected some 5.1 million people throughout the Himalayan region.[3] Contrary to the claims of her family and community that she had struggled with her vision since childhood, Chandni bibi insists that the earthquake made her completely blind. She describes this experience as a "taking away of light, brightness and illumination." In order to complicate the victim/survivor binary routinely presented in academic, humanitarian, and other interventionist discourses on disaster survivors, I juxtapose the seemingly mundane details of Chandni bibi's daily life with the calm, incremental, accretive violence of natural disasters (Nixon 2011). In this way, I reveal the "ordinariness" of survival—which is rarely achieved through some grand transcendent gesture (Das 2007). Rather, Chandni bibi's story is an achingly human one, mired in quotidian details. By revealing how she understands her encounter with the earthquake, I provide an alternative to interpreting her experiences in purely clinical and reductive terms.

This paper is based on a series of interviews and ethnographic research conducted with Chandni bibi at her home in Siran Valley.[4] Siran is one of Northern Pakistan's several forgotten valleys, hidden among the cracks and crevices of the lesser known Himalayan region. It rarely appears on any map and is rather unceremoniously absorbed into the boundaries of the larger Khyber Paktunkhwa province. Siran is dispersed into numerous sparsely populated, smaller villages. Modest houses with mud and corrugated iron sheet roofs dot its mountainscapes.[5] To an outsider these houses appear out of place, but they are rather strategically placed based on local understandings of acceptable topography, flat enough to construct a homestead. The terrain is rugged and homes are connected via narrow, makeshift mountain pathways. Residents overcome this apparent lack of connectivity with considerable ease, and do not let the trivialities of topography interfere with everyday life.[6]

Admittedly, I arrive in the valley with at least some disciplinary baggage, troubled by an unresolved past as a humanitarian worker in similar spaces (Aijazi 2014). I am here to understand social repair and remaking after natural disasters (Aijazi 2015). I have identified Chandni bibi using conventional markers of vulnerability such as "disability," "extreme poverty," and "old age," arbitrary categories commonly used to demarcate and sift through target populations after humanitarian emergencies. Coincidentally, Chandni bibi is also considered "highly vulnerable" by

FIG. 1. Pictured on the immediate right, Chandni bibi's home in Siran Valley. Photographs are included after obtaining her consent.

her community because she is blind, single, and "beyond marriageable age." She also lived through the earthquake. After obtaining permission from her and from her family, I enter their home. She is not entirely comfortable with my presence. I ask her name. She hesitates. "My name is Chandni, the earthquake extinguished the light of my eyes" (Chandni bibi, unpublished data).

Who Is Chandni bibi?

Quiet laughter and an introspective silence—which should not be mistaken for a failure in communication—steadily punctuate our interviews. Chandni bibi's quietness can be understood as a deliberate reflection on the astonishment and incredulity of being interviewed and the peculiar insistence of our questions.

Centrality of Home

Home is a necessary constant for Chandni bibi (fig. 1). It reflects the materiality of a familiar space and actively structures her social relations and everyday life. Home and its implied constancy allow Chandni bibi to remain anchored in the very same house and village where she was born.

Once managed by her parents, Chandni bibi's younger brother now heads the household, which includes his wife and their children. Chandni bibi explains: "We have been living here since the beginning with our parents; we have no other place to call home." Their home is at a distance from other members of their caste and extended family:

> We are the only ones here. Our relatives used to live close to us before the earthquake but moved away after it. Now they rarely come to visit us. When they do visit us, we enjoy their company. They tell us about their lives and we share with them some of our stories. I have not been to their house in over two years. (Chandni bibi, unpublished data)

The limited degree to which Chandni bibi and her household are embedded in their caste and extended family signals the fragile nature of their village social networks. It also highlights the extent of the disruption that followed the 2005 earthquake, which in addition to causing material destruction and loss of life, also reorganized social relationships. This is a particularly important consequence for Chandni bibi, who due to her visual impairment is unable to visit her now dispersed social relations. Chandni bibi's home, however, continues to serve as a nucleus for her relatives and also for other village women operating outside the micropolitics of caste configurations: "There are no places as such in the village which are easily accessible by women [without intense public scrutiny] or where I can go. The women and girls come here to our house and sit with us" (Chandni bibi, unpublished data).

Relationships of Care

Chandni bibi's attachment to her home is partially cemented by memories of her parents. Her mother died when she was very young and Chandni bibi only offers a limited conscious recollection of her *ammi* (mother):

> I was very young, I wasn't very old [when my mother died]. I could not even walk; I could not get from one point to the other [pointing at two opposite corners of the room]. Maybe I could have walked just a little bit. When *ammi* died, I was perhaps three years old [gesturing with her hand how tall she must have been]. (Chandni bibi, unpublished data)

Chandni bibi describes the transitions in the household with the loss of her parents: "My mother used to look after me, then she died. After her death, *abbu* [my father] took care of me. When he also died, *bhai* [my brother] took over the responsibility of looking after me. Abbu died of old age." Chandni bibi describes her relationships via the functionality of care, defining both her parents and brother in terms of their responsibilities in looking after her. She does not explicitly elaborate on any emotional attachments with her parents, but her love for them is apparent throughout our interviews: "After the death of my parents, my life became very constricted." Chandni bibi also speaks about her brother and his wife in a similar fashion:

> After *abbu*'s death, *bhai* took care of me. I live with him, I have no place else to go, he is my only brother. Who else will take care of me, if not him? He feeds me and buys me clothes. During the day, he works on daily wages [as an unskilled laborer], and in the night he comes home with tea and sugar; this is how he does it. When I need something such as clothes, shoes etc., I ask him. He then gets them for me. I was very happy when he got married. I was glad that now a *bhabi* [sister-in-law] would enter the family who will also look after me. Abbu arranged for his marriage and found him a bride; *ammi* was already dead. Bhai takes care of me; otherwise, I will just die. (Chandni bibi, unpublished data)

Chandni bibi is very concerned about her self-preservation. This is accentuated by fears of her visual impairment, being unmarried, the death of her parents, and the isolation of living far from any other relatives. From her life experiences and perhaps from the general nature of a patriarchal society, Chandni bibi has internalized that she must always be taken care of. She has calibrated her relationships, including with her sister-in-law, in similar approximations.

Chandni bibi uses the collective of the family to speak about her self. Her notion of family is inextricably tied to home both as a place of uninterrupted residence and also as a space of familial continuity. When initially asked who lives in the house, she replied: "Myself, *bhai*, *ammi*, and *abbu*." Throughout our interviews, Chandni bibi often speaks in plural pronouns, referring to the collective of the family (*ammi*, *abbu*, and *bhai*), which forms an important component of her identity.

Unfortunately, after the earthquake familial ties beyond the immediate household did not translate into any form of assistance or comfort, further reinforcing Chandni bibi's reliance on her brother. She shared with us her disappointment: "The Rabb [Allah, the Sustainer of life] is a witness! My brother is the only one who looks after me, no *chacha* [father's brother] or *mamoo* [mother's brother], not even the neighbors, nobody" (Chandni bibi, unpublished data).

Everyday Life

Chandni bibi's daily life closely revolves around her home. She spends her time reading *namaz* (Islamic prayers offered five times a day), warming herself by the fireplace (which doubles as a stove), and resting on the *charpoy* (traditional bed). She explains, "This is my routine; it is not much. This is how my life passes. I also pick up the children. I can't really do any real work, just remain sitting all day long." She expands on her relationship with her brother's children, "Their mother leaves them at home so I look after them. I like them. They don't bother me as such, they are sometimes naughty, but my time passes. I guess there is little pleasure in my life."

Chandni bibi looks after her brother's children and is therefore a caregiver as well as a care receiver. This awards her a place of responsibility within the household, allowing her to partake tangibly in homemaking. Chandni bibi, therefore, occupies a relational position of accountability, necessary for remaining embedded within the household.

Being quite aware of her limited mobility, Chandni bibi shares some spaces accessible to her outside the house: "I sit here [pointing toward a tree], I come outside and sit under this tree to enjoy the sunshine and think, to comfort my heart" (fig. 2).

Occasionally, Chandni bibi also visits her sister-in-law's mother. These visits placate her heart, she explains:

> There is no other place that I can get to. Sometimes my heart feels constricted [I feel unsettled]. To feel better and more grounded I go to her house. She is my *chachi* [my father's sister in addition to being my sister-in-law's mother]. She is a good person. I don't give or take anything from her. We just sit together and talk, then I come back home. Visiting her makes my heart feels better. (Chandni bibi, unpublished data)

Chandni bibi inhabits the surrounding geography as best as she can. She frequents spaces outside of her home, even though they may be in the immediate vicinity. She also invests in relationships—such as with her aunt and her brother's children—as a means of keeping herself grounded and

FIG. 2. Chandni bibi's space for deep contemplation.

anchored within the familiarity and continuity of the family unit. Since she is unable to visit other relatives, Chandni bibi places great importance on being able to visit her *chachi*. These visits provide her with the possibility of forming meaningful connections with others at her own volition. More importantly, Chandni bibi is deeply invested in the project of taking care of her heart. This involves praying, forming meaningful and codependent relationships, and finding spaces near or around her home where she can be outdoors and engage in reflective contemplation.

Revelations of Snow and Rain

Winters are a complex phenomenon for the residents of Siran Valley, including Chandni bibi. The challenging season reveals important insights into her life, such as her spirituality, complex relationships with her brother and home, and the material and existential experiences of the extreme season. According to Chandni bibi, winters are the most difficult time of the year. Winters restrict her mobility, already constrained by her visual impairment and the difficult topography, cementing Chandni bibi to her home in a rather ambivalent relationship:

When there is heavy rain and snow, life becomes very difficult. Other people can get out of their homes and move around while I remain stuck in this room. I feel very unsettled but I keep my heart strong and do *sabar*. The sunshine feels good, in the winters. It is not that I can go places in any case, but when it rains my heart sinks. I feel worried. (Chandni bibi, unpublished data)

Sabar is Arabic for patience, and is the Islamic spiritual practice of remaining steadfast and not relinquishing hope in the face of adversity. It is the working of the heart and spirit (as opposed to the body and mind). Islamic traditions repeatedly instruct believers to practice *sabar*, and narrate numerous stories of overwhelming oppression and structural constraints through which prophets and pious people emerged stronger by remaining steadfast in their beliefs, both political and spiritual. Chandni bibi describes her life during winters as a concrete embodiment of *sabar*.[7] Chandni bibi contends that the cold interferes with both her vision and mobility:

My eyes don't open in the winters, even right now I have difficulties keeping my eyes open. In the summers when it is warm, one can at least step outside; go here and there. But in winters my eyes remain sealed shut, even right now my head hurts. (Chandni bibi, unpublished data)

Chandni bibi quickly grounds herself back into the concreteness of her experiences indicating that the winter months pose a combination of material and existential threats: "If during winters one wears warm clothes and warm socks then one can get by and it is not so bad, but if these all are not available then how can one survive the winters?"

Even though Chandni bibi is grateful to her brother for providing her with the basic necessities of life, including allowing her to stay in his home and remain established within the family unit, the tensions that punctuate their relationship are also evident. When asked why she never sought treatment for her blindness, from either a medical doctor or traditional/ spiritual healer, Chandni bibi responded:

Ever since my eyes lost their light, I have not sought any treatment. Well, *ammi* and *abbu* have died, so who is there to ask otherwise? My brother is good to me, but he also has his own children, which he must take care of. He brings his wage home, feeds himself and also feeds me as well as his children. Perhaps there is a cure for my blindness, but I do not have the means [to afford it]. (Chandni bibi, unpublished data)

The Earthquake

The 2005 earthquake was an event of unprecedented magnitude, rupturing common beliefs about the physical and social worlds. Survivors were forced to confront displacement and large numbers of deaths; loss of property, livestock, and food reserves; and the destruction of livelihoods and agricultural lands. In addition, the earthquake ruptured confidence in the permanence and stability of the physical and social worlds and the protections they previously guaranteed. Chandni bibi recalls her memory of the earthquake:

> We were sitting outside in the courtyard, sifting through the corn, when the mountains started to quiver. We ran down to the banks of the Siran River. We spent the next few days there by the river under the stars. We did not go back home because we were scared the roof might collapse on us in our sleep. The possibility of the mountains collapsing terrified me. What if there is a rockslide? What if the house fell? Several village houses had completely crumbled, there was dust everywhere and it turned very dark, I was very scared. Our animals died, the fodder we had collected for winters, the boxes where we store corn, our fields, our home, they were all crushed by the mountains. I don't know why the earthquake occurred, only Allah knows. It is part of His workings. I don't know of these mysteries. (Chandni bibi, unpublished data)

A Changed Life

Chandni bibi insists that when she was a little girl she could see rather clearly and would play in the village just like other children: "I could make out everything, every little detail." She describes her routine before the disaster:

> I used to enjoy sweeping the floors and making *roti* [flat bread]. I could easily get around, no problem! I would get meals ready for the family, remove any rocks in the field brought down by the landslide, even plough the ground getting it ready in time for planting season. I would wake up in the morning, make chai, sweep the floors, make *roti*, get the meals ready. (Chandni bibi, unpublished data)

The earthquake had profound consequences for Chandni bibi, as she holds the event responsible for the loss of her vision. She contends, "Yes! My eyesight escaped during the earthquake. Now I can barely keep my eyes open. The earthquake forced the light out of my eyes. What can be more jarring than that?" Chandni bibi elaborates:

> When a person closes their eyes, what is left? Absolutely nothing, just darkness, this is how my life has changed. My eyes are my biggest afflic-tion. I am unable to feel happiness anymore. When the day of *Eid* comes [Islamic day of celebration] I feel upset, I cannot freely go out into the world and even attend a wedding. (Chandni bibi, unpublished data)

Survival as Embodiment

For Chandni bibi, the most significant consequence of the earthquake was the complete loss of her vision. Other community members were fairly certain that Chandni bibi had difficulties with her vision since childhood. Her family also suggested this was the case, though they acknowledged that her vision became significantly worse after the earthquake. Through-out our conversations, however, Chandni bibi insists that the earthquake is responsible for her blindness. She delineates in detail how the earth-quake and its resulting damage to her eyesight impacted her ability to con-tribute to the household—essential for maintaining her place in the home.

Instead of ascertaining the actual causes of Chandni bibi's blindness or validating the factual nature of her claims, I focus on her insistence that her blindness was a direct consequence of the earthquake. Paul Connerton has long argued that societies and individuals remember in multiple ways, including through the incorporation of social memory into the human body (1989). In her blindness, Chandni bibi embodies the social experience of the earthquake, where "bodily memory, biogra-phy, and social history merged" (Kleinman and Kleinman 1994, 714). Drawing on Kleinman and Kleinman, it is possible to read Chandni bi-bi's experience of constantly carrying the burden of the earthquake with her as a way of ensuring that the event is not disremembered and there-fore rendered insignificant. I understand Chandni bibi's engagement with this active process of remembering as a way of manifesting the so-cial and personal experience of the earthquake in the loss of her vision. While other earthquake survivors may have tried to forget the disaster to facilitate a return to a life of normalcy, I argue that Chandni bibi carries the memory of the event with her at all times.

Another important way Chandni bibi navigates the uncertainties of the future and embodies her survival is through her spirituality and investment in taking care of her heart:

> I like to offer my *namaz* [prayers], I read them with the full attention of my heart, I feel peace. I do not enjoy any act more then praying. I pray that Allah keeps us all in safety and under His protection. I pray that my eyes regain their vision and light. I do not ask for anything else. I am hopeful about my eyes, that my vision comes back, the light returns to my eyes. Then my life will pass smoothly. I just hope Allah gives me this much, because He is actually the only one who can give me such a gift. (Chandni bibi, unpublished data)

Chandni bibi hopes to regain her eyesight, so she can live life on her own terms and participate in the important task of homemaking. Through her spirituality, practices of prayer, and *sabar* she is able to maintain hopes and desires for the future, and invest in the act of living in ways that matter deeply (Kleinman 1999). Her efforts toward taking care of her heart are in line with her aspirations for the future. She elaborates:

> [If I regain my vision] I will continue to live with my brother. I am longing to immerse myself in the surrounding environment, to go visit my relatives, but without any light in my eyes I cannot do any of these. I just wish Allah can return my vision. This is my heart's desire. If I can get my eyes back, that will be gold for me. (Chandni bibi, unpublished data)

Closure

Chandni bibi is deeply spiritual and identifies as a devout Muslim woman. It is important that we don't separate her practice and embodiment of Islam from her unique cultural, social, and political context. Rather, by emphasizing her spirituality and commitment to Islam, I have attempted to demonstrate how Chandni bibi reinhabits daily life, providing us with important insights on the mundane vocation of survival.[8]

Speculating on Chandni bibi's loss of vision, a staff member of the World Food Programme remarked that perhaps she is deficient in some essential micronutrient, insisting on a purely physiological reason for her blindness, which may be rectified by a targeted micronutrient intervention. On the other hand, those in the medical establishment insist that her blindness is most likely a symptom of post-traumatic stress disorder and suggest that she requires an immediate psychological assessment. This may be true, however, I am interested in presenting Chandni bibi's complex engagement with the 2005 earthquake without imposing any predefined parameters, which could limit our interpretations of her experiences. Instead of focusing on the event (the disaster) as a state of exception external to her immediate reality and lifeworld, I have focused on how the earthquake and its lingering effects continue to unfold in Chandni bibi's daily life, and more importantly, how she navigates these enduring consequences as rooted within her own vulnerabilities. In reading Chandni bibi's experiences of the earthquake against the nuanced features of her daily life (home, family, spirituality, navigation of the harsh winters), it becomes possible to conclude that she embodies the social and personal experience of the earthquake in her blindness. Carrying the burden of the experience of the earthquake in this way ensures that the event will never be forgotten and rendered insignificant. For Chandni bibi, continuation of life and survivability are not dependent on the erasure and reappropriation of her past experiences, but rather on embracing these experiences. I maintain that Chandni bibi's loss of vision is an important, necessary, and valid way for her to process the spectacular experience of the earthquake and the stabilities of the physical and social worlds it challenged.

Chandni bibi's insistence that the earthquake was responsible for the loss of her vision indicates that disasters are lived, experienced, and embodied in multiple ways. She challenges the very category of the static *disaster survivor*, a socially constructed identity dependent on limiting "human experiences of disruption to sterile, laboratory states" and disallowing "disrupted bodies from articulating their experiences in other expressions, styles and embodiments" (Aijazi 2015, 22). Interestingly, Chandni bibi's somatic response to the earthquake is reflective of similar claims made by other disaster survivors in the valley. Several survivors reported that since the earthquake, they have had difficulty recalling immediate tasks and recent conversations, indicating a rupture in short-term memory. Others complained of a marked increase in body pains, aches, and stomach ulcers. At least one other long-term resident of the valley whom I interviewed reported a rapid decline in his vision. Like Chandni bibi, he attributes his visual impairment to the 2005 earthquake.

What does such an enrichment of the disaster subject offer us? For one, it decenters the mental health, human rights, and other emancipatory interventionist agendas—which heavily rely on the active oversimplification of the disaster subject in order to demonstrate a seamless fit between identifiable survivor needs and planned assistance. If social scientists and humanitarian practitioners assess human actions and experiences in an exclusively clinical way, they risk being denied an understanding of the many less obvious and/or idiosyncratic ways survivors react to and cope with disruption.

What can the interventionist machinery *really* offer Chandni bibi? In order to answer this question, it is necessary to locate Chandni bibi within the broader context of humanitarian assistance and disaster recovery, which constitute the principal international and national response to the catastrophe. Siran received considerable attention in the aftermath of the earthquake. As one NGO manager reported, "Donors were throwing money left, center, and right. They would come to our office and beg us to take on projects" (Anees Ahmad, unpublished data). Chandni bibi is a beneficiary. During displacement, her household received food rations and financial compensation for rebuilding their home.[9] Chandni bibi's household was often selected for assistance by humanitarian agencies, since her compounded vulnerabilities, especially her blindness, made her the quintessential "helpless victim." While the humanitarian machinery closed their file on Siran just two years after the earthquake—wrongfully signaling recovery (or the drying up of international funds)—I show that Chandni bibi continues to struggle through the lingering consequences of the earthquake. There has been no recovery for her: "My eyes didn't have light after the earthquake, they still don't [nothing has changed]" (Chandni bibi, unpublished data).

Acknowledgments

This research would not have been possible without the assistance of my research staff: Ambreen Khan, Mubashir Nawaz Khan, and our skillful driver Aurangzaib. I acknowledge Haashar Association, a grassroots organization working in Pakistan's extreme North, for hosting my research. Financial support for this work was received from the USAID-funded Competitive Grants Program—a joint initiative of the Planning Commission of Pakistan and the Pakistan Strategy Support Program; International Food Policy Research Institute (IFPRI); the International

Development Research Center (IDRC); the United Nations Office for the Coordination of Humanitarian Affairs (OCHA); and the Liu Institute for Global Issues, University of British Columbia. This research was given ethics review approval by the University of British Columbia Behavioural Research Ethics Board.

Omer Aijazi is a PhD candidate at the University of British Columbia. A former humanitarian, his research examines social repair after natural disasters as informed by the lived experiences of disaster survivors in two remote Himalayan valleys in Northern Pakistan.

Notes

1. I use the pronoun "we" to reflect my complicity with the academic establishment despite Pepper's (2006) warnings of the deception of a false consensus.
2. "Bibi" is used to address women in Pakistan and is typically paired with a given name. In addition to implying respect, "bibi" also structures social interactions between opposite genders by predefining these exchanges as strictly nonsexual and distant, denying any forms of possible intimacy.
3. Natural disasters are frequent in Northern Pakistan. In 2010, monsoon floods ravaged the region again, affecting some twenty million people across the country. A large flood also devastated Siran in 1992, details of which are poorly documented. These are in addition to frequently recurring, smaller events including seasonal landslides, snowstorms, flash floods, and glacier melts.
4. Fieldwork was conducted during November and December 2014. A total of three sets of interviews were conducted with Chandni bibi. Each set lasted from sixty to one hundred twenty minutes. In accordance with local expectations of gender segregation, a female research assistant conducted these interviews in the local Hindko language. Each successive interview was based on the responses received in the previous round. I meticulously reviewed each round of interviews and depending on participant responses, drafted follow-up questions and sought clarification on previous responses where required. This allowed a feedback loop between the primary researcher (myself) and the research subject. Chandni bibi's sister-in-law and brother were also occasionally consulted. Interviews were supplemented with elaborate ethnographic methods including participant observations and walks conducted with Chandni bibi by the primary researcher as well as the female research assistant. All research transactions took place in Chandni bibi's home. In addition, for at least two months, I was embedded within Chandni

bibi's village in Siran, and conducted similar interviews with other residents, village elders, and humanitarian aid workers. Chandni bibi's name has been changed to protect her identity.

5. These iron sheets are remnants of the intense humanitarian action that took place in the wake of the 2005 earthquake. While this temporarily brought Siran into the national and international spotlight, the valley quickly faded into the background as a result of an equally rapid humanitarian withdrawal.

6. It is important to understand that the geography of the region intimately shapes everyday life and structures notions of community and belonging, setting residents apart from mainland Pakistan. In the absence of any central spaces, which could serve as a focal point for locals, familial units organized into immediate and extended households form the standard parameters of one's social world and relationships. Complex caste and tribal relations further exacerbate this sense of fragmentation.

7. It should be noted that the 2005 earthquake also occurred at the onset of the winter season.

8. I explore in more detail Islam and agentival capacity after natural disasters in another paper. See Aijazi and Panjwani 2015.

9. The money was spent on legal proceedings challenging the local landlords, who, being the legal owners of her family's land, demanded that the reconstruction money should be given to them. Due to a shortage of funds, Chandni bibi's house never reached completion, and unlike some of her neighbors, the roof of her home is still made of mud instead of iron sheets.

Works Cited

Agamben, Giorgio. 1998. *Homo Sacer: Sovereign Power and Bare Life.* Translated by Daniel Heller-Roazen. Stanford, CA: Stanford University Press.

Aijazi, Omer. 2014. "The Imaginations of Humanitarian Assistance: A Machete to Counter the Crazy Forest of Varying Trajectories." *UnderCurrents: Journal of Critical Environmental Studies* 18: 46–51.

———. 2015. "Theorizing a Social Repair Orientation to Disaster Recovery: Developing Insights for Disaster Recovery Policy and Programming." *Global Social Welfare* 2 (1): 15–28.

Aijazi, Omer, and Dilnoor Panjwani. 2015. "Religion in Spaces of Social Disruption: Re-Reading the Public Transcript of Disaster Relief in Pakistan." *International Journal of Mass Emergencies and Disasters* 33 (1): 28–54.

Baines, Erin, and Lara Rosenoff Gauvin. 2014. "Motherhood and Social Repair after War and Displacement in Northern Uganda." *Journal of Refugee Studies* 27 (2): 282–300.

Bouris, Erica. 2007. *Complex Political Victims*. Bloomfield, CT: Kumarian Press.

Connerton, Paul. 1989. *How Societies Remember*. Cambridge: Cambridge University Press.

Das, Veena. 2007. *Life and Words: Violence and the Descent into the Ordinary*. Berkeley, CA: University of California Press.

Fassin, Didier, and Richard Rechtman. 2009. *The Empire of Trauma: An Inquiry into the Condition of Victimhood*. Princeton, NJ: Princeton University Press.

Finnström, Sverker. 2008. *Living with Bad Surroundings: War, History, and Everyday Moments in Northern Uganda*. Durham, NC: Duke University Press.

Kleinman, Arthur. 1999. "Experience and Its Moral Modes: Culture, Human Conditions, and Disorder." In *The Tanner Lectures on Human Values*, edited by G. B. Peterson. Salt Lake City: University of Utah Press.

———. 2006. *What Really Matters: Living a Moral Life Amidst Uncertainty and Danger*. Oxford: Oxford University Press.

Kleinman, Arthur, Veena Das, and Margaret Lock. 1996. Introduction to *Daedalus* 125 (1): xi–xx.

Kleinman, Arthur, and Joan Kleinman. 1994. "How Bodies Remember: Social Memory and Bodily Experience of Criticism, Resistance, and Delegitimation following China's Cultural Revolution." *New Literary History* 25 (3): 707–23.

Malkki, Liisa. H. 1996. "Speechless Emissaries: Refugees, Humanitarianism, and Dehistoricization." *Cultural Anthropology* 11 (3): 377–404.

McGown, Rima Berns. 2003. "Writing Across Difference: Standing on Authentic Ground." *Journal of Muslim Minority Affairs* 23 (1): 163–71.

Nixon, Rob. 2011. *Slow Violence and the Environmentalism of the Poor*. Cambridge, MA: Harvard University Press.

Peppers, Cathy. 2006. "The Dangerous Pronoun: An Ecopoetics of 'We.'" *International Journal of the Arts in Society* 1 (2): 93–100.

Swartz, Sally. 2006. "The Third Voice: Writing Case-notes." *Feminism & Psychology* 16 (4): 427–44.

"In This Told-Backward Biography": Marianne Moore Against Survival in Her Queer Archival Poetry

Elien Arckens

Artists usually design their works to be preserved for future generations. In the same way, we observe previous artworks in order to understand contemporary cultural productions. This twofold dynamic, which ensures both the survival of our artistic patrimony and a continuity of its production, is not as endemic to art as often thought. Artists can choose to break with traditions, or can refuse to follow artistic conventions. The phrase "I'd rather die than . . . " is often exclaimed by the artistic outcasts of this world. Think of Roy Lichtenstein's 1963 painting *Drowning Girl*, alternatively titled *I Don't Care! I'd Rather Sink*, which is a thematic depiction of such an extreme refusal. Yet, I believe that there is one poet in particular who—surprisingly—enriches our engagement with these questions of artistic production, queerness, and survival.

Marianne Moore, feminist and queer poet, was a meticulous observer, an obsessive collector. Throughout her life, she believed that to feel deeply one had to see clearly, and she perceived the world with precision and critical acuity. Above all, she collected with equal dedication the written materials from that observed world. Gathering quotations from a diversity of sources, most often nonliterary or even quotidian, it was the rule rather than the exception that she twisted the quoted material's original phrasing or meaning. Her experimental poetry contains catalogues of collected fragments and is representative of collage. It is a testimony, an archive of what she considered valuable and worthwhile for future remembrance. Yet, I argue, her poetic archive, which has a rather atypical design, testifies against the ideology of survival. Even though her poems have often been called "acts of survival," Moore does not look at the past as a talisman

WSQ: Women's Studies Quarterly 44: 1 & 2 (Spring/Summer 2016)

for the future, and her queer archival poem-collections attest to anxiety over—rather than faith in—inheritance, continuity, and memory.[1]

As the most impersonal and cagey of her already impersonally modernist generation, Moore figures as an exceptional representative of queer archival poetry. As I will indicate, hers is a poetics that opposes the legacy of the closet and queer literature's subsequent urge to "come out," "open the box," and "break the silence" via personal testimonies. Her writings are not confessional—let alone autobiographical—and there is not even a critical consensus about Moore's queerness in the first place. She never married, nor did she have any lesbian relationships, and her personal letters attest only to a couple of inconsiderable college crushes. However, I draw on Eve Kosofsky Sedgwick's definition of queer as "the open mesh of possibilities, gaps, overlaps, dissonances and resonances, lapses and excesses of meaning when the constituent elements of anyone's gender, of anyone's sexuality aren't made (or can't be made) to signify monolithically" (1993, 8).

In multiple ways, Moore lives and writes according to this less rigid model of sexuality. Not until her mother's death in 1947, when Moore was already sixty, had she ever lived on her own, or written a poem without her mother's consent. During her childhood and continuing in later family correspondence, a playful game of animal nicknaming began, in which Marianne masculinized as "Gator," "Basilisk," "Weasel," "Uncle (Fangs)," "Mouse," or "Rat." She would later adopt this purposefully cross gendering practice into her poetics. In her poetic menagerie of queer animals, the dragon is the most remarkable. Moore herself once admitted in "O, to Be a Dragon" that she would like to be one, "of silkworm size or immense," preferably "almost invisible" but a decidedly "felicitous phenomenon" (1967, 177). This dragon, as a nongendered combatant, offers a clue to the eccentric woman who thrives behind the tame, reserved exterior. It is this visible-invisible and gendered-nongendered discrepancy that contributes to Moore's idiosyncratic queerness.

A "queer archive," as established by Ann Cvetkovich, refers to any mechanism that collects information and is "composed of material practices that challenge traditional conceptions of history and understand the quest for history as a psychic need rather than a science" (2003, 268). Cvetkovich further argues that the queer archivist resembles "the fan or the collector whose attachment to objects is often fetishistic, idiosyncratic or obsessional" (253). Nonetheless, the queer archivist distinguishes him/herself from a scientifically driven, historical archivist in his/her personal need for a testimony. A testimony may not be in itself a scientific catalog, but the instinct behind assorting the (often psychological) materials can be of a methodical nature. A collection becomes a testimony when the collected material resembles the archivist's interests, and hence testifies to his/her personality. Consequently, the queer archive becomes an autobiographical memoir. Historic interest in a problematic past is an endemic feature of most queer literature. As I will later indicate, queer collectors can build different views of the past or—as in Moore's case—hold these different views simultaneously. By collecting a wide range of mostly marginal "ephemera," the queer archivist is especially interested in outmoded or backward styles, and the often sentimental popular culture, to create this personal "archive of feelings" (243–44). In this way, the queer archive is close to camp, itself a queer medium of art (Love 2007, 7). All in all, the psychic need to record the often-problematic gay and lesbian past results in a remarkably emotional archive.

Above all, the queer archive moves beyond Jacques Derrida's deconstructed archive, for it offers a symptomatic reading that analyzes the presence of ideology in Derrida's text. In *Archive Fever,* Derrida claims that the death drive is inherent in all archival work, which incites not only forgetfulness or the annihilation of memory but eventually renders any archive impossible: "The archive always works, and *a priori,* against itself" (1995, 14). Archive fever impedes the archival desire, for it simultaneously causes the contradictory impulse to preserve as well as to destroy. Hence, Derrida calls this specific death drive *"le mal d'archive,"* or "archive fever" (14). The archive, driven by archive fever, is inseparable from a negativity that questions social orders in the form of a "repetition compulsion," which refers to the compulsive acts of endless postponement that produce an indefinite deferral of meaning, identity, and collective history (14). Despite the fact that Derrida sees the archive as memorializing the memory it simultaneously annihilates, he still believes that the archive will open onto the future. As Lee Edelman points out, *Archive Fever* disputes the binary of life and death, opting instead for the alternatives of living on and living after (2011, 155–56). Moreover, Derrida's argument, supported by an anecdote about a Bible that was passed on from Freud's grandfather to his father, is still dependent on a father-son relationship, in which the grandfather, through a return from the past, turns his son into an archive that passes on patrimonial/paternal inheritance (Cvetkovich 2003, 268). Derrida deconstructs the life/death dichotomy, but only to offer a survival of patrimonial inheritance, whereas the queer archivist problematizes the very ideology of survival itself.

Moreover, the queer quest for historical detail and accuracy allows for a return not from but *to* the past. Even more, the queer's specifically "overwhelming desire to *feel historical*," as Christopher Nealon indicates, implies a desire to make public and collective what is often painfully private (2001, 8). The use of archives, as private acts made public, are then perfect mediums of expression for the queer poet, even if this feverish expression of a queer identity results simultaneously in the concealment of sexually "secret passions" (Derrida 1995, 63). Derrida, however, still adheres to a world in which "the Child" is futurity's guarantor that signifies survival, even though that survival remains inseparable from the death drive's negativity. Edelman, on the other hand, has argued that the queer becomes, through its abject status as unproductive and antisocial, a threat to survival and to "the guarantor of futurity": the Child (2004, 11–12).[2] Consequently, reproductive futurism's figural Child, who passes down the queer archive, may signify survival, but the queer (child) sustaining that figure can never survive itself, destined as it is to voice others' texts (2011, 156). In her poems, Moore complicates this queer's relation to survival. Circular repetition instead of narrative progress, a proliferation of incoherent voices instead of vocal consistency, and the use of archival history as meant for historic reproduction instead of future production are what make Moore's poetry an act of queer archival work that testifies against the ideology of survival.

However, Moore's queer archive is not autobiographical, not even personal, and, despite Cvetkovich's claim, neither is it based on any sort of "psychic need." Even though Moore describes her poetry as "a little anthology of statements that took my fancy—phrasings that I liked" (1987, 551), these statements reflect on public and political matters. Her documentary obsession is expressive of her scientific, rather than poetic or psychic, precision. In a column for *The Dial*, Moore once described poetry as "the science of assorting and the art of investing an assortment with dignity" (1987, 182). Her poetics oppose the legacy of the closet, as her celibacy is not hiding another sexual identity, but is a sexuality in itself. Nevertheless, secrecy is not to be mistaken for silence: "The deepest feeling always shows itself in silence; / not in silence but restraint" ("Silence").

Her poems are best read as "personal-impersonal expressions of appearance" ("People's Surroundings"). Moore's obsessive archive fever is ambiguously "personal-impersonal," yet results in a poetry that is resistant to any autobiographical or sexual expression.

Moore's poems show the queer collector's interest in the past, even though this is an interest that, as Heather Love has argued, is based on "the challenge to engage with the past without being destroyed by it" (2007, 1). This might be the very reason why Moore engineers an aesthetic of distorted, quasi-untraceable quotations. In this, she adheres to both Ann Cvetkovich's and Carolyn Dinshaw's queer views of the past that, respectively, radicalize and resist conventional history. Like Cvetkovich, Moore's poems express a "passionate desire to claim the fact of history" (2003, 242), but like Dinshaw, she resists conventional history's linearity and causality. Dinshaw sees the queer desire for history as a desire for a different sort of past, generated by what she calls a "postdisenchanted temporal perspective" that represents an extensive now, but that "rejects the necessity of revealed truth at the end of time or as the meaning of all time" (2007, 185). In her poetry, Moore represents a desire, or as she describes it, "a capacity for fact" ("An Octopus"), while simultaneously adhering to a poetics of multitemporality, multivocality, and what Edelman calls a "symptomatic repetition" that refuses to follow temporal, linear logic (2011, 188). This echoes Julia Kristeva's distinction between linear and monumental/cyclical time. In *Women's Time*, Kristeva associates cyclical time with anteriority, memory, and the cycles of female reproductive fertility without insisting on actual reproduction (1981, 17). Moore's queer engagement with the cultural past both radicalizes and resists its linearity by distorting its causality and refusing to give the reader any final, moral resolution at the end of her poems.

My reading of Moore's archival poem-collections focuses on her last volume, *Tell Me, Tell Me: Granite, Steel, and Other Topics* (1966), as this later work is most clearly preoccupied with shapeless circularity and queer inconsistency in poetic lyricism. She also becomes increasingly obsessed with the poetic play of concealment, how one can at once "reveal / and veil / a peacock-tail," ("Arthur Mitchell"), and how "you have been deceived into thinking that you have progressed" ("An Octopus"). Above all, especially in *Tell Me, Tell Me*—note the contrast with a more active "Tell My Story"—Moore takes on the role of the child to whom stories are told, and who gives voice to the past. With this considered, I disagree with

Susan McCabe, who argues that Moore—given her successful production of queer variation without actual propagation—would be representative of the "survival of the queerly fit" (2009, 547). I argue instead that in *Tell Me, Tell Me*, Moore, like the child, may signify survival but that she and her queer archive can never actually survive because of the negativity inherent in archiving others' texts.

Celebrated Celibate

From 1952 onward—the year she won the Bollingen Prize, the National Book Award, and the Pulitzer Prize—Moore became a public celebrity. This was also a period marked by her public celibacy.[3] Her status as celibate spinster additionally defines her queer experience as one of "anachronism" (Freeman 2000, 729) and "temporal asynchrony" (Dinshaw 2007, 190), as well as defining her general sense of backwardness, for if Moore looks at the future, it is always in the form of a reanimated past. This historical backwardness is particularly charged for the queer subject, who has been regarded as backward because of his/her deviancy. It becomes even more charged when the queer subject adopts the sexual model and political identity of celibate, given celibacy's association with belatedness. Not very worldly altogether, they seem the embodiment of bygone times. It is crucial, however, to nuance celibacy's belatedness and to define Moore, as Benjamin Kahan does, not as intrinsically outmoded and old-fashioned but as adopting a celibate temporality that is *marked* by the past (Kahan 2008, 514). Above all, celibacy's very status of anachronism comes from the idea that it is associated with figures *from* the past, whereas Moore's celibacy is of a temporality that looks *toward* the past. The disruption caused by celibacy's anachronism nonetheless compels us, as Elizabeth Freeman suggests, "to reimagine our historical categories" (2007, 742). While I follow Kahan when he suggests that Moore's poetics refuse to follow the accepted order of life and lyric, I do not agree with his statement that Moore rewrites the past and its belatedness "as guides for the future" (2008, 515). Neither do I believe that Moore lives only in the past, suffering from an anxiety over future's progressions, for in that case she would not have experienced her celibacy as empowering: "What of chastity? It confers a particular strength" (Moore 1987, 503). But I do follow critics such as Edelman and Freeman, who stress that the queer, and especially the celibate as queer, remains inseparable from negativity toward survival because, as anachronisms, the time of their sexual identity is focused on the past.

Celibacy follows a retroactive temporality that magnifies the "repetition compulsion" inherent in archive fever, as the intermingling of past and present lead to a cyclical time in which repetitions can no longer be separated from each other. As such, celibacy postpones survival through intertextuality and reversed progress. In *Tell Me, Tell Me*, Moore begins with endings and ends with beginnings. In fact, reverse chronology is the principal system of ordering in *Tell Me, Tell Me*, which begins with the 1966 poem "Granite and Steel" and ends with the 1957 poem "Sun." Throughout the volume, and within poems, she practices what she describes in the title poem as a poetics of "the told-backward biography" ("Tell Me, Tell Me"). For instance, in "Old Amusement Park," she portrays this park, as the subtitle states, "Before it became LaGuardia Airport." Now, she can present this outmoded park from a retroactive perspective, "when the triumph is reflective / and confusion, retroactive" (1966, 13). Between the volume's poems this perspective is also perceivable. For instance, there is no direct reference given to the poem's subject, the Brooklyn Bridge, in "Granite and Steel" except for an indirect hint to its designer, John Roebling. Only in the next poem, "In Lieu of the Lyre," which is about an entirely different subject, is Roebling explicitly linked to his bridge:

> or "catenary and triangle together hold the span in place"
>   (of a bridge),
> or a too often forgotten surely relevant thing, that Roebling cable
>   was invented by John A. Roebling

> (1966, 8)

Throughout the volume, linearity is twisted, causality contorted, and the overall progress is one of retroactive temporality. Celibates, like asexual people, have something estranging, and although celibacy is not to be mistaken for secrecy, it is closely related to obscurity. The apparent lack of sexual desire is often seen as inhuman or hyperrational, and hence as a nonentity, rather than as a distinctive sexuality on its own.[4] Moore, specifically, takes pleasure in, or as she describes it in the 1948 talk "Humility, Concentration, and Gusto," shares a "gusto" for difficulty and "obscurity." In her 1966 volume, one also finds a short essay titled "A Burning Desire to Be Explicit." In the first sentence, Moore describes her writing style:

> Always, in whatever I wrote—prose or verse—I have had a burning de-
> sire to be explicit; beset always, however carefully I had written, by the
> charge of obscurity. (1966, 5)

"Explicit" could refer to Moore's desire to be verbally accurate or, as Benjamin Kahan highlights, to the queer desire to be sexually explicit (2008,
521). A motif for this pleasure in obscurity can be found in "the knot," a figure that recurs throughout the volume. Moore mentions it for the first time
in the poem "To a Giraffe," as she hints at the "emotionally-tied-in-knots
animal"; then in "Charity Overcoming Envy" as "The Gordian knot need
not be cut"; and once more in the title-poem "Tell Me, Tell Me":

> to flee; by engineering strategy—
> the viper's traffic-knot—flee
> to metaphysical newmown hay,
> honeysuckle, or woods fragrance.
>
> (1966, 44)

In "Charity Overcoming Envy," the "Gordian Knot" refers to a legend of
Phrygian Gordium and is used as a metaphor for dealing with an intractable problem. If one intends to cut the Gordian Knot, one tries to solve
the problem by either cheating or thinking outside the box (or closet). As
it does not have to be cut in this situation, since "Destiny is not devising
a plot" and so "the problem is mastered" ("Charity Overcoming Envy"),
there apparently is no "box" or "closet" behind which something is hidden. The craftily queer solution is the knot itself, for pleasure can be found
in obscurity, and queerness does not reside in an unraveled knot but in
the knot's very negativity. I agree with Kahan, who sees the knot as an
image of nonreproduction, for it could allude to "a knotted phallus, a tied
tongue, and tied fallopian tubes," which are "impediments to sexual acts"
that eventually stop all progress (2008, 523). This image of nonproduction and antisurvival, however, is Moore's very own "engineering strategy" that allows her to flee away to her own queer space of "metaphysical
newmown hay, / honeysuckle, or woods fragrance." In the volume, knots
represent obstacles of nonproduction that in their very negativity allow for
the queer's existence. Yet the proof of that existence—the queer archive—
cannot promise future propagation.

Camp Citationality and Performativity

The queer archivist's retroactive temporality is enhanced by intertextuality and citationality, which is not only an aspect of the queer archive but also of camp. She gives voice to numerous sayings by citing—often unmarked, and if marked, often incorrectly. Moore herself repeatedly had to elucidate this citational aesthetics:

> "Why the many quotation marks?" I am asked. Pardon my saying more than once, when a thing has been said so well that it could not be said better, why paraphrase it? Hence my writing is, if not a cabinet of fossils, a kind of collection of flies in amber. (1987, 551)

In accordance with the first half of the volume's title, *Tell Me, Tell Me,* Moore's cabinet of fossils is the result of prior stories told to her. She herself performs the role of the (queer) Child whose "collections of flies in amber" may signify survival, but cannot ultimately survive because of the queer archive's inherent death drive. In this, the queer archive holds a camp quality, a style usually associated with the homosexual scene. In accordance with Keith Harvey's arguments, I see Moore's citationality as a form of verbal camp that can manipulate interaction, here with prior texts, resulting in irony (Harvey 2002, 1145). Moreover, in "Notes on 'Camp,'" Susan Sontag mentions under "Note 10" that:

> Camp sees everything in quotation marks. It's not a lamp, but a "lamp"; not a woman, but a "woman." To perceive Camp in objects and persons is to understand Being-as-Playing-a-Role. It is the farthest extension, in sensibility, of the metaphor of life as theater. (1979, 280)

Moore, who is "Being-as-Playing-a-Role" of the Child, gives voice to pre-existing texts that, in being compulsively repeated and distorted, become ironic echoes of the past. Camp, with its interest in popular and outmoded fashions, is a backward art (Love 2007, 7). Consequently, in a queer archive, one can build a *retroactive* "queer performativity" (Freeman 2000, 728–29). Moore's performativity is not progressive, as in Judith Butler's formulation, but through citationality, it presents repetitions with a backward-looking force. In Moore's poetry, the importance given to descriptive detail in citations transcends the role such detail plays as historical evidence of the factual truth. As such, Moore's citationality as performance neither allows for a perfect reconstruction nor derails into postmodern parody. Moore's poetry instead functions as a kind of anachronism that, according to Freeman's definition, "disrupt[s] what might otherwise be a seamless, point-by-point retelling of a prior text" (2000, 734).

This implies that the citational performativity found in her queer archive relies on precision, although this precision is inflicted with subversion. In "Carnegie Hall: Rescued," for instance, the poetic speaker lauds the rescue of the famous music hall, by way of thanking "Saint Diogenes / supreme commander" in quotation marks:

> "It spreads," the campaign—carried on
>   by long-distance telephone,
>   with "Saint Diogenes
>   supreme commander."
>   At the fifty-ninth minute
>   of the eleventh hour, a rescuer
> Makes room for Mr. Carnegie's
> music hall . . .
>
>   (1966, 40)

Detailed description alternates with obfuscation. Why would "'It spreads'" be put in quotation marks? Whom is she citing, and why these two indeterminate words in the first place? Similarly, by referring to "a rescuer," suspense is maintained, but not before having said that this particular rescuer arrived "At the fifty-ninth minute / of the eleventh hour." Twelve o'clock, in other words. It seems vital that we remember that particular time and that it happened not just by a regular phone call but a "long-distance" one, while "the campaign" and its "rescuer" remain undefined and, so, unremembered. For who is this Saint Diogenes? In Moore's "Notes and Acknowledgements," inserted at the end of the volume, she mentions that lines three and four, "with 'Saint Diogenes / supreme commander," come from the article "The Talk of the Town" from the April 9, 1960 issue of *The New Yorker*. However, if one compares the poem to its source, it becomes clear that she did not cite only this line, or cite this line in full. In the article, nothing is said about "Saint Diogenes." Yet, next to "supreme commander" she also copies without mention the lines "long-distance telephone," and "at the fifty-ninth minute of the eleventh hour," as well as references to Paderewski, Tchaikovsky, and Gilels in the next stanza. Moore refers to these artists only because they were mentioned in the article. In a poem about rescuing one of New York's most valuable music halls, and thus about preserving cultural inheritance, her precision—"Tchaikovsky, of course / on the opening / night, 1891;"—is imbued with ambiguity—"With Andrew C. and Mr. R., / 'our spearhead, Mr. Star'"—and with the past:

> "When very young my dream
>   was of pure glory."
> Must he say "was" of his "light
>   dream," which confirms our glittering story?
>
> (1966, 41)

Referring here to Jean Cocteau's "Preface to the Past," what she scrutinizes in Cocteau's play with time and verb forms, she herself does in a previous stanza, "Mr. Carnegie's / music hall, which by degrees / became (becomes) / our music stronghold" (40). Moreover, her reference to the homosexual writer Cocteau is striking, especially if we keep in mind that Sontag classified him within her camp notes (1979, 278). All in all, Moore seems intent on us knowing about the survival of Carnegie Hall, yet the given details concern trivialities whereas the true core of what ought to be remembered is not mentioned.

Moore's desire for accuracy results in impairment, ultimately destroying what it would preserve. In other words, the archive is built on contradictions. Moreover, the queer archive can only exist *because* of its contradictions. A major contradiction is the camp distinction between artificial and authentic. Once again, it is a distinction that revolves around details, and how details that were originally intended to reinforce realism eventually create *sur*realism. Susan McCabe describes Moore's technique of classification as one of "gender-crossing taxonomies," which allow her to render "the hypervariant" (2009, 561–62). Moore's description of Yul's sister in the poem "Rescue with Yul Brynner" is based on such a hybrid classification:

> —twin of an enchantress—
> elephant-borne dancer in silver-spangled dress,
> swirled aloft by trunk, with star-tipped wand, Tamara,
>
> (1966, 39)

This diversity of elephants in dresses with swirling trunks blurs the divide between authentic and artificial. Moore aligns her archive once again with camp, which can be seen as the "love of the unnatural: of artifice and exaggeration" (Sontag 1979, 275). Her camp interests range from old amusement parks and Carnegie's Music Hall, to baseball, giraffes, and Yul Brynner, but is this what she ultimately wishes to memorize?

Biography: Remember Me (Not)?

The volume's last two poems, "Saint Valentine" and "Sun," deal most explicitly with this question of remembrance, memory, and hence, survival. In "Saint Valentine," Moore contemplates whether her "memento," her queer archive, will supplant the object (re-)collected:

> If those remembered by you
> are to think of you and not me,
> it seems to me that the memento
> ....
> should have a name beginning with "V,"

> (1966, 45)

Moore here once more performs the role of the (queer) Child, who questions the paternal inheritance of this particular saint. Yet, as argued before, if we read celibacy not as an unfulfilled desire but as the anachronous fulfillment of desire itself (Kahan 2008, 522), Moore's desire manifests in the textual "gusto" of her writing: "Any valentine that is *written* / Is as the *vendange* to the vine" ("Saint Valentine"). Looking for the right "V," she eventually finds the word, "Verse—unabashedly bold—is appropriate." Despite the homage to Saint Valentine, it is her own "Verse" that she wishes to have remembered. In "Sun," the last poem of the volume, preservation and forgetfulness are intertwined. In an italicized preface to the poem, she states: "Hope and Fear accost him." At the beginning, Moore cites John Skelton without reference, "'No man may him hyde / From Deth hollow-eyed,'" after which she immediately counters his statement by saying, "For us, this inconvenient truth does not suffice" ("Sun"). It is not a coincidence that Moore ends this poem, and as such, her volume, with the line, "Insurgent feet shall not outrun / multiplied flames, O Sun." This prophetical declaration repeats and so confirms the beginning. Nothing has progressed, and no moral meaning is added at the end. It is a perfect example of Dinshaw's "postdisenchanted temporal perspective," a temporal experience that "opens up to an expansive now, but [that] . . . rejects the necessity of revealed truth at the end of time" (2007, 185–86). The queer archivist does not collect so as to find an all-encompassing resolution that might show the way to a brighter future. On the contrary, in this volume Moore recounts everything told, yet also immediately counters those memories.

The biography Moore recounts throughout the volume has a retroactive, "told-backward" temporality that is typical of archives. As Derrida suggests, archives, unlike histories, are temporally motivated not so much by present linearity as by the logic of the future perfect: "what *will have been* and *ought to* or *should be in the future*" (1981, 32). The past represented by Moore is "a set of Doppler effects, diversions, dispersals, swerves, and forking paths" (Kahan 2008, 525), or, as she describes in the poem "Tell Me, Tell Me," a "told-backward biography":

> In this told-backward biography
> . . . .
> the tailor's tale ended captivity
>   in two senses. Besides having told
> of a coat which made the tailor's fortune,
>   it rescued a reader
>   from being driven mad by a scold.
>
> (1966, 44)

Whose biography is told backward, and to whom does "the scold" refer? In the original story, captive mice save the tailor of Gloucester by helping him make a cerise coat *after* they are set free. However, in the story told by Moore, the poetic speaker is looking for "refuge" and tells the already "rescued tailor of Gloucester" that, having helped him, "I [she] am going to flee; by engineering strategy—" (1966, 44). The backward biography as told by the scold—by Moore?—seems like a metaphor for the repression of queers as mice, "who 'breathed inconsistency and drank / contradiction'" (1966, 43). They dress others, allowing for their *présence*—as in charisma—and presence, whereas they themselves remain "captive" inside the confinement of the queer closet. This captivity can be seen as the classical spinster's image, or, the way I read it, as a self-chosen identity. According to my reading, celibacy's confinement becomes an image of freedom and independence. As such, we acquire a "told-backward biography" that ends with renewed freedom, but begins with an imperative death wish:

> Tell me, tell me
>> Where might there be a refuge for me
>> From egocentricity
>> . . . .
>> and obliterate continuity?
>
> (1966, 43)

Moore wants to be liberated from the "egocentricity" of heteronormative family's "continuity" and propagation. She flees into "methaphysical new-mown hay, honeysuckle, *or* woods fragrance" ("Tell Me, Tell Me," emphasis mine). But what do these elements have in common? In the volume's essay, "A Burning Desire to Be Explicit," Moore recounts how a member at a women's club once asked her what "metaphysical newmown hay" actually meant. Moore replied by explaining, "'Oh, something like a sudden whiff of fragrance in contrast with the doggedly continuous opposition to spontaneous conversation that had gone before'" ("A Burning Desire"). These elements, as fragrances, then share in the suddenness and fleetingness of their presence. Moreover, and in accordance with Edelman's "logic of the "or," this adverb tells of the queer excess beyond the "or," disorienting the otherwise strict divide between captivity (death) and freedom (life) (Edelman 2011, 150–51, 165). Fleeing into the excessive fleetingness of queer fragrances allows her to bisect and disorient familial continuity as promised by the "egocentric" Child.

Moore embraces backwardness by exploring memory as survival, yet, according to Derridean logic, loses memory again in the act of archiving. Memory is driven by the will to survive, just as much as the archive is nourished by the destructive death drive in archive fever. The queer archivist in Moore is, because of her looking backward, not at all interested in future continuity. Even though the second part of the volume's title sounds industrial, *Granite, Steel, and Other Topics*, and the first poems are partly dedicated to the Brooklyn Bridge, a paramount image of America's progression, Moore warns against the dangers of progress and familial "egocentricity" ("Tell Me, Tell Me"). Additionally, despite the many references to "rescue"—two poems have it in their titles, "Rescue with Yul Brynner" and "Carnegie Hall: Rescued," and in "Tell Me, Tell Me," rescue from captivity is the main theme—she does not talk of it in the sense of futurity and survival. What the queer archive is rescued from is the very disentangled continuity inherent in heteronormative propagation. The backward trajectory, the retroactive temporality, and the anxiety of memory eventually transcend the simple binary between life and death. Instead, Moore offers us the logic of the "or" as the fetishization of difference and as the disruption of survival's logic: "life or death?" (Edelman 2011, 165). Her queer archive simultaneously offers all contrasting assets that life, death, remembrance, or forgetfulness entail. No final resolution can be made, as the death drive in archive fever will always and a priori destroy what it intends to memorialize. By embracing this negativity, by giving in to the archive's death drive, and by "'breath[ing] inconsistency and dr[inking] / contradiction,'" Moore—as reproductive futurism's figural Child—could give, "in this told-backward biography," nothing more than an *impression* of survival ("Tell Me, Tell Me").

It is this very impression around which the larger debate revolves. We might not know who "Brad" is in Lichtenstein's painting, and neither does Moore wish to have us remember anything except for distorted trivialities. But, however much these queer details ultimately destroy the memory Moore wishes them to preserve, there is, at the very least, an impression of survival that lasts. Because, of course Lichtenstein's *Drowning Girl* cares, and of course Moore would wish that her queer archival poetry continue to be read and, hence, survive its writer. In the end, Moore's experimental poetry has shown that to be "against survival"—which is not the same as having an imperative death wish—is about expressing a "gusto" for life and literature so deeply felt that its inherent death drive can destroy everything, except for that impression.

Elien Arckens is a researcher in the department of English Literature, Ghent University (Belgium), and a member of the RAP-team (Research on Authorship in Performance). Her field of focus is in Marianne Moore studies, as well as feminist theory.

Notes

1. The greatest adherent of the survival perspective in Moore's poetry is her biographer, Linda Leavell, whose latest book is aptly titled *Holding On Upside Down: The Life and Work of Marianne Moore* (2013).
2. In *No Future*, Lee Edelman distinguishes between the Child as an ideologi-

cal fantasy of reproductive futurism and the child as biological entity which
functions as a substrate for the former.

3. Marianne Moore, though loved for her exuberance by her contemporaries,
was equally often characterized for her "spinsterly aversion" (Ezra Pound,
cited by Heuving 1992, 18), and R. P. Blackmur once even exclaimed that
"no poet has been so chaste" (cited by Leavell 2013, xi).

4. In his latest book, *Celibacies: American Modernism & Sexual Life* (2013), Benjamin Kahan sheds new light on the history and perception of asexuality and
celibacy, arguing it to be a proper sexuality of its own.

Works Cited

Cvetkovich, Ann. 2003. *An Archive of Feelings: Trauma, Sexuality, and Lesbian
Public Cultures*. Durham, NC: Duke University Press.

Derrida, Jacques. 1995. "Archive Fever: A Freudian Impression." Translated by E.
Prenowitz. *Diacritics* 25 (2): 9–63.

Dinshaw, Carolyn, Lee Edelman, Roderick A. Ferguson, Carla Freccero,
Elizabeth Freeman, Judith Halberstam, Annamarie Jagose, Christopher
S. Nealon, Tan Hoang Nguyen. 2007. "Theorizing Queer Temporalities:
A Roundtable Discussion." *GLQ: A Journal of Lesbian and Gay Studies* 13
(2/3): 177–95.

Edelman, Lee. 2004. *No Future: Queer Theory and the Death Drive*. Durham, NC:
Duke University Press.

———. 2011. "Against Survival: Queerness in a Time That's Out of Joint."
Shakespeare Quarterly 62 (2): 148–69.

Freeman, Elizabeth. 2000. "Packing History, Count(er)ing Generations." *New
Literary History* 31 (4): 727–44.

Harvey, Keith. 2002. "Camp Talk and Citationality: A Queer Take on 'Authentic'
and 'Represented' Utterance." *Journal of Pragmatics* 34 (9): 1114–65.

Heuving, Jeanne. 1992. *Omissions are Not Accidents: Gender in the Art of
Marianne Moore*. Detroit: Wayne State University Press.

Kahan, Benjamin. 2008. "'The Viper's Traffic-Knot': Celibacy and Queerness in
the 'Late' Marianne Moore." *GLQ: A Journal of Lesbian and Gay Studies* 14
(4): 509–35.

———. 2013. *Celibacies: American Modernism & Sexual Life*. Durham, NC: Duke
University Press.

Kristeva, Julia. 1981. "Women's Time." Translated by A. Jardine and H. Blake.
Signs 7 (1): 13–35.

Leavell, Linda. 2013. *Holding on Upside Down: The Life and Work of Marianne
Moore*. New York: Farrar, Straus and Giroux.

Love, Heather. 2007. *Feeling Backward: Loss and the Politics of Queer History.* Cambridge, MA: Harvard University Press.

McCabe, Susan. 2009. "Survival of the Queerly Fit: Darwin, Marianne Moore, and Elizabeth Bishop." *Twentieth-Century Literature* 55 (4): 547–71.

Moore, Marianne. 1966. *Tell Me, Tell Me: Granite, Steel, and Other Topics.* New York: The Viking Press.

———. 1967. *The Complete Poems of Marianne Moore.* London: Faber and Faber.

———. 1987. *The Complete Prose of Marianne Moore.* Edited by P. C. Willis. London: Faber and Faber.

Nealon, Christopher. 2001. *Foundlings: Lesbian and Gay Historical Emotion before Stonewall.* Durham, NC: Duke University Press.

Sedgwick, Eve Kosofsky. 1993. *Tendencies.* Durham, NC: Duke University Press.

Sontag, Susan. 1979. "Notes on 'Camp.'" In *Against Interpretation And Other Essays.* New York: Dell.

The Subjects of Survival: The Anti-Intersectional Routes of Breast Cancer

Amy L. Brandzel

"You look better with hair." This was my grandmother's response when she saw me shortly after I had completed chemotherapy. And because she was dealing with Alzheimer's disease, this observation was repeated each time she saw me. My mother was worried that if I showed up on my grandmother's front door with a bald head, it would necessarily burden my grandmother with the requisite anxiety and fear that I might be dying of cancer. But my grandmother was far too superficial for that (I take after my grandmother), and her matter-of-fact tone that I might consider growing hair as an aesthetic preference entertained me every time. And yet, within my genderqueer communities, many seem to disagree with my grandmother. I was "cruised on" by queers during my chemotherapy more than any time before, and sadly, ever since. With the addition of a leather accessory, I could pretty much guarantee a wink or a look by a passing queer. And given my white, middle-class, Nebraskan background, being seen as a punkish queer was a delight indeed.

The bald head was only the first of many opportunities for gender-queerness and coalitional subjectivity brought on by the deadly prognosis. Alongside horrific chronic pain from treatment, a likely death from cancer at some point in the not so distant future, and a highly tenuous journey on the tenure track, breast cancer allowed for a wide array of opportunities to embody some of the many intersectionalities of lived experience.

I'm in good company. Some of the most inspiring feminist scholars have lived with and negotiated the constraints and conventions of breast cancer. Audre Lorde set the tone when she railed against the "imposed silence" of breast cancer, particularly as manifest in the demand that breast

WSQ: Women's Studies Quarterly 44: 1 & 2 (Spring/Summer 2016) © 2016 by Amy L. Brandzel.

cancer patients wear prostheses and wigs in order to cover over the violence of breast cancer in U.S. society (1997, 7). Eve Kosofsky Sedgwick offered us the playful suggestion that breast cancer might be one of the most profound opportunities for an "adventure in applied deconstruction" (1993, 12). And more recently, S. Lochlann Jain described how challenging it is for a butch lesbian to endure the "relentless hyper- and heterosexualization of the disease" (2007, 506).

What brings these scholars together is not merely their feminist and queer critiques of the ways in which breast cancer is represented and contorted through the breast cancer industrial complex. They also share a longing and heartfelt search for agentic subject positions in which they can model and forge their own terms of survival. As Lorde observed, "Off and on I keep thinking. I have cancer. I'm a black lesbian feminist poet, how am I going to do this now? Where are the models for what I'm supposed to be in this situation? But there were none. That is it, Audre. You're on your own" (1997, 28). And Jain, in a similar though less intersectional vein, pointed out that across the hyper-heterosexualization of the disease, "There is simply no subject position available for the cancer butch" (2007, 521). And as Sedgwick expresses, in an exasperated tone, "I can't tell you how many people—women, men, gay, straight, feminists, gender traditionalists—have said or implied to me that my proper recourse for counsel, encouragement, solidarity in dealing with breast cancer would be (i.e., I infer, *had better be*) other women in their most essential identity as women" (1992, 202–3). Each of these scholars, in their own way, wrestles with the limited and contorted terms of survival subjectivity as produced by hegemonic breast cancer discourses. Throughout mainstream breast cancer, survival has been routed into a white, normative, heterogendered, ableist subjectivity.

But in my experience, the anti-intersectional subject position offered by hegemonic breast cancer takes work. The breast cancer industry, in all of its postfeminist glory, works endlessly and strategically to guide breast cancer patients around and away from the obvious intersectionalities and multiple subjectivities of embodied vulnerability. Women of color scholarship has consistently critiqued the violence of racialized, gendered, and sexualized normativities, whereby white heterosexual women are marked as the normative referents for feminism and more. This scholarship has also linked these hegemonic discursive regimes to operations of subjectivity, whereby single-axis analyses contort subjectivities into autonomous, individualistic, unified, and universalized subjects of consciousness. In her famous review of *This Bridge Called My Back*, Norma Alarcón argued that a careful engagement with literature by women of color reveals the ways in which multiple subjectivities are erased and silenced through linguistic and political conventions that require allegiance to mono-systems of thought, as well as the disavowal of relational dialogues and experiences (1990). As she observes, "By 'forgetting' or refusing to take into account that we are culturally constituted in and through language in complex ways and not just engendered in a homogeneous situation, the Anglo-American subject of consciousness cannot come to terms with her (his) own class-biased ethnocentrism" (1990, 363). Alarcón's description of the white feminist disavowal of multiple subjectivities is an exceptionally on-point description of the current state of the breast cancer subject as produced by the hegemonic breast cancer movement.

While "survival is messy" (to quote the introduction to this special issue), the breast cancer industry exerts an exorbitant amount of time, effort, and dollars to clean up that mess. Within the rhetoric and structures of breast cancer, survival is sanitized and constricted to a particularly distinct, anti-intersectional, unitary subject position. Breast cancer patients are constantly detoured away from inevitable intersectional connections to transgender embodiments, queered affects, disabled communities, and the racialized, classed, and able-bodied operations of precarity. But of course, how can we not look at the obsessively pink ribbons and good cheer within all of those "races for the cure" and not see that they are desperately running from something? Underneath the surface of breast cancer rhetoric lies an anxiety that the intersectionalities of gender, race, sexuality, and dis/ablity will be exposed.

Intersectional Potentials, and Lack Thereof

Reflecting on the potential of breast cancer activism in 1990, Barbara Brenner warned that the movement was at a critical crossroads (2002). Recounting the history of breast cancer activism, Brenner detailed the ways in which breast cancer patients increasingly critiqued mainstream cancer organizations and the medical establishment in the 1960s and 1970s for disappearing and isolating their experiences of breast cancer. Support groups, such as Y-ME, were borne from the intransigence of the American Cancer Society to offer spaces for patients to talk openly about their experiences. And feminist activist groups, such as Breast Cancer Action, were dedicated to political analyses that could dissect gender discrimination, environmental racisms, and the troubling nexus of corporations and national cancer organizations. But in reviewing the state of breast cancer activism as of 1990, Brenner offered a prescient warning: even though breast cancer itself "knows no boundaries of race, ethnicity, or social class," breast cancer activisms were dominated by white, middle-class women (2002, 346). Brenner linked intersectionality with the potential success of the movement, arguing that the eradication of the breast cancer epidemic requires that the movement address its most daunting challenge, the lack of racial and economic diversity.

Brenner was not alone in hoping for a truly feminist—as in intersectional—breast cancer movement. In 1992, Alisa Solomon argued that the radical potential of the breast cancer movement rested in what she saw was a newly emerging coalition between breast cancer activists and environmental activists. This merger could challenge the increasing neoliberal detour around the ways in which environmental toxins have impacted the development of cancer. Elaborating on this radical potential, medical anthropologist Mary K. Anglin claimed that the environmental justice movement, especially informed via analyses of environmental racisms, could propel the breast cancer movement into a coalition that would "address the compounding of the violence of breast cancer and other diseases by the sociopolitical processes in which race, ethnicity, nationality, class, and gender are embedded in the U.S." (1998, 203).

And yet, as of 2015, breast cancer activism has become the epitome of disconnected, anti-intersectional activism. With the assistance of major breast cancer charities like the Susan G. Komen Foundation, breast cancer activism is dominated by white, middle-class, heterosexual womanhood. This activism consistently evades and neglects the connections between breast cancer and systemic operations of power, inequalities, and normative social relations. As Samantha King observes, breast cancer "activists" are "discouraged from questioning the underlying structures and guiding assumptions of the cancer-industrial complex" (2006, 104). As Barbara Ehrenreich pointedly notes, the breast cancer movement's apolitical stance merely recites the "chorus of sentimentality and good cheer; after all, breast cancer would hardly be the darling of corporate America if its complexion changed from pink to green" (2001, 48).

For some scholars, the movement's lack of systemic and intersectional analysis is explained by its hegemonic demographic (Brenner 2002; Cart-wright 1998; Kaufert 1998; King 2006; Klawiter 2008). That is, the white, middle-class, heterosexuality of the majority of breast cancer activists forecloses the possibility of richer, smarter, and more political analyses. As King argues:

> The historically entrenched homogenous demographic makeup of the movement goes some way to explaining the particular agenda it has em-braced and the fact that issues relating to forms of oppression based on class, sexual identity, or race have been marginalized in favor of a careful and nonthreatening focus on women (not feminists) as a constituency and breast cancer as a single issue that is presented as a mainly scientific, rather than economic, environmental, or social problem. (2006, 3)

Within this framing, the dominance of normatively privileged identities of breast cancer activists therefore explains and excuses the lack of intersec-tional and politically astute analyses. Some scholars even use this logic to explain their own anti-intersectional analyses of the breast cancer move-ment, implying that the dominance of whiteness thereby explains the scholar's own inability to negotiate racial difference within their own work (Klawiter 2008, xxvii, 4).

Even when women of color are present, the white-centeredness of hegemonic breast cancer appears to be a train that cannot be stopped. Looking back at 1990s activism, Patricia Kaufert observes the troubling fact that "despite [the influence of] Audre Lorde and the African Amer-ican Breast Cancer Alliance, despite its commitment to inclusivity, the breast cancer movement was not really in touch with the problems and issues faced by women who were not middle-class, not insured, [and] not white." Kaufert then relates the white normativity of breast cancer to the white normativity of women's studies. As she says, "The relatively narrow class base of the breast cancer movement is not unusual. Accusations that someone, whether scholar or activist, has ignored or neglected the 'other' woman are endemic within women's studies" (1998, 304).

And yet, if we return to Barbara Brenner's warning twenty-five years ago, the white-centeredness of breast cancer activism was not a foregone conclusion. Brenner, a white Jewish lesbian leader in the movement, was one of many feminist activists that was attuned to and echoed the call for intersectional analyses from women of color feminisms. Involved in Breast Cancer Action (an avowedly feminist organization that continues to call out the various forms of "pinkwashing" in corporate sponsorship and subterfuge via the ubiquitous pink ribbon), Brenner was one of many feminist activists dedicated to systemic analyses of breast cancer, such as the nexus of racialized and gendered discrimination within medical institutions. And as others pointed out, the various coalitions across health and environmental activisms created plenty of space to make breast cancer activism a systemic-focused practice. These coalitions represented activists who were dedicated to making connections across racialized, gendered, sexualized, and classed experiences and perspectives on breast cancer.

At one level, we cannot afford to rest with such a narrative, whereby the white-centeredness of some becomes an explanation for the white-centeredness of many. Intersectionality is as much a call for shared responsibility about the need for making intersectional connections as it is a call for multiple and diverse perspectives. Hence, the lack of intersectionality within hegemonic breast cancer is not a foreclosed conclusion that can be excused or explained away by the various axes of privilege that many of these activists embody.

At another level, this story of how hegemonic breast cancer became so very antifeminist and anti-intersectional covers over numerous vocal and voracious feminist and antiracist breast cancer activists and organizations across racialized locations and perspectives. While Breast Cancer Action is one of the few national organizations that lambaste the breast cancer industrial complex, numerous local organizations offer feminist analyses and activisms against the mainstream discourses of breast cancer (Anglin 1998; Anglin 2006; Brenner 2002; Fishman 2000; Kaufert 1998; King 2006; Klawiter 2008). And responding to the lacunas in mainstream breast cancer activisms, numerous organizations focus exclusively on the particular needs of women of color breast cancer survivors, both at the national and local levels.

For example, the national Sisters Network Inc., founded in 1994, focuses on the needs of breast cancer survivors within African American communities. Not only do they hold national conferences and support local chapters, they address the fact that breast cancer in the African American community is more deadly than in any other racial group. Young African American women are in extreme danger, and many African American women's initial diagnosis happens at very advanced stages of the disease. The Sisters Network has numerous initiatives focused on addressing these disparities, such as the "Teens 4 Pink" (focused on teaching young African

American women about breast health), the "Young Sisters Initiative" (creating coalitional opportunities for young women with breast cancer), and the "Gift for Life Block Walk" (whereby volunteers canvas neighborhoods to provide information on breast cancer).

Many Asian and Pacific Islander organizations work to counter the troubling ways in which the racialized category of "Asian American" is used within national breast cancer statistics. For many years now, national breast cancer statistics suggest that Asian American women have the lowest incidence of the disease and the lowest death rates. And yet, hidden within the category of "Asian American" is the frightening fact that Native Hawaiian and other Pacific Islander women have the highest rates of death from breast cancer. The "Asian American" category, then, obscures the fact that many women swept under this large, incongruent racialized rug have exceptionally high rates of devastating breast cancers. Therefore, organizations such as the Asian & Pacific Islander American Health Forum run a variety of initiatives attempting to counter the dangerous miscommunications of U.S. breast cancer statistics.

The fact that these organizations exist, and have existed for quite some time, reminds us that the anti-intersectionalities of hegemonic breast cancer do not take place within a vacuum. Women of color, queer, and feminist activists and organizations are present within the scholarly debates, local and national hearings, conference spaces, online chat rooms, and even the dominant breast cancer organizations themselves that actively choose to negate or ignore these intersectional and political analyses, contributions, and priorities.

One of the most important insights that some scholars have offered regarding the "success" of the breast cancer movement is that its mainstreaming has been a purposeful and willful choice to capitalize on privileged normativities. That is, the most dominant representations of breast cancer "survivors" are the result of careful and selective sculpting by some breast cancer activists who choose to distance themselves from more threatening representations. Many scholars argue, for example, that while the roots of breast cancer activism can be found in AIDS activism, some breast cancer activists capitalized on the privileged normativities of white middle-class heterofemininity as a means to offer a less scary, more righteous cause (King 2006; Kaufert 1998). Compared to the representations of AIDS as the deadly contagion of gay sex, not to mention the radical tactics of queer activists, breast cancer was a far more palatable and worthy disease. According to Kaufert, "The moral worthiness of the breast cancer victim became the subtext: the young mother dying with breast cancer contrasted against the public stereotype of the AIDS patient, gay, male, and radical" (1998, 303).

The "worthiness" of breast cancer survivors is directly linked to their whiteness. Samantha King points out, for example, that breast cancer activists have consciously chosen to represent themselves as white saintly mothers worthy of cherishing and saving. In a fantastic analysis of the National Football League's (NFL) "Real Men Wear Pink" breast cancer awareness campaign, King argues that the affiliation of professional football players with inappropriate and violent black heteromasculinity offered an essential foil in order to further bolster the sanctity of white, middle-class, motherly breast cancer survivors. Inappropriate black heteromasculinity is, as the Moynihan report and hegemonic narratives continue to tell us, the fault of black mothers. As King observes, "Unlike the welfare queen—the quintessential antimother and the symbol of all that threatens moral guardianship, selflessness, and good health on which nationally sanctioned motherhood depends—the breast cancer survivors we see in Real Men Wear Pink and in discourse of breast cancer more broadly are the embodiment of white middle-class nationally sanctioned motherhood" (2006, 23). Saving white womanhood from breast cancer, then, becomes a means to save U.S. society as a whole.

And yet, the white saintliness of breast cancer survivors has necessarily had to wrestle with the fear and anxiety of its potentially feminist-leanings. Mainstream breast cancer activism appears to have some pseudo-feminist elements: it centers and celebrates the visibilities of women with breast cancer, it critiques patriarchal medical regimes, and it organizes a form of "sisterhood" that invites breast cancer patients and potential breast cancer patients (i.e., all "women") to unite. But as Ehrenreich points out, "there is nothing very feminist—in an ideological or activist sense—about the mainstream of breast-cancer culture today" (2001, 47). But, again, this distancing from feminism is carefully sculpted. As Klawiter documents, the Komen Foundation actively worked to dissociate themselves from feminist breast cancer organizations that were led by those rowdy lesbians/feminists (2008, 139).

The anti-intersectional, apolitical priorities of hegemonic breast cancer are *active choices* that organizations and activists make to direct the narrative of breast cancer survival away from feminist intersectionality, and toward a particularly neoliberal (i.e. privileged and individualized) white hyper-heterofemininity. While intersectional analyses can be hard work, especially due to the limits of hegemonic language structures, the reverse must also be understood; anti-intersectionalities, such as represented by hegemonic breast cancer activisms, take serious effort, labor, and time.

Gender Trouble

Breast cancer is one of many disease paradigms dominated by the biopolitical discourse of risk. According to Klawiter, current medical discourse—especially as dominated by various surveillance and disease detection regimes—locates all adult women on "an expansive disease continuum" (2008, xxviii). Through statistical measures, social science, and medical studies on detection, disease progression, and survival, populations of "women" are variably marked as "risky subjects." What determines a "woman's" risk for breast cancer includes: being female, being over the age of fifty-five, having breast cancer in your family, beginning menstruation before the age of twelve, not going through childbirth before your midtwenties, being overweight, and drinking alcohol. While those are the most common risk categories, literature has increasingly emphasized racial categories, noting that white women are more likely to be diagnosed with breast cancer, black women are more likely to die from breast cancer, and Asian American women are least likely to be diagnosed with and die from breast cancer.[1]

The discourse of risk disguises multiple levels of violence. While the risk of breast cancer for those deemed "female" or "woman" appears to be self-explanatory, we might hope that at some point in the not-so-distant future medical oncology catches up with gender theorists in order to offer more specificity. Men, transmen, and gender nonconforming people develop breast cancer, and while gender might appear to offer an easy shorthand, what is actually meant by "female" or "women" is people with developed breast duct cells. And despite the overwhelming disinformation in the mainstream media about breast cancer, heredity and genetics only account for a very small number of breast cancer diagnoses every year. This disjuncture demonstrates the ways in which "at risk" categories are less about statistical probabilities and more about common ways of sorting populations.

Racialized categories of risk to breast cancer further anti-intersectional knowledge and conceal the violence of racialized categories themselves. As mentioned earlier, the unstable category "Asian American" obscures the extreme vulnerability of Pacific Islander and Indigenous women throughout the Pacific. And to suggest that white women are more likely to be diagnosed with breast cancer requires the critical caveat that this is mostly due to the classed and racialized privileges of white women to seek out, feel comfortable with, and be able to afford medical treatment. Women of color, especially those located within communities that have been violated by medical experiments, are far less likely to search for or find authority in medical institutions (Anglin 2006; Fishman 2000). Statistics of risk rarely, if ever, include any intersectional connections (even those as simple as the nexus of race and age) and completely negate critical categories such as economic class and geographic location. In these ways, the lack of intersectionality within the discourse of risk results in dangerous misperceptions as to which bodies are the most vulnerable to death and illness (Fishman 2000, 191–92).

The discourse of risk directs our attention away from environmental and social factors and toward the myth that individualized behavior can make or break your chances with breast cancer. Within risk factor rhetoric, "whatever has caused it, you did it" (Anglin 1998, 191). Despite the huge debate around whether or not early detection really does save lives, "There is a subtle message," according to breast cancer activist Judith Brady, "that if you're a good girl and get your mammogram, you won't be punished with breast cancer" (Solomon 1992, 161). Considering the various so-called factors fixated on gender, proper and timely reproduction, and body weight, what remains "risky" are sexual autonomy, the refusal of feminized labor, and normative standards of beauty. As breast cancer surgeon Susan Love observes, the discourse of risk factors "smacks of the attitude that if women would stay home and have babies like they're supposed to, they wouldn't get breast cancer" (Solomon 1992, 160).

The ubiquities of pink ribbons and good cheer within the breast cancer industry have only made things worse. If you add up all of the various socially mediated messages that cancer is caused by cranky attitudes, anger, and resentment, then it is hard to miss the message that feminists, lesbians, and women of color make the quintessential victims of breast cancer. Women of color, especially when pointing out white privilege or racist paradigms, are constantly accused of being angry. And feminists, as symbolized by the man-hating lesbian stereotype, are unable to take a joke or lighten up because they are so unwaveringly fixated on critique. Living at the intersections of these typologies, Lorde received the message loud and clear that anger-via-critique causes cancer. In a moving passage in *The Cancer Journals*, Lorde attempts to dislodge the message that had clearly started to embed itself in her soul:

> Was I wrong to be working so hard against the oppressions afflicting women and Black people? Was I in error to be speaking out against our silent passivity and the cynicism of a mechanized and inhuman civilization that is destroying our earth and those who live upon it? Was I really fighting the spread of radiation, racism, woman-slaughter, chemical invasion of our food, pollution to our environment, the abuse and psychic destruction of our young, merely to avoid dealing with my first and greatest responsibility—to be happy? (1997, 76)

And as she continues to grapple with the idea that a critical worldview causes cancer, she argues that ignorance is not a luxury women of color can afford. To ignore the reality that their "daily lives are stitched with violence and with hatred . . . can mean destruction." In the end, she asserts, "We are equally destroyed by false happiness and false breasts, and the passive acceptance of false values that corrupt our lives and distort our experience" (1997, 78).

And yet, three decades later, we are even more immersed in the discourse that happiness/ignorance heals. As Ehrenreich points out, while U.S. society is saturated with claims that the best means for social advancement merely requires "a good attitude," she had no idea how thorough "relentless brightsiding" could be until she was diagnosed with breast cancer (2001; 2009). Breast cancer is the land of good cheer, and the demand "smile or die" has been purposefully and carefully orchestrated as such. And as Maren Klawiter documents so well, breast cancer activism became mainstream, corporatized, and widely successful (in terms of dollars raised) when organizations such as the Komen Foundation managed to funnel a "culture of optimism" into a form of "consensus activism"(Klawiter 2008, 134). The consensus, however, is forged through decoupling breast cancer from death and dying, thereby creating that *happy place*, or "that sweet spot in all American women where soap opera fan and feminist meet" (Goldman 1997).

The culture of optimism within breast cancer is not only especially virulent, it is also relentlessly feminized. Ehrenreich argues that the "ultrafeminine theme of the breast cancer 'marketplace'" is an effort to infantilize women with breast cancer, thereby working to (re)consolidate femininity into "a state of arrested development" (2001, 46). Other critics and scholars have argued that the hyperfeminization of breast cancer stems from some type of well-intentioned desire to "return" the femininity that is supposedly lost through the experience of mastectomy and hair loss (Crompvoets 2012). S. Lochlann Jain, however, sees the feminine hype as an active effort to (re)produce and police the social constructions of gender (2007, 506). But might we go one step further, to see the ways in which the obsession with pink shtick is a desperate effort to constrain the gender trouble that breast cancer necessarily embodies? Put differently, might the fear be that all breast cancer patients really are budding feminists, on the brink of seeing behind the curtain of white, gendered, heteronormativity that the breast cancer industry works so hard to uphold?

Leave it to one of the founders of queer theory, Eve Sedgwick, to remind us of the radical potential lost and found within the breast-cancered body. Sedgwick's scholarship is as famous for her work on queer performativity and sexual ambiguity as it is for her ability to unsettle the status quo. Even through the pain and violence of treatment, Sedgwick could not help but see her embodiment as potentially multiplicitous. As she reflects:

> A dizzying array of gender challenges and experiments comes with the initiations of surgery, of chemotherapy, of hormone therapy. Just getting dressed in the morning means deciding how many breasts I will be able to recognize myself if I am wearing (a voice in me keeps whispering, three). . . . I have never felt less stability in my gender, age, and racial identities; nor, anxious and full of the shreds of dread, shame, and mourning as this process is, have I ever felt more of a mind to explore and exploit every possibility." (1992, 204)

The drag that Sedgwick negotiates here is not unique. The stripping down of the body in breast cancer treatment highlights the ways in which gendered, racialized, and sexualized performativities are opportunities for negotiation as much as they are violent demands for conformity.

But of course, Sedgwick's playfulness coincided with the agony of having to maneuver the gendered gauntlet of breast cancer medicalization. Reflecting on her breast cancer diagnosis, she famously observed, "Shit, now I guess I really must be a woman" (1992, 202). Sedgwick's newfound "womanness" via breast cancer was not about a loss of femininity, or the lack of the heterosexual male gaze, via mastectomy, wigs, and so forth. Rather, it was from the gendering of breast cancer treatment itself. From having to direct oneself to the "Women's Cancer" wing of the hospital, through the welcome wagon of the "Look Good, Feel Better" campaign (full of complimentary wigs, makeup, and beauty tips), and across the numerous presumptive conversations with medical staff about what type of reconstruction or prosthesis you should have, the medical network of breast cancer genders you at every turn in order to demand that you are, must be, a "woman."

This might be a good time to admit that I do not identify as a woman (or a man). It took a while, but it finally clicked. For many years while teaching gender and queer studies, I had only incorporated gender theory into my own life at the most basic levels: as a transgender ally, a gender theorist, and a poststructuralist queer feminist critic. But the privilege and audacity of merely teaching gender theory rather than practicing it caught up with me. And so I finally "got it" and announced to my students, to my colleagues, to myself: my so-called identification as "female" is just one category mistake among many. And while I've fallen prey to the mistaken presumption that I am this gendered being numerous times in the past, and might easily do so again in the future, I am taking responsibility for the privileges incurred by such a normative misunderstanding. To be clear, this is not a coming-out narrative; I am not transgender. I am merely a gender theorist finally practicing what I preach.

The timing was funny. A few months after my epiphany, I was diagnosed with Stage III (now IV) breast cancer and was thrown into the relentless gendered circuit of breast cancer treatment. I was met with representatives from the "Look Good, Feel Better" campaign to learn about the free merchandise and various tutorials that were readily available to help me *relearn* my femininity. I was given extensive information on reconstruction surgery, temporary prostheses, and how to find more permanent breast prostheses once I had healed from my surgery. And even when I brought in extensive information on transmen's top surgeries for my surgeon to study, she continued to think her goal was to create a surface that would prepare me for reconstruction or prosthesis. My multiple tutorials on gender theory to the nursing staff, my detailed request for top surgery-ish mastectomy, and even my infamous furrowed brow, could not stop the good-willed intentions that repeatedly told me, in one way or another, that I had nothing to worry about because I always was and will remain a woman.

Even shopping for the various accoutrements of breast cancer incessantly routes you away from connections to transgender embodiments. While insurance covers some of the cost of buying a wig and/or prosthesis from one of the many mastectomy boutiques, you can save a lot of money by shopping for the same items at any transgender-oriented retailer. For a fifth of the price, and with a lot more options to choose from (especially regarding skin tones for prostheses), you can experience the playful humor of transwomen and see the ways in which this might be an opportunity, as much as it is a life threatening experience. And yet, informational kits from breast cancer institutions will point patients toward the more hetero-feminized option of mastectomy boutiques in order to assure patients that their essentialized gender identity remains stable.

In the midst of an essay dedicated to explaining how there are no subject positions available to her as a "cancer butch," Jain offers the following caveat in a footnote: "Before anyone panics, I am not saying that women get reconstructions because they are homophobic" (2007, 533 FN 47). But I beg to differ. The obsession with reconstruction and prostheses demonstrates the nexus of transphobia and homophobia within breast cancer. Jain's observation that there is a "relentless hyper- and heterosexualization of the disease" makes it clear that it is impossible to parse out sexual anxieties from gendered ones. Whether explicit or implicit, breast cancer is saturated with the fear that breast cancer patients will lose their (hetero)femininity and might end up looking like, or relating to, lesbians, feminists, and/or transgender people. Even if a diagnosis of breast cancer itself appears to be a confirmation of the antifeminist message that "biology is destiny," breast cancer's naturalization relies upon incessant repetition and imitation in order to reproduce itself. The heavy-handedness of breast cancer activism and treatment is due to the need to quash the intersectional feminist possibilities—the gender troubles—that come with breast-cancered embodiments.

Dissing Disability

Illness autobiographies are everywhere: the Internet, magazines, monographs, anthologies, plays, Lifetime movies, poetry, and more. As literary scholars note, these biographies share similar narrative arcs. Many of the "autopathographies," for example, begin by describing the ways in which an illness or disease creates a crisis of identity, a crisis that is eventually sutured once the author comes to a new and enlightened consciousness (Couser 1997; Waples 2013). Breast cancer narratives follow similar trajectories, with a few added gendered plot devices, such as shopping for wigs and/or prostheses, the revelation of and coming to terms with the new breast(s)/chest, and the discovery of sisterhood in breast cancer support groups along the way (Waples 2013; Price Herndl 2006; Ryan 2004). But what astonishes me is that these various illness narratives rarely acknowledge how their (supposedly new, perhaps temporary) embodiments might allow them to consider the ways in which able-bodiedness is a violent normalization regime. Put differently, in all of the coming-to-consciousness, how can formerly able-bodied people continue to refuse to see the ways they are connected to a large, various, and active disabled community?

This neglect does not go both ways. Disability studies and activists do think about the interconnections across and between illness, impairment, and disability. As Rosemarie Garland-Thomson argues, disability activism is best served by seeing the ways in which diverse experiences and states are "grouped together under the medical-scientific rubric of abnormality and its accompanying cultural sentence of inferiority" (2005, 1558). Including able-bodiedness as a primary vector in the intersectionalities of social difference allows us to begin making the connections. As Kim Hall observes:

> Seemingly unrelated technologies such as orthopedic shoes, cosmetic surgery, hearing aids, diet and exercise regimes, prosthetic limbs, anti-depressants, Viagra, and genital surgeries designed to correct intersexed bodies all seek to transform deviant bodies, bodies that threaten to blur and, thus, undermine organizing binaries of social life (such as those defining dominant conceptions of gender and racial identity) into docile bodies that reinforce dominant cultural norms of gendered, raced, and classed bodily function and appearance. (2002, vii)

This is why, more often than not, disability studies and activists call for fluid definitions of disability in order to expose the linkages across the various possible displacements from normative able-bodied/mindedness. But this more open-ended, generous, and inclusive definition of disability is also about survival. As Eli Clare so eloquently describes:

> I am looking for friends and allies, for communities where the gawking, gaping, staring finally turns to something else, something true to

the bone. Places where strength gets to be softened and tempered, love honed and stretched. Where gender is known as more than a simple binary. Where we encourage each other to swish and swagger, limp and roll, and learn the language of pride. Places where our bodies begin to become home. (2003, 261)

And yet, despite the generous spirit of disability activists and scholars, typical illness narratives in general, and the breast cancer industry in particular, refuse the gift of coalition (Kafer 2013). Rather, they mark illness as a temporary moment that merely provides the gift of enlightened perspective, an enlightenment that is fulfilled once they overcome the temporary obstacle of disease or illness. This distancing from disability is, at one level, motored by the fear of stigma and the possibility of acquiring a new axis of disadvantaged identity (Coleman 2006, 142). But at another level, anxiety and disdain for relationality with disabled communities stems from the fear and knowledge that able-bodiedness is a privileged and *temporary* status (Siebers 2006). That is, bodies begin, and often end, in various stages of disability and dependency. Shunning disabled communities, then, becomes a protective mode of denying the precarity of material life.

I will admit that being baldheaded in public was harder than I expected. Despite the gender play and the queer attention, there were so many more looks of pity: the lower lip quiver, the sorrowful eyebrows, and those too-bad-for-you (thank-god-you're-not-me) looks were excruciating. There are ways in which the association with extreme vulnerability and precariousness overshadowed the playful opportunities. And even when Jain is reflecting on how she might enjoy the hot queer potential of being a baldheaded rocker lesbian, she is trapped by baldheadedness's connotation with near death. As Jain reflects, "Though a shaven head, and even breastlessness, is a completely conceivable choice for a person like me (queer, out, athletic, relatively confident), the fact that I was bald from cancer supplanted using baldness or a flat chest to express identity" (2013, 210).

In their social science study of whether lesbians choose to have breast reconstructions, Lisa R. Rubin and Molly Tanenbaum wanted to see if lesbians are more resilient to pressures to conform to hegemonic hyperfemininity (2011). Some of the lesbians they interviewed felt pressure to conform to a different image: the one-breasted warrior image, as most notably represented by Deena Metzger's famous image, "The Warrior," from

1977. Also known as the "tree poster," the image (photographed by Hella Hammid) shows Metzger with outstretched arms, bearing her left breast and a colorful tattoo tracing the mastectomy scar over the right side of her chest. As Rubin and Tanenbaum observe, "over time this iconic image had also come to represent a 'right' way for strong women to handle cancer, and some participants expressed feelings of inadequacy for not choosing that option" (2011, 407). Moreover, while many participants described their knowledge and experience with gender play, others pointed out how the mastectomy actually brought up deep wounds and struggles with normative femininity. But what struck the scholars as most shocking were the ways in which arguments in favor of reconstruction presented by lesbian participants actually revealed a deeply ingrained fear of being associated with disability. And so, while they were looking for the ways in which lesbians might be resistant to a heteronormative gaze, they argued that "another privileged and controlling gaze—the 'able-bodied' gaze—may be at least as important to understand [that] women's reconstruction decisions" are also motivated by "fears associated with the imperfect, fragile, and mortal body" (2011, 410).

But this observation is only news to breast cancer patients that refuse to acknowledge their own disabled embodiment. One of the most curious elements of having breast cancer is the way many bystanders' sympathy is clearly coupled with a sense of relief. While it is rare to have a friend, colleague, or loved one actually say the words, "better you than me," their self-centered relief is written all over their faces. And as many breast cancer scholars have noted, that anxiety works both ways. That is, many breast cancer communities are engrossed within the chorus of "why me?" (as represented by the name of one of the first breast cancer support organizations, Y-ME). But these refusals, displacements, and laments are merely another way of naming the ways illness, like disability, works through a system of comparative valuing and devaluing.

The question "why me?" is saturated in privilege. Reflecting on her experience with breast cancer communities' lament, Sedgwick could not help but make the connection: do people who have been marked by the state (or other institutions) as socially dead or terminally precarious—such as those living with AIDS, or the impoverished—have the luxury of such a question?

"Why me?" was not something it could have occurred to me to ask in a world where so many companions of my own age were already dealing with fear, debilitation, and death. I wonder, too, whether it characterizes the responses of urban women of color forced by violence, by drugs, by state indifference or hostility, by AIDS and other illnesses, into familiarity with the rhythms of early death. (Sedgwick 1993, 14)

The refusal to recognize alliances with and affinities toward disabled communities is part of a larger practice of devaluing differences, and it's concomitant disavowal of privilege. People are differentially and comparatively exposed to injury, violence, poverty, indebtedness, and death through discourses and operations of precarity and disposability. As Athena Athanasiou and Judith Butler explain, "dispossessed subjectivities" (whether rendered "subhuman or hauntingly all-too-human") are produced through the "various modalities of valuelessness, such as social death, abandonment, impoverishment, state and individual racism, fascism, homophobia, sexual assault, militarism, malnutrition, industrial accidents, workplace injuries, privatization, and liberal governmentalization of aversion and empathy" (2013, 18–19). The disabled are an integral part of the larger accumulation of dispossessed subjectivities, and the un/intentional distancing on the part of cancer communities is one more layer of insult upon injury.

Coming to Terms with Audre Lorde

As it should be, feminists continue to grapple with Audre Lorde's work on breast cancer. As Jain points out, "The academic literature tends to take Audre Lorde as the primary feminist theorist of breast cancer, and her 1980 *Cancer Journals* remains, nearly three decades out, the final word on breast cancer and gender theory" (2007, 507). Mary DeShazer argues that Lorde's legacy is profound, as her work provided the catalyst for feminist health activists and health narratives, and that it continues to be a resource for leading feminist activists (2013, 40). G. Thomas Couser, in his groundbreaking literary analysis of the illness narrative genre, argues that Lorde's *Cancer Journals* stands out for merging personal engagements with politically engaged analyses (1997, 50–51). And yet, if Lorde remains the "final word on breast cancer," why haven't breast cancer narratives or feminist scholarship on breast cancer fully engaged with the intersectional, structural and embodied analyses that Lorde so ably demonstrated?

More often than not, feminist theorists pose the question as to whether or not Lorde's analysis is "still relevant" and/or "needs updating" (Jain 2007; King 2006; Pickens 2014; Price Herndl 2002). King argues, for example, that Lorde's critiques are still quite germane. While Lorde's call for a removal of the individualized stigma of breast cancer has been somewhat answered, Lorde's warning as to how the demand to look on the bright side of things can disappear structural inequalities "is more relevant now than ever before" (King 2006, 102). King argues for an urgent return to Lorde, especially in order to account for and be accountable to "broader struggles where breast cancer is just a part" (114).

Jain argues that the majority of Lorde's calls remain prescient; breast prostheses and wigs still conceal the violence of breast cancer, environmental causes of breast cancer are still ignored, patriarchal medical systems are still in place, and breast cancer is an even larger epidemic now than it was in Lorde's time (Jain 2007, 508). But Jain is troubled by the ways in which Lorde's call for the visibility of breast cancer patients—especially in regard to her call for breast cancer "warriors" to engage the public—has become more problematic than Lorde could have anticipated. According to Jain, the breast cancer movement's success in making breast cancer visible has now made breast cancer ubiquitous, so much so that it has become an expected part of everyday life for women. In Ehrenreich's terms, breast cancer has become "a normal marker in the life cycle, like menopause or graying hair" (2001, 49). Jain's brilliant insight is that the ubiquity of breast cancer imagery, especially through the pink ribbon and cheerful races for the cure, has covered over the carnage of breast cancer.

In one of her essays on breast cancer, Diane Price Herndl openly admits that her goal is to create an avowedly "theoretical version of self-justification" in order for her to "com[e] to terms with not living up to Audre Lorde" (2002, 144). Similar to the lesbians in the Rubin and Tanenbaum study on reconstruction, Price Herndl wrestles with feminist peer pressure (as represented by Lorde) to refuse reconstruction in order to make the viciousness of breast cancer visible. Grappling with her own internal feminist dialogue and with Lorde, Price Herndl attempts to describe her own breast reconstruction as the creation of a "postmodern feminist body." This body is possible because "things have changed" and "Lorde's mission to make breast cancer visible, to give it a voice, has succeeded" (2002, 149–150). This visibility then, creates the space for people to choose to get reconstructions, wear prostheses, or even refuse these operations altogether.

True, things have changed. Breast reconstruction is far more advanced and more widely available now than it was during Lorde's day. [2] Mastectomy boutiques are now an actual business model, with many available throughout major cities and across the Internet. But questions remain about what types of "choices" people can make. Despite the vast numbers of mastectomy products and consumers, mastectomy bras continue to presume that breast cancer patients have two breast forms, or need at least one prosthesis pocket to even out their chest. Going single-breasted is not a "choice" in the sense that there are no bras that support such a need—unless you can afford a customized specialty bra (Pickens 2014, 140; Saywell et al. 2000, 53). There are very few images of people who "choose" to be seen as single-breasted, which is why some breast cancer patients find political affinity in anyone who dares to buck the status quo (Klawiter 2008, 182; Saywell et al. 2000, 53–54). As one remarks, "Every time I see someone who flaunts the fact that she has one lump, not two, I feel like cheering" (Saywell et al. 2000, 54).

How might these avowedly feminist engagements with Lorde be purposefully routing themselves around her intersectional critiques of breast cancer? In other words, why are all of these attempts to engage with Audre Lorde evading her arguments about the ways in which white normativity, heterofemininity, able-bodiedness, and environmental racism work in concert to disappear the structural productions of and experiences of breast cancer? If we are going to come to terms with Lorde, shouldn't we consider *her terms,* as outlined in *The Cancer Journals* and echoed throughout her oeuvre as a whole? It takes work (as in effort) to read and engage with Lorde's *Cancer Journals* while ignoring or evading her detailed descriptions of how racial, sexual, and gender differences function together to forge her experience as a black lesbian with breast cancer. The visibility that Lorde asked for was never a mere recovery of a breast-cancered body without shame; the visibility that she asked for, demanded, was the visibility of breast cancer patients to each other, across and within difference. The political action she called for was not a pink-ribboned race; it was a one-breasted army that showed up at Congress demanding the investigation of the environmental toxins in mass meat production. The prosthesis was not a mere instrument to cover over women's experiences with breast cancer; for Lorde, the prosthesis was the symbolic representation of the erasure of human diversity and frailty (Pickens 2014, 140). And finally, the subjectivity Lorde sought was not a temporarily sick apolitical white femininity, but an antiracist, feminist, queer woman of color activist-artist who would serve as a role model for others. She wrote *The Cancer Journals* to refuse to let cancer be "yet another imposed silence" and "tool of separation and powerlessness" (7). But this is exactly what breast cancer remains.

What is it about breast cancer—the experience, the movement, and the politics—that works so desperately to move away from the interconnections of lived experience, the intersectionalities of structural power, and the multidimensionality of embodiment? Because even though the breast-cancered body is one particular example of a relational embodiment, it is continuously pushed away from the potential experiential alliance with those "whose proper place is non-being" (Butler and Athanasiou 2013, 19). Throughout my own journey living with breast cancer, I've never felt so dis/connected. We must come to terms with Lorde, because our survival depends upon it.

Amy L. Brandzel is an assistant professor of American studies and women studies at the University of New Mexico. Their work examines how normative knowledge systems enact violence (rhetorical, emotional, corporeal, social, and institutional) on nonnormative bodies, practices, behaviors, and forms of affiliation.

Notes

1. Numerous organizations, medical institutions, and government agencies repeat these narratives on risk factors. See, for example, Breastcancer.org 2015; the American Cancer Society 2015; and Centers for Disease Control and Prevention 2015. A few organizations attempt to disrupt this narrative, such as Breast Cancer Action (2004).
2. It remains a bit unclear how many patients choose to undergo reconstruction surgeries. Some studies suggest that only about 25 to 35 percent of patients choose reconstruction, while other studies suggest that number is a little over 50 percent (Morrow 2014). Some studies suggest the numbers of patients choosing reconstruction have increased over time, while others suggest it has decreased (Jagsi et al. 2014).

Works Cited

Alarcón, Norma. 1990. "The Theoretical Subject(s) of *This Bridge Called My Back* and Anglo-American Feminism." In *Making Face, Making Soul: Haciendo Caras,* edited by Gloria Anzaldúa, 356–69. San Francisco: Aunt Lute Books.

American Cancer Society. 2015. "What Are the Risk Factors for Breast Cancer?" Last modified August 19. http://www.cancer.org/cancer/breastcancer/detailedguide/breast-cancer-risk-factors.

Anglin, Mary K. 1998. "Dismantling the Master's House: Cancer Activists, Discourses of Prevention, and Environmental Justice." *Identities* 5 (2): 183–217.

———. 2006. "Whose Health? Whose Justice? Examining Quality of Care and Breast Cancer Activism through the Intersections of Gender, Race, Ethnicity, and Class." In *Gender, Race, Class, and Health: Intersectional Approaches,* edited by Amy Shulz and Leith Mullings, 213–341. San Francisco: Josey-Bass.

Breastcancer.org. 2015. "Breast Cancer Risk Factors." Accessed September 15. http://www.breastcancer.org/risk/factors.

Breast Cancer Action. 2004. "What You Should Know about Breast Cancer Risk." Accessed September 15, 2015. http://archive.bcaction.org/index.php?page=bcrisk.

Brenner, Barbara. 2002. "Sister Support: Women Create a Breast Cancer Movement." In *Breast Cancer: Society Shapes an Epidemic,* edited by Anne S. Kasper and Susan J. Ferguson, 325–55. New York: Palgrave Macmillan.

Butler, Judith, and Athena Athanasiou. 2013. *Dispossession: The Performative in the Political.* Cambridge, UK: Polity Press.

Cartwright, Lisa. 1998. "Community and the Public Body in Breast Cancer Media Activism." *Cultural Studies* 12 (2): 117–38.

Centers for Disease Control and Prevention. 2015. "What Are the Risk Factors for Breast Cancer?" Last modified November 17. http://www.cdc.gov/cancer/breast/basic_info/risk_factors.htm.

Clare, Eli. 2003. "Gawking, Gaping, Staring." *GLQ: A Journal of Lesbian and Gay Studies* 9 (1): 257–61.

Coleman, Lerita M. 2006. "Stigma: An Enigma Demystified." In *The Disability Studies Reader,* edited by Lennard J. Davis, 141–52. New York: Routledge.

Couser, G. Thomas. 1997. *Recovering Bodies: Illness, Disability, and Life-Writing.* Madison, WI: University of Wisconsin Press.

Crompvoets, Samantha. 2012. "Prosthetic Fantasies: Loss, Recovery, and the Marketing of Wholeness After Breast Cancer." *Social Semiotics* 22 (1): 107–20.

DeShazer, Mary K. 2013. *Mammographies: The Cultural Discourses of Breast Cancer Narratives.* Ann Arbor, MI: University of Michigan Press.

Ehrenreich, Barbara. 2001. "Welcome To Cancerland." *Harper's Magazine,* 43–53.

———. 2009. *Bright-sided: How the Relentless Promotion of Positive Thinking Has Undermined America.* New York: Metropolitan Books.

Fishman, Jennifer. 2000. "Assessing Breast Cancer: Risk, Science, and Environmental Racism in an 'At Risk' Community." In *Ideologies of Breast Cancer: Feminist Perspectives,* edited by Laura Potts, 182–204. New York: St. Martin's Press.

Garland-Thomson, Rosemarie. 2005. "Feminist Disability Studies." *Signs* 30 (2): 1557–87.

Goldman, Debra. 1997. "The Consumer Republic: Illness as Metaphor." *Adweek,* November 3. http://www.adweek.com/news/advertising/consumer-republic-22813.

Hall, Kim Q. 2002. "Feminism, Disability, and Embodiment." *NWSA Journal* 14 (3): vii-xiii.

Jagsi, Reshma, Jing Jiang, Adeyiza O. Momoh, Amy Alderman, Sharon H. Giordano, Thomas A. Buchholz, Steven J. Kronowitz, and Benjamin D. Smith. 2014. "Trends and Variation in Use of Breast Reconstruction in Patients with Breast Cancer Undergoing Mastectomy in the United States." *Journal of Clinical Oncology* 32: 919–26.

Jain, S. Lochlann. 2007. "Cancer Butch." *Cultural Anthropology* 22 (4): 501–38.

———. 2013. *Malignant: How Cancer Becomes Us.* Berkeley, CA: University of California Press.

Kafer, Alison. 2013. *Feminist, Queer, Crip.* Bloomington, IN: Indiana University Press.

Kaufert, Patricia. 1998. "Women, Resistance, and the Breast Cancer Movement." In *Pragmatic Women and Body Politics,* edited by Margaret Lock and Patricia Kaufert, 287–309. Cambridge: Cambridge University Press.

King, Samantha. 2006. *Pink Ribbons, Inc: Breast Cancer and the Politics of Philanthropy.* Minneapolis, MN: University of Minnesota Press.

Klawiter, Maren. 2008. *The Biopolitics of Breast Cancer: Changing Cultures of Disease and Activism.* Minneapolis, MN: University of Minnesota Press.

Lorde, Audre. 1997. *The Cancer Journals: Special Edition.* San Francisco: Aunt Lute Books.

Morrow, Monica, Yun Li, Amy K. Alderman, Reshma Jagsi, Ann S. Hamilton, John J. Graff, Sarah T. Hawley, and Steven J. Katz. 2014. "Access to Breast Reconstruction After Mastectomy and Patient Perspectives on Reconstruction Decision Making." *JAMA Surgery* 149 (10): 1015–21.

Pickens, Theri A. 2014. *New Body Politics: Narrating Arab and Black Identity in the Contemporary United States*. New York: Routledge.

Price Herndl, Diane. 2002. "Reconstructing the Posthuman Feminist Body Twenty Years after Audre Lorde's *Cancer Journals*." In *Disability Studies: Enabling the Humanities*, edited by Sharon L. Snyder, Brenda Jo Brueggemann, and Rosemarie Garland-Thomson, 144–55. New York: The Modern Language Association.

———. 2006. "Our Breasts, Our Selves: Identity, Community, and Ethics in Cancer Autobiographies." *Signs* 32 (1): 221–45.

Rubin, Lisa R., and Molly Tanenbaum. 2011. "'Does That Make Me a Woman?': Breast Cancer, Mastectomy, and Breast Reconstruction Decisions Among Sexual Minority Women." *Psychology of Women Quarterly* 35 (3): 401–14.

Ryan, Cynthia. 2004. "Am I Not a Woman? The Rhetoric of Breast Cancer Stories in African American Women's Popular Periodicals." *Journal of Medical Humanities* 25 (2): 129–50.

Saywell, Cherise, Lisa Beattie, and Lesley Henderson. 2000. "Sexualized Illness: The Newsworthy Body in Media Representations of Breast Cancer." In *Ideologies of Breast Cancer: Feminist Perspectives*, edited by Laura Potts, 37–62. New York: St. Martin's Press.

Sedgwick, Eve Kosofsky. 1992. "White Glasses." *The Yale Journal of Criticism* 5 (3): 193–208.

———. 1993. *Tendencies*. Durham, NC: Duke University Press.

Siebers, Tobin. 2006. "Disability in Theory: From Social Constructionism to the New Realism of the Body." In *The Disability Studies Reader*, edited by Lennard J. Davis, 173–83. New York: Routledge.

Solomon, Alisa. 1992. "The Politics of Breast Cancer." *Camera Obscura* 28: 157–77.

Waples, Emily. 2013. "Emplotted Bodies: Breast Cancer, Feminism, and the Future." *Tulsa Studies in Women's Literature* 33 (1): 47–70.

Vision and Precarity in Marjane Satrapi's *Persepolis*

Golnar Nabizadeh

What does it mean to survive, and when, and how, does survival matter? As the editors of this special issue have suggested, "To survive is messy, elaborate, layered," contingent as it is on biological, political, and material conditions that support life or liveliness. The claim for the renewed centrality of survival in modern times rests on the recognition of widespread threats to human life, social, and physical environments brought about by political violence, social persecution, and ecological crises. Domestic violence, the right to abortion, and equal pay are only a few of the additional issues that disproportionately impact women's lives. Survival is always contingent on the unfolding of an event's horizon and is shaped by evolving circumstances rather than guaranteed. The term itself is used in a variety of contexts: capital-S "Survivor," situated historically, may refer to a person who survived the Holocaust; in popular contemporary culture, the term refers to a reality game show franchise where contestants must "survive" in seemingly difficult and "exotic" settings. Ranging from the profound to the superficial, "survival" is multiply inflected in contemporary culture, and more often than not, these inflections overlap and contradict one another. Survival is marked by precarity and persistence, two qualities that also mark the text under analysis in this article.

With these permutations in mind, in this paper I explore the multiple modalities of survival in Marjane Satrapi's "autographic" memoir, *Persepolis* (2003/4). Influenced by Art Spiegelman's *Maus* (1996) and David B.'s *Epileptic* (2002), Satrapi's comic skillfully addresses difficult subjects through an iconic visual style. Like both Spiegelman and B., Satrapi uses the comic form to explore the relationship between personal memories

WSQ: Women's Studies Quarterly 44: 1 & 2 (Spring/Summer 2016) © 2016 by Golnar Nabizadeh.

and cultural history. In this respect, I suggest that *Persepolis* significantly contributes to feminist cultural histories, because Satrapi's story is told through a female and Iranian perspective, two descriptors that have been—at least historically —infrequently linked within Western discourses, including feminist conversations.[1]

Narrating Women's Lives

I use the term "autographic" in reference to Gillian Whitlock and Anna Poletti's neologism in a special issue of *Biography*. Leveraging Leigh Gilmore's conceptual term "autobiographics" in her landmark study on feminist self-representation (1994), Whitlock and Poletti broadly define "autographics" as "[l]ife narrative fabricated in and through drawing and design using various technologies, modes, and materials" (2008, v). As one mode of autographic writing, comics offer what I call here a "frame of recognition" for the subjects they portray. By "frame of recognition," I mean first the physical frame—usually in the form of a line—that encloses images and words in comics, and second, the way that these frames are figuratively deployed to redress overdetermined narratives of marginalized subjectivities, including women's lives. In women's life writing, the work of comics is particularly significant because of the personalized field of vision that the form promotes. As Hillary Chute suggests, "The types of challenges we see in women's graphic narrative are not found anywhere else—or anywhere else in a *post*-avant-garde horizon," and part of the political significance of these images lies in their complexity and avoidance of an "obviously 'correct' feminist politics" (2010, 4–5, emphasis in original). The reader can observe the subtleties of narrating womanhood in *Persepolis* with its careful unraveling of cross-cultural codes and expectations.

Since the 1970s, women's life writing has gained richness and depth from the production of graphic memoirs such as the underground anthology, *Wimmen's Comix Collective* (1972–1992), and more recently, Alison Bechdel's *Fun Home: A Family Tragi-Comic* (2006), Julie Doucet's *My New York Diary* (1999), and Aline Kominsky-Crumb's *Need More Love* (2007). These works demonstrate the ability of visual narratives to agitate, inform, and unsettle assumptions about women's lives and their histories, while representing those histories in new and visually arresting ways. Bechdel, for example, meticulously traces over old diary entries to re-historicize her childhood, while Kominsky-Crumb utilizes a mixed-media format to chart the conflicting messages she received as a young woman about femininity and sexuality. In each case, the author's personal approach to narration informs the aesthetic design of the text. The complex feelings in each autobiographical work, such as feelings of shame and guilt about sexuality, suicide, and disease, are literally given space for visualization, a process that generates creative interventions into understanding survival and subjectivity. The comic's form, then, itself a medium that has gained wider acceptance only in recent decades, seems an ideal platform through which to explore these affective constellations.

Within this context, one can evaluate the significance *Persepolis* holds in extending the visual vocabulary of autobiographic narratives. Satrapi's vibrant drawings attest to the contradictions, complications, and demands of survival and highlight the diversity of women's lives in Iran to augment the visual archive. Satrapi clarifies the commemorative function of the work in the book's preface, stating, "I also don't want those Iranians who lost their lives in prisons defending freedom . . . or who were forced to leave their families and flee their homeland to be forgotten" (Satrapi 2003, ellipsis in original). Through its emphasis on the importance of witnessing, the narrative elevates counter-historical narratives that are mostly unknown by a Western reading public, such as Iran's political history in the twentieth century, the mass executions of political prisoners following the 1979 Revolution, and other losses that populate its pages. At the same time, the story attests to the conditions under which survival persists, often unexpectedly. *Persepolis* thus reminds the reader of the precarity of survival, a condition that is always contingent on the unfolding of circumstances—political, social, material—and the ways in which liveliness can be encountered under the most difficult circumstances.

Satrapi's text, then, bears witness to those lives lost or disavowed in official historical records, both in Iran and in the West. Figured as a work of witnessing, the text commemorates individuals who have perished and whose lives stand in, symbolically, for the thousands who were victims of war and revolution. Like photography, the hand-drawn narrative records an indexical mark in the midst of death—and here, the mark is linked directly to the hand of its creator, rather than the surface of the photographic plate or digital screen. This physical tracing bears the imprint of survival, the "I am here" of articulation expressed through the material line of the text. In this way, the text expands the visual archive by depicting events that have been rarely captured through other visual media such as photography or film. This visual intimacy is, I argue, particularly powerful in women's storytelling, because it tends to the ambiguities between appearance and reality in playful, provocative, and painful ways. This article explores the ways in which the text depicts strategies for survival under repressive circumstances, particularly in relation to women's lives. In this regard, I analyze the role of witnessing in the text and the representation of violence, Satrapi's "miraculous" survival after she attempts suicide, the ways in which trauma generates nonlinear narratives, and the interrelationship between humor and mourning as a creative strategy of survival.

Remembrance and Aesthetics in *Persepolis*

Throughout *Persepolis*, Marjane and other characters repeatedly emphasize the importance of remembering lost lives, both in the text's present and in retrospect. The political import of the text is thus heightened, not only because of the narrative proper, but also because of the self-conscious futurity of the narrative, as acts of remembrance ricochet between past, present, and future audiences of the story. Translated from French, the first English edition of *Persepolis* consists of two volumes: *Persepolis: The Story of a Childhood*, and *Persepolis 2: The Story of a Return*.

The first volume depicts the author's childhood avatar—Marji's—early life in Iran, set against the 1979 Revolution and the Iran-Iraq War, which raged for almost eight years between 1980 and 1988. As the story commences, the reader is introduced to Marji as a schoolgirl, the daughter of middle-class intellectuals, whose class has recently been compelled to wear the veil under the dictates of the new Islamic Government. The first volume traces the contours of Marji's life and her growing political consciousness across domestic and public domains subject to heavy surveillance by the new regime. From its opening pages, her story depicts the tensions that permeate daily life after the 1979 Revolution. This is perhaps best exemplified by the introduction of the mandatory hijab described in the book's opening sequence. Throughout the story, Satrapi depicts these and other restrictions on women's attire, modes of conduct, and demeanor, and also the ways in which these incursions are challenged by the female (and male) characters in her work. In the opening pages, for example, Satrapi depicts her classmates playing with their headscarves as skipping ropes, which foregrounds forms of civil resistance in adulthood. All too soon, we learn of traumatic events in Marji's life, such as the execution of her beloved uncle Anoosh, and the devastating human cost of the Iran-Iraq War. Eventually, to secure their daughter's survival outside this fraught setting, Marji's parents send her abroad to Vienna.

Persepolis 2 thus opens with fourteen-year-old Marjane—the author's adolescent avatar—describing her arrival in Vienna in 1984. Marjane has come to Austria with the "idea of leaving a religious Iran for an open and secular Europe" (Satrapi 2004, 1). During her years there, these ideas are tested as Marjane faces other challenges to her survival, including heartbreak, racism, and physical and psychic homelessness. After being homeless for several months and surviving severe bronchitis, Marjane decides to return to Iran. While in Vienna, she pretends that she is French, rather than Iranian, with the *récitatif*: "Being Iranian was a heavy burden to bear at the time" (195). Marjane's disavowal of her Iranian identity is inverted after her return to Tehran, where her experiences overseas alienate her from her friends. Feeling increasingly isolated, and after turning to a number of mental health professionals without experiencing any improvement, Marjane attempts suicide twice. Her improbable survival (her doctor exclaims, "It must be a miracle!") initiates a shift in Marjane's sense of self; she decides that she "was not made to die" and trains as an aerobics instructor before completing a course at the College of Art in Tehran. This volume closes the narrative of *Persepolis*, as Marjane permanently leaves Iran for France in 1994 having been accepted into the School of Decorative Arts in Strasbourg.

Satrapi's visual style is informed by her training in fine arts in Iran and Europe and incorporates distinct influences, such as German Expressionist film, as well as traditional elements in Iranian "miniature" paintings. Several critics deemed *Persepolis* "naive" and "unskilled" upon its publication. Yet it is precisely this lack of artfulness that provides the narrative with its affective power. As Nima Naghibi and Andrew O'Malley posit, the presumed naïveté of Satrapi's illustrations frequently camouflages the complex politics in the narrative, along with the use of a medium associated "primarily with either low-brow or juvenile readers and narratives" (2005, 234). Naghibi and O'Malley point to Dana Heller's work in identifying the subversive potential of comics or cartoons— including as a feminist strategy—because of the way in which messages can be infused, or camouflaged, into these forms that are generally considered nonthreatening (2003, 31). Indeed, this potentiality dovetails usefully with the iconic capacity of comics, which as comics theorist Scott

McCloud has noted, encourages readers to project themselves onto the characters they encounter. By utilizing an abstracted, nonrealistic mode of representation, Satrapi augments the significance of minor details through what Scott McCloud calls their "iconic abstraction" (1993, 54). Satrapi's "simplified" visual style enlivens the narrative, because it conveys the traumatic memories therein. Rather than seeking to represent the past through a photographic likeness, Satrapi's visual style allows the reader to project their identification with the text precisely through its simplicity.

The text is rendered in stark black-and-white images. Satrapi has explained that she grappled with how to depict violence in *Persepolis*, given that representations of violent events have become "so normal, so banal," despite their depiction of occurrences which in themselves are "not normal" at all (Hajdu 2004, 35). Satrapi suggests that for readers who can readily access images that portray violence in hyperreal detail to come across more of the same in the novel might only contribute to the banality that haunts modern images of violence. Satrapi thus chooses to depict the horror of violence through a different visual mode. Instead of vivid color, she uses black and white to paint her images of bloodshed, stating, "Black and white makes [violence] more abstract and more interesting" (Hajdu 2004, 35). As Ann Cvetkovich observes, the use of black and white in *Persepolis* demonstrates "testimony's power to provide forms of truth that are emotional rather than factual" (2008, 114). Here, the reader is afforded access to affective truths that have been written out of formal historical narratives.

Indeed, the narrative structure of the work is itself subject to this testimonial impulse. Chute suggests that "[i]mages in comics appear in fragments, just as they do in actual recollection; this fragmentation, in particular, is a prominent feature of traumatic memory" (2010, 4). Indeed, this fragmentation is also evident in the co-constitutive relationship between the *récitatif*—the authorial narrative—and the diegetic text, usually in the form of speech bubbles, so that most graphic narratives are polyphonic in structure, creating space for past and present to jostle alongside one another on the same page and frequently in the same panel. This oscillation is complicated further by the images that accompany the written word, and the slippages in between, which generate multiple layers of meaning. These attributes are evident in *Persepolis*, with its dramatic yet playful invocation of a story that moves between past and present to reveal the complexities of physical and psychic survival.

In the history of comics, the material survival of such texts is itself a relatively recent phenomenon. In the early twentieth century, comics, at least in the North American tradition, were ephemera, designed to last only for immediate consumption in Sunday newspapers. It was only from the middle of the twentieth century on that comics, a particular mode of graphic narratives, could be printed on better quality stock as printing and production costs decreased. As a material work, *Persepolis* will persist in circulation beyond the lifetime of its creator and, indeed, its critics. Throughout its pages, survival is evident across several orders, all of which demonstrate the precarious nature of this condition. On one hand, we have the survival of the main character and author, who attempts suicide, as relayed within the text. That Marjane's survival is unexpected is indicated through the word "miraculous" in the story, used by Marjane, her doctors, and her therapists. Its unlikeliness re-instills a liveliness where once there was little. On the other hand, we encounter representations of individuals who have perished under horrific circumstances and who are memorialized within the pages of Satrapi's work. Marjane's Uncle Anoosh, her neighbor, Neda, and family friends Siamak Jari and Mohsen Shakiba, are immortalized through the narrative—image and text—that now remains intact beyond each of their respective lifespans. The commemoration of each life stands in for the broader recognition in Satrapi's preface to the memory of millions of individuals who have perished in Iran's recent history and whom Satrapi insists must not be forgotten. As we will see, this injunction is repeatedly invoked throughout *Persepolis*.

A Crisis of Witnessing

Satrapi defines *Persepolis* as a text that bears witness. In an interview, she explains: "I was born in a country in a certain time, and I was witness to many things. I was a witness to a revolution. I was a witness to war. I was witness to a huge emigration. I was a witness when I came back" (Leith 2004). Cathy Caruth offers a useful definition of testimony, one that resonates with Marjane's quest to "not forget": "To *testify*—to *vow to tell*, to *promise* and produce one's own speech as material evidence for truth—is to accomplish a *speech act*, rather than to simply formulate a statement" (1995, 17, emphasis in original). Satrapi alternatively occupies the position of a primary and secondary witness (observing events first hand, and remediating the past through imagined memories respectively), and the production of *Persepolis* is a testament to Satrapi's traumatic survival. As Caruth suggests, traumatic survival can be understood in relation to the "temporality of the missed event," and in this context may be signposted by a complicated engagement with the past, possibly in the form of a "responsibility or a command" (2006, 3). Marjane internalizes a responsibility toward the past and its contents, and forms of remembrance permeate the text.

The reader encounters instances where family and friends perish under the hand of the new regime or in the course of the Iran-Iraq War. These traumas are injurious for Marjane, and the first volume of *Persepolis* is studded with these multiple forms of loss. In the episode entitled "The Heroes," the reader learns that three thousand political prisoners were released following the Shah's deposition and that Marji's family "knew two of them" (2003, 47). Below a panoramic frame, which shows prisoners being released from imprisonment, the reader is presented with two panels that resemble identity cards for Siamak Jari and Mohsen Shakiba, both of whom are friends of the Satrapi family. The details that accompany each panel catalogue their names, dates of birth, and dates of incarceration and release. The detailing concludes, "Political Conviction: Communist," and this text stands immediately above their shadows, which stretch deep into the panel's depth of field against an otherwise white background.

As part of the expressionist idiom of *Persepolis*, these panels provide one example of the way Satrapi uses monochromatic contrast to amplify the dramatic tension of the narrative. Read in the context of the previous episode, in which Marji learns about the kinds of torture that Communist revolutionaries faced under the Shah's regime, the shadows resemble tombstones, acknowledging the fate of many revolutionaries executed under the Shah's regime. On another level, the men's shadows herald the near future in their strong resemblance to the *chador* that many women would don under the Islamic Regime. Thus the celebrations following the Shah's exile, represented in a full-page panel with a cheering population (Satrapi 2003, 42), turn out to be premature, as the new regime increasingly curtails the fundamental rights and freedoms of its citizens. The shadows in the "identity card" panel also foreground the fates of both men, as Mohsen is soon found murdered in his home (65) and Siamak's sister is "executed in his place" as he and his family cross the border "hidden among a flock of sheep" (66).

Visuality of Death

Persepolis thus continually underscores the inherent instability of survival, as the narrative is hewn from a keen appreciation of what it means to
survive or perish in the face of this instability. In one sequence devoid of
speech or *récitatif*, a young man falls to his death from a rooftop after the
"morality police" storm a party, scattering its occupants in all directions.
The sequence builds in tension as the reader follows the chase across
moonlit rooftops. The police eventually gain ground and the man attempts
to jump from one rooftop to the next, but fails. The final panel in this sequence depicts the moon shining above the rooftops, and I suggest that
the reader can project the role of the "silent witness" onto the moon. In
Satrapi's visuality of death, there tends to be a figure or object that remains
present either within or beyond the panel in which death or loss occurs.
In the rooftop example, I suggest that the moon, whose light is present
throughout the scene (and on which the sequence ends), occupies a position similar to the reader—a constant presence watching the story unfold.
The visuality of death throughout the text thus involves an afterimage,
through the act of witnessing or recall. Thus visuality is brought to bear on
death in a way that emphasizes remembrance.

As Satrapi writes in her preface to the book, "I also don't want those
Iranians who lost their lives in prisons defending freedom . . . or who were
forced to leave their families and flee their homeland to be forgotten. One
can forgive but one should never forget" (2003). This promise is repeatedly relayed in the text itself, by different characters and by Marjane herself.
As she prepares to leave Iran as a fourteen-year-old her father exclaims,
"Don't ever forget who you are!" This time, Marji breaks the fourth wall
and replies, "No. I won't ever forget" (148).

The solemnity of Marji's expression is enhanced by the white "reflection" light, which seems to enshrine her image as an icon. Her gaze meets
the reader's as a reminder that both she and the reader are literary witnesses to the events that have been depicted in the preceding pages. The meeting of Marji's gaze with that of the reader produces an oscillation between
the two positions, as the reader encounters Marji, who is watching the
reader observe her. The narrative moment bears precisely on both movements: Marji speaks to the reader on behalf of Iranians from her genera-

tion and that of her parents, and in doing so she breaks the implied world of the text and interrupts its temporal setting. The reader is thus called into a direct relationship to the text, through Marji's "outward" gaze. Satrapi uses this technique sparingly throughout *Persepolis*, and the material lines of the artist's hand are used to establish and disrupt the gaze. In the example discussed here, the encounter between Marji and the reader brings the episode to a close, and its position in the bottom right-hand corner of the page reinforces this act of closure.

Notably, the imperative to bear witness does not—or perhaps cannot—always demand a faithful interpretation of temporality. As Satrapi described in an interview for the *International Journal of Comic Arts*, beyond the desire of storytelling, "there's something extra when you position yourself as a witness: you also have to re-orient your mind" (quoted in Chute 2010, 166). I suggest that this becomes particularly relevant in traumatic circumstances where survival announces itself as a conditional circumstance. For example, Art Spiegelman's *In the Shadow of No Towers* (2004) describes the author's impressions of the attacks on the World Trade Center and his struggle in the aftermath of this event. The work is printed on thick, oversized card stock and uses an episodic structure. With regard to this structure Spiegelman has explained that he could only bear to create one double-page spread per monthly basis, as he feared that his survival was not guaranteed beyond each deadline. Accordingly, every episode carries the date span in which it was created, a reminder of the material limits to the role of the witness. These examples from Satrapi and Spiegelman demonstrate narrative reorientation in response to trauma and the ways in which the conditionality of survival finds itself expressed through the disruption of everyday temporal frameworks. In each case, the reader is presented with an attempt on the part of the narrator to make sense of the insensible.

In an episode of *Persepolis* entitled "The Bracelet," for example, the reader learns about the death of Neda Baba-Levy, Marji's Jewish friend and neighbor, who is killed by a bomb blast (Satrapi 2003, 142). While her mother uncomfortably suggests that the Baba-Levy's might have left home on the Sabbath, Marji realizes the devastating truth when she sees Neda's hand partially exposed under the building rubble. In particular, she recognizes the bracelet the wrist wears and is able to identify the body part, horrifyingly, as belonging to Neda.

The episode ends with her explanation, "No scream in the world could have relieved my suffering and my anger," adorning a solid black panel (Satrapi 2003, 142). This panel sequence presents the reader with what Marji would perhaps see with her eyes covered. In *Persepolis*, this event takes place when Marji is twelve. However, Satrapi has explained that this event actually took place when she was eighteen, after her return from Austria to Iran. She explains, "The feeling of seeing a bomb falling [at any time] is the same. . . . Who cares if it happened at this time or another time?" (Roberts 2015). Satrapi's statement describes the way that traumatic events can disrupt "everyday" interpretive frameworks. The devastating impact of "seeing a bomb falling" remains the same, regardless of whether this event is witnessed at the age of twelve or eighteen. Indeed, one can suggest that the chronological inaccuracy of the event serves to emphasize the way in which narrative frameworks can "hold" traumas that might otherwise be dismissed. In turn, the discontinuous narration attests to the difficulties of survival because it seeks to make sense of an extraordinary event that cannot be understood within ordinary, chronological, historical narratives.[2] The double trauma of living through war and revolution, and witnessing this carnage thus rearranges the linear placement of the event.

Witnessing itself can trouble the demands of survival, and we see the disturbance that the necessity of reorientation provokes in the text. Overwhelmed by the affective landscape in Tehran, Marjane's attempts to communicate her experiences in Vienna to her family and friends are not successful. This failure is compounded by Marjane's sensitivity to the suffering of Iranians directly impacted by the war, and her shame for her absence. Upon her return to Iran from Vienna, her father explains the significant losses that have befallen large sections of the Iranian population, including mass executions. Following this exchange, Marjane decides, "I would never tell them anything about my Austrian life. They had suffered enough as it was" (Satrapi 2004, 103).

Another scene demonstrates the contradictory expectations she must navigate on her return. This conflict is revealed through a particular conversation: her friends ask whether she enjoyed having sex while living abroad and Marjane replies, "It depends who it's with," implicitly revealing that she has had more than one sexual partner. Her friends are outraged at this response, which challenges their perceptions of appropriate sexual behavior and confirms their ideas of what it means to live in the West. Rather than hear Marjane's story for its intended meaning, one friend asks her accusingly, "[Then] what's the difference between you and a whore???" (Satrapi 2004, 116). This experience leaves Marjane "even more depressed" (117), an affective state depicted across four panels by a black background that increasingly descends around her crumpling stature (114). On her mother's advice, she turns to a succession of therapists and doctors. Satrapi depicts three of these appointments in three consecutive frames. In each scene, Marjane offers different explanations for her depression, but does not secure meaningful responses from her listeners. In the second frame, for example, she explains, "When I was in Vienna . . . I was reduced to nothing. I thought that in coming back to Iran, this would change," to which the therapist's response is depicted as an ellipsis, " . . . " (117). The last doctor she sees prescribes medication, which only causes her to vacillate between numbness and a trancelike consciousness (118).

Marjane fantasizes how family and friends might tend to her in Iran. She imagines explaining that she suffered in Vienna, and envisions them compassionately showering her with treats as tokens of their understanding for her ordeals (113). This sequence constitutes a rare occasion in *Persepolis* where the written and visual messages directly reinforce one another with no irony. This sequence allows the reader access to Marjane's fantasy, which provides an important rendering of Marjane's desire to be understood. Here, the lexicon of survival is understood through fantasy, and the latter allows Satrapi to demonstrate the difficulties of navigating cross-cultural expectations, particularly in relation to women's lives.

Humor and Survival

There is evidence that Marjane's ability to survive the unbearable earlier in her life occurs partly through the use of humor. In an episode from *Persepolis* entitled "The Key," for example, the *récitatif* explains that soon after the Revolution, Marji and her classmates must line up "twice a day to mourn the war dead" and as funeral marches are played, they beat their breasts in a show of grief (Satrapi 2003, 95). (It is worth noting that classes were segregated along heteronormative gender lines following the Revolution.)

In this page-size panel, the girls are depicted at the moment their hands make contact with their chests, and the jagged lines around their hands represents the force of impact. Against a black background, their expressions—fixed in a glaze of enforced mourning—create a stark image of shallow grief. Here, the tessellated contours of the girls' hijabs correlate with the oppressive conditions of this prescribed mourning. The flat design of this panel speaks to the flattened affect that the schoolgirls express in this public display of grief. As she does in the earlier example of women subverting enforced dress in the public domain, Satrapi draws attention to the way in which this apparent compliance with authorial forces contains resistance.

The shallow performative modality of grief antithetically attests to the largely unconscious grief the girls feel under the strictures of the Islamic regime. As they adjust to the new ritual of mourning which becomes part of the fabric of school life, the students begin to parody this display of enforced grieving. Marji in particular parrots popular phrases associated with this form of public mourning. For example, in one panel, she writhes on the ground, and cheekily answers her teacher's question, "What are you doing?" with, "I'm suffering, can't you see?" (2003, 97). Within the space of a few frames, then, the narrative moves from depicting the conventions of mourning to its ridicule. The comedic element is frequently produced through the divergent messages delivered by the written text on one hand and the image on the other. This dual codification is a significant feature of comics because it allows each message to retain its integrity while it is read against the other. Similarly, when the class must decorate their classroom for the anniversary of the Revolution, the girls use toilet paper as garlands and remain united in their contravention by not revealing who instigated the prank. Again, the element of farce allows for a play of (and on) mourning to be enacted, for which the teacher reprimands the class. Within the precarity of their circumstances, the girls find resistance, and persistence, through parody.

Much like the heterodoxy of mourning, these acts of ridicule reside outside social conventions as they caricature "serious" performances deployed to enforce the legitimacy of the regime through their repetition. The parodic mode, then, speaks to a strategy of making difficult things "bearable" and allowing the girls to subsume their intimate grief beneath its ritualized performance. At the same time, the cathartic impact of these humorous scenes does not shore up the painful memories that are being recalled but allows them to be explored through the tender relief that child's play offers. The use of humor connects *Persepolis* to other autographic works, such as Kominsky-Crumb's *Need More Love*, Bechdel's *Fun Home*, and Spiegelman's *Maus, In the Shadow of No Towers*, and *Breakdowns* (2008), among others. In each of these works, humor is used in a variety of ways such as parody, slapstick, and wry commentary.

Conclusion

Survival finds itself expressed and contained through a multiplicity of forms—forms that are irreducible and creative, embedded as they are in historical, political, and cultural specificities. The intersections between visual and verbal content instantiate multiple meanings that mimic everyday slippages between appearances and reality in relation to material and discursive registers. Satrapi's *Persepolis* demonstrates the ways in which comics and graphic novels powerfully attest to and imagine strategies for survival in women's life writing. The author's autobiographical text is cast in black and white—which immediately sets the scene for the memories that form the focus of each episode. In turn, the episodes demonstrate the wide range of affective strategies that are essential for survival, such as grief, anger, and humor. What we see within the pages of *Persepolis* is not that storytelling is curtailed by the demands of survival but rather that storytelling *is* survival. The imperative to remember the past is nestled within each episode, as Satrapi narrates the words used by family and friends to animate their memories for the reader. In this process, it is an affective fidelity to the past that is privileged rather than a temporal one. This is not to suggest that Satrapi simply presents an ad hoc narrative, far from it, but rather that her narrative provides a counter-historical account of Iran post-1979 through its autobiographical focus.

Women's life writing has benefited from the entry of comics and graphic novels into the field. The simultaneous delivery of written and visual messages means that the reader must interpret both, and the construction of meaning will depend on the subtle interplay between both modes of communication. I suggest that this interplay is particularly significant in women's life writing, because the visual domain of comics allows the author to imagine invisible worlds and states of being through her hand. This provides a distinct contrast to the ways in which women's lived experiences have been historically silenced. Moreover, the highly personalized hand drawn images allow authors such as Satrapi to intimately connect their bodies with the histories they are representing. In *Persepolis*, Satrapi has combined these narrative and aesthetic dimensions to produce a text that offers important insights into the multiple modalities of survival in women's lives.

Golnar Nabizadeh is an honorary research fellow at the University of Western Australia. Her fields of research include visual culture, trauma narratives, and memory studies.

She has previously published on the work of Alison Bechdel, Shaun Tan, and adaptation in contemporary Australian art. She has a monograph forthcoming with Ashgate Publishing, entitled *Representation and Memory in Graphic Novels* (2017).

Notes

1. There are, of course, exceptions to this assertion, particularly in relation to Iranian women's life writing in an Anglo-American context, including *Reading Lolita in Tehran* by Azar Nafisi (2008); Tara Bahrampour, *To See and See Again: A Life in Iran and America* (1999); Azadeh Moaveni, *Lipstick Jihad: A Memoir of Growing Up Iranian in America and American in Iran* (2006); Firoozeh Dumas, *Funny in Farsi: A Memoir of Growing Up Iranian in America* (2003); and Gelareh Asayesh, *Saffron Sky: A Life Between Iran and America* (1999); as well as Nobel Laureate Shirin Ebadi's memoir, *Iran Awakening: One Woman's Journey to Reclaim Her Life and Country* (2006). In the context of mainstream comics, Miriam Kent explores the creation of Marvel Comic's teenage Muslim Pakistani hero Kamala Khan in "Unveiling Marvels: Ms. Marvel and the Reception of the New Muslim Superheroine" (2015).

2. My reading of this scene is indebted to Dori Laub's landmark essay on "Bearing Witness, or the Vicissitudes of Witnessing," in which he recounts a female patient's description of an explosion in Auschwitz. While I am not seeking to compare the trauma perpetuated by the Holocaust with the trauma that Satrapi describes in her narrative, Laub's sensitive reading of his patient's erroneous recollection about the details of the explosion (four, rather than one chimney exploding) is a useful analogue for the current discussion. Rather than discounting the patient's memory as incorrect, and therefore invalid, Laub suggests that the woman was testifying to something more radical within the confines of Auschwitz than the explosion itself. He suggests that her testimony concerned "the reality of an unimaginable occurrence," or in other words, "She was testifying not simply to empirical historical facts, but to the very secret of survival and of resistance to extermination" (1992, 61).

Works Cited

Asayesh, Galareh. 1999. *Saffron Sky*. Boston: Beacon Press.

B., David. 2002. *Epileptic*. Seattle: Fantagraphics.

Bahrampour, Tara. 1999. *To See and See Again*. Berkeley, CA: University of California Press.

Bechdel, Alison. 2006. *Fun Home*. New York: Houghton Mifflin.

Caruth, Cathy. 1995. Introduction to *Trauma: Explorations in Memory,* edited by Cathy Caruth, 3–12. Baltimore, MD: The Johns Hopkins University Press.

———. 2006. "An Introduction to Trauma, Memory, and Testimony." *Reading On* 1(1): 1–3.

Chute, Hillary. 2008. "The Texture of Retracing in Marjane Satrapi's *Persepolis*." *WSQ* 36 (1/2): 92–110.

———. 2010. *Graphic Women: Life Narrative and Contemporary Comics*. New York: Columbia University Press.

Cvetkovich, Ann. 2008. "Drawing the Archive in Alison Bechdel's *Fun Home*." *WSQ* 36 (1/2): 111–28.

Doucet, Julie. 2004. *My New York Diary*. Quebec: Drawn & Quarterly.

Dumas, Firoozeh. 2003. *Funny in Farsi*. New York: Villard Books.

Ebadi, Shirin. 2006. *Iran Awakening*. New York: Random House.

Gilmore, Leigh. 1994. *Autobiographics: A Feminist Theory of Women's Self-Representation*. Ithaca, NY: Cornell University Press.

Hajdu, David. 2004. "Persian Miniatures." *BookForum*, Oct/Nov, 32–35.

Heller, Dana A. 2003. "*Hothead Paisan*: Clearing a Space for a Lesbian Feminist Folklore." *New York Folklore* 19 (1): 27–44.

Kent, Miriam. 2015. "Unveiling Marvels: Ms. Marvel and the Reception of the New Muslim Superheroine." *Feminist Media Studies* 15 (3): 522–38.

Kominsky-Crumb, Aline. 2007. *Need More Love*. London: MQ Publications.

Laub, Dori. 1992. "Bearing Witness, or the Vicissitudes of Witnessing." In *Testimony: Crises of Witnessing in Literature, Psychoanalysis and History*, edited by Shoshanna Felman and Dori Laub, 57–74. New York: Routledge.

Leith, Sam. 2004. "A Writer's Life: Marjane Satrapi." *Telegraph*, December 12.

McCloud, Scott. 1993. *Understanding Comics: The Invisible Art*. New York: Kitchen Sink Press.

Moaveni, Azadeh. 2005. *Lipstick Jihad*. New York: PublicAffairs.

Nafisi, Azar. 2003. *Reading Lolita in Tehran*. New York: Random House.

Naghibi, Nima, and Andrew O'Malley. 2005. "Estranging the Familiar: 'East' and 'West' in Satrapi's *Persepolis*." *ESC: English Studies in Canada* 31 (2/3): 223–47.

Robbins, Trina. 2016. *The Complete Wimmen's Comix*. Seattle: Fantagraphics.

Roberts, Sheila. 2015. "Marjane Satrapi Interview, *Persepolis*." MoviesOnline. Accessed March 1. http://www.moviesonline.ca/movienews_13781.html.

Satrapi, Marjane. 2003. *Persepolis: The Story of a Childhood*. Translated by Anjali Singh. New York: Pantheon.

———. 2004. *Persepolis 2: The Story of a Return*. Transated by L'Association. New York: Pantheon.

Spiegelman, Art. 1996. *The Complete Maus*. New York: Pantheon.

———. 2004. *In the Shadow of No Times*. New York: Pantheon.

Whitlock, Gillian, and Anna Poletti. 2008. "Self-Regarding Art." *Biography: An Interdisciplinary Quarterly* 31 (1): v–xxiii.

PART III. **THE MESH: SURVIVAL IN-BETWEEN**

Ornamenting the Unthinkable: Visualizing Survival under Occupation

Rebecca A. Adelman and Wendy Kozol

Repetitive, messy, and often hard to see: survival is rarely photogenic. Relative to spectacular scenes of violent dying or heroic living that comprise familiar images of military conflict, survival may look rather dull, if it appears at all. Militarized violence typically becomes visible in mortality, but survival blurs the distinctions between life and death in the precarious environments that war creates, thus eluding or confounding predominant visual modalities for representing war zones. Related to this, survival is often illegible in politicized wartime fantasies about life and death, an incomprehensibility rooted in its deviation from mythologized visions of living and dying. In part, mainstream news media may find it difficult to depict survival—and consequently, distant spectators may find survival difficult to envision—because it is ubiquitous and temporally expansive. Dramatic events lend themselves to capture in single-frame photographs or short film clips, while the ongoing task of surviving war lasts as long, or longer, than the conflict itself, a duration that is inimical to the narrative constraints of news media and entertainment genres.

Wartime survival is the maintenance of life in an extreme form of what Lauren Berlant characterizes as "crisis ordinariness" (2011, 10), a concept that encapsulates the everyday traumas and forms of precarity generated by the current global political economy. Structural violence nourishes crisis ordinariness, while circumscribing its visibility through corporate and state control of the media. Yet as generative as the idea of "crisis ordinariness" is, the "crisis" that modifies the "ordinariness" in this evocative phrase also risks overshadowing it. To focus too narrowly on abiding

WSQ: Women's Studies Quarterly **44**: 1 & 2 (Spring/Summer 2016) © 2016 by Rebecca A. Adelman and Wendy Kozol. All rights reserved.

crisis (or interlocking crises) is to risk overlooking the active, inventive, everyday survival strategies that crisis elicits, and the ways that those innovations mitigate the crisis that begets them. Shifting our gaze away from crisis, we look here to a visual document of livable forms of ordinariness that emerge in fissures within the protracted crisis of militarized violence.

Confronting survival in visual cultures of war often requires departing from ideological absolutes (for sometimes the work of survival is ugly) and fantasies about resistance (for sometimes the work of survival is primarily utilitarian). Instead, this visual departure opens up alternative critical, political, and spectatorial possibilities. Here, we consider the interweaving of survival, catastrophe, and ordinariness in the needlepoint artwork of Esther Nisenthal Krinitz to illustrate this potential. Krinitz, who lived through the Nazi occupation of Poland, juxtaposes the luscious materiality and pastoral settings of thirty-six fabric collage and embroidered panels with a visual narrative of surviving genocidal violence (Krinitz and Steinhardt 2005). Arresting both for its virtuosic level of detail and frank rendition of the occupation and attendant traumas, Krinitz's needlework ornaments the conjunction of the horrific and the quotidian. This jarring combination confronts viewers even as the haptic richness and sensory elegance of her craft pulls us toward spectatorial pleasures.

Building on Eve Kosofsky Sedgwick's insistence on the importance of reparative practices that work to ameliorate the traumatic impacts of structural violence, we consider how the sensory lure of Krinitz's needlepoint grates against knowledge about the miseries these scenes depict (2003, 144). Reparative practices, as Sedgwick defines them, constitute the "many ways selves and communities succeed in extracting sustenance from the objects of a culture—even of a culture whose avowed desire has often been not to sustain them" (150–51). Through an exploration of the haptic and visual aspects of Krinitz's reparative artistic practice, we argue that her creations visualize survival as a process of extracting sustenance from an imperiled material world. Critical attention to the reparative dimensions of this extractive work, in turn, reframes feminist studies away from a preoccupation with the victimization of women in wartime.

We locate our critical project at the intersection of apparently irreconcilable phenomena: indexical representation, militarized violence, and survival within war zones. In "Ornamenting the Unthinkable," we address the surprising, and often unstable, recombinations that occur at this seemingly incommensurable junction. Before analyzing Krinitz's work, we set forth a conceptual framework for a feminist study of visual practices that depict survival in militarized environments. This framework informs our subsequent engagement with Krinitz's art and underpins our concluding reflections on the spectatorial dilemmas that it provokes. These dilemmas are rooted, we suggest, in the tension between appreciating the work as she surely wished (for it is lavish, even sumptuous), and resisting the temptation to drift so far into the profound loveliness of the needlework that we forget the intractability of crisis and trauma.

Gender and the Invisibility of the Nonspectacular

Survival in the context of militarized violence is the process of continually navigating phenomena that are essentially incompatible but coexist all the time: the maintenance of life in an environment engineered to *immiserate* or extinguish it. Stringing together one breath, another, and another yet again. Finding food, preparing it, eating it. Drifting off to sleep, waking some time later. Working or struggling to find work. Cleaning. Quiet intimacies, and little joys. All of this plays out on a fabric of suffering that unfolds around rather more spectacular injuries and deaths. This kind of living—in war zones, through state-sanctioned violence, or under occupation by enemy forces—is characterized by temporal extendedness and experiential repetitiousness, which makes the work of survival exhausting and often inhospitable to visual representation. Pitched below the register of the spectacular, survival is exponentially more common than familiar images of conflict would suggest. Indeed, it is nearly impossible to quantify the number of people affected by—and hence compelled to survive—militarized violence; even expansive casualty counts do not capture the way that such casualties ripple outward to impact families, children, and other kinship networks.[1]

Grindingly constant rather than episodically intense (like the violence of combat or airstrikes), survival is difficult to identify and compress into a narrative, and so is rarely made visible by the news media. In many ways, it is much easier to account for dying in war than living continually in and through it, and death is surely a more obvious target for visual representation. We turn to Krinitz's needlepoint precisely because she depicts survival so keenly—vibrant colors and textures anchor her stories in an animate lifeworld filled with natural and human features: trees, clothing, livestock, rain, wagons, farmers, soldiers, tools, haystacks, matzos, clouds, fences, and rivers. Most scholars who study visual cultures of war focus—not incorrectly—on representational strategies that make extreme suffering clear, knowable, and affecting to spectators. Or, conversely, they focus on how image-making technologies militate against such clarity. Many insist that seeing distant suffering can affectively move viewers beyond personal or national self-interest toward political action. On the other side, social critics have long decried mainstream news reporting for its voyeurism and promotion of hegemonic politics,[2] and for self-censorship that limits and distorts the flow of information (Taylor 1998). Motivating these debates are questions about how to represent the material, juridical, and political vulnerabilities that place certain populations at risk.

In a notable departure from this scholarly debate on representations of extreme suffering, Patricia Zimmermann's analysis of 1990s politically oriented independent filmmakers stands out for her explorations of how their films navigate personal and political subjectivities in relation to traumatic national and transnational histories (2000, 53). In these films, exemplified by Rebecca Baron's *okay bye-bye* (1998) and Rea Tajiri's *History and Memory* (1991), autobiographical documentarians cross genre boundaries to incorporate personal memories, found objects, and fictive elements in a complex intertwining of history and subjectivity. The historicizing lens of these films re-envisions visual relationships between subjectivity and the global political economy; yet for all their innovations, they do not access the dreary, quotidian struggles of survival.

Questioning the "real" of history—a practice fundamental to much work in feminist and cultural studies—also recurs in persistent and often intractable debates in visual culture studies about whether it is possible to represent massive traumas like the Holocaust and other state-sanctioned violence or terrorist attacks.[3] We suggest inverting the question, to trouble the relative invisibility of survival: Has survival, perhaps, seemed too small to represent? In *The Future of the Image*, Jacques Rancière posits that the question of whether something is representable should not be framed as a yes-or-no inquiry. Instead, he suggests querying the epistemic circumstances in which representability is determined by asking, "Under what conditions might it be said that certain things cannot be represented? Under what conditions can an unrepresentable phenomenon . . . be given a specific conceptual shape?" (2007, 109). If power dynamics organize and sustain the divisions between what can and cannot be seen, then introducing a feminist orientation into Rancière's question illuminates the gender politics operative in the representation and visibility of survival. Survival often happens in (presumably feminine) domestic spaces, a further explanation for its systematic exclusion from representations of war zones. Prominent visual archives of the Holocaust document women's victimization at the expense of images of women's survival strategies. Krinitz notably evades these visual traps, capturing the asphyxiating genocidal violence that insinuates itself into every corner of existence, while also showcasing the ingenuity required, and expended, to sustain life.

Broadly speaking, feminists who study militarized violence have shuttled between critical attention to conditions of gender victimization and celebratory explorations of agency, resistance, and activism. But how to represent the temporal expansiveness and lived complexity of survival without either idealizing or trivializing the struggles of the everyday? Women's testimonials have long been the centerpiece of feminist scholars' and activists' work; yet some raise concerns about the dangers of overidentification through social categories like gender, while ignoring the myriad factors constituting trauma survivors' agency (Grewal 2005; Hesford 2011). Rey Chow, for instance, critiques both Westerners' desire for the *authentic survivor*, the "passive victim on display," and paternalistic claims that alternative images restore "true subjectivity," for both can be assimilated into the colonizer's gaze (1996, 123). She argues that the search for an "authentic" subject of violence may serve to "enric[h] ourselves precisely with what can be called the surplus value of the oppressed" (124). Images of survival, lacking unequivocal visual stories of either resistance or immiseration, refuse spectators such gratification.

Critics like Judith Butler have demonstrated that Western nation-states like the United States and globally dominant media franchises deploy discursive strategies that elide the suffering of others and render their lives ungrievable (Butler 2004; 2009). Yet the remedy for this is not simply to make the suffering of others more visible. Asma Abbas argues that such displays typically benefit the privileged, who inhabit a sensorium that demands a "performance of suffering" and relegates sufferers to the status of objects to appease the interests of onlookers (2010). Accordingly, we look elsewhere to explore how representations of survival that envision circumscribed flourishing in spite of immiseration might facilitate the recognition of grievable lives, thus emphasizing the necessity of visual practices whose efficacy is not contingent on the display and consumption of spectacular injury.

Feminist cultural studies methodologies frequently proceed from critiques of exploitative media spectacles to alternative cultural practices that (apparently) depict empowerment.[4] Such a reading would likely emphasize Krinitz's choice of needlepoint, and her innovative use of this conventionally gendered medium. This is an important dimension of her artwork, but we propose a different optic to capture its profound connection to quotidian struggles for survival. We do this in the hope of advancing feminist conversations beyond the now predictable methodological, theoretical, and rhetorical trajectory that moves from a critique of (past) victimization to a progressive narrative about present (or future) empowerment. In other words, where is it possible to take a feminist critique beyond this redemptive paradigm, which cannot account for the endless and nonteleological work of survival, and thus risks misattributing a political impetus to it? Our feminist reading of Krinitz's artistic practice identifies it as a form of survival and a negotiation against—but never entirely free from—the political and social violences endemic to military occupations.

Flourishing in Catastrophe

Unlike the indexical imprint of a photograph, Krinitz's needlepoint depicts survival iconically, giving it material shape, weight, texture, fiber, and presence in time. By rendering the brutal conditions of survival in forms that are far from realistic (even as they are very detailed), Krinitz depicts the lifeworlds where she found resources for her survival. This corpus of thirty-six fabric panels illustrates her life before, during, and after the Nazi occupation of Poland.[5] Constructed through embroidery, other forms of needlework, and fabric collage, these panels vary in size (most are nineteen to forty-five inches per side) and aesthetic and narrative complexity, as they aggregate into a startling record of phenomena that scholars of visual culture often insist cannot be faithfully documented.[6]

Defining aesthetics expansively as "sensory perception and all of the diverse ways in which images and the work of representation engage it," Mark Reinhardt challenges critics who worry about the risks of "aestheticizing" or beautifying violence and suffering (2007, 23). Instead, he insists that aesthetic strategies can function to encourage "both critical engagement and a kind of metacritical reflection" rather than distancing subjects by turning them into gilded objects of suffering (26). The haptic intensity and ornamentality of Krinitz's needlepoint create aesthetic and narrative juxtapositions that, we argue, invite metacritical reflection on conditions of survival amid the horrors of war. In doing so, these panels are also a bold affront to predominant and problematically gendered patterns of Holocaust remembrance in which, as James E. Young writes, "photographers, curators, historians, and museumgoers continue to turn women into objects of memory, idealized casts of perfect suffering and victimization" (2009, 1778). Considering the prevalent figure of the mourning woman in atrocity photography, Marta Zarzycka argues that this figure "replaces the un-picturable character of trauma and loss with a recognizable scene" (2014, 64). In contrast, Krinitz's radically different vision, realized with a virtuoso's skill in vibrant materiality, is suffused with collective and individual traumas resulting from genocidal actions, but is not delimited by them—for her productivity defies assimilation into familiar narratives of paralyzing suffering, loss, and melancholy.

When Nazi soldiers came to her family's small village of Mniszek, Poland, in October 1942 and ordered the inhabitants onto a train bound for a death camp, fifteen-year-old Esther refused to go, escaping instead with her twelve-year-old sister Mania. Permanently separated from their parents, older brother, and two younger sisters, Esther and Mania changed their names and masqueraded as Polish Catholic farm girls. Esther and Mania are the beguiling protagonists of many of the panels, but these are more than pictures of girlish derring-do: both content and form depict the mechanics of survival. The panels follow the sisters' journey from their village to the home of Stefan, an acquaintance of their parents who hid them briefly but evicted them because of the risk posed to his family and property if they were discovered. Subsequent panels illustrate their movements from place to place until another farmer hired them to work on his land, which they did until Poland's liberation. The narrative continues after liberation, showing Esther and Mania's travels to the Maidanek concentration camp in a futile search for their family, after which Esther attached herself to the Polish and Russian armies that led her to Germany under their auspices. Reuniting once again with her sister, they then spent time in a displaced persons camp in Germany, which resulted in marriages and emigration: Mania and her husband to Palestine, Esther and hers to Brooklyn, near his family.

Unlike the more familiar dynamic, whereby outsiders represent victims of atrocity, Krinitz is both the creator and agent of these scenes, and their inventiveness and deliberate labor-intensiveness refute any sense that she is merely a victim of history. Trained as a dressmaker but not as an artist, Krinitz might be classified as an "outsider" or "visionary" artist.[7] Outsider artists, in Daniel Wojcik's description, are "people with no formal artistic training, who are isolated from dominant culture and the mainstream art world, and who create art that is idiosyncratic or without precedent" (2008, 179).[8] Many scholars, including Wojcik, note that outsider art is often rooted in or expressive of personal loss or struggle (187). Yet this critical frame risks occluding the broader political significance of such work—a risk especially keen when the artists are women—by making it seem solipsistically therapeutic. Conceptualizing outsider art in such a way obscures its engagements with social and political forms of power—a common strategy for trivializing women's experiences and critiques.

In its connections to domesticity, utility, and the ordinariness of women's household chores, the medium of needlework is experientially and structurally similar to survival. The repetition (or drudgery) of sewing innumerable tiny stitches reenacts the constant, incremental micropolitics of survival. Moreover, the apparently unremarkable nature of needlework in general is uncannily resonant with Krinitz's experience of occupation, in which she and Mania often "hid in plain sight" (Shapiro-Perl 2012, 234). Against the prevailing imperative for absolute gravitas in creative work on the Holocaust (Langford 2013, 112), the almost cartoonish and haptic liveliness of the panels compels a different way of looking. In a critical appreciation of art whose production is reliant upon physically demanding "fabrication," Paula Owen argues that such works are "grounded, repeated physical responses to an unstable environment rather than assertions of ideological prowess" (2011, 95). This is not to say that Krinitz's art is apolitical, but rather that, like the work of survival, it is not primarily political. The politics that might adhere to her conjoining of memory and history, of ideology and materiality, are central to but not definitive of her creative process, its products, or the survival that it represents. This is not artwork that is "merely" a personal, therapeutic, autobiographical exercise; rather, it showcases the intricate ways that living and politics enmesh in the daily survival of occupation.

Moreover, the intense corporeality of Krinitz's art reinserts female embodiment into Holocaust remembrance. Anyone who has ever handled needle and thread would appreciate the physical experience of doing such exacting needlework—the countless fingertip pricks, the tiredness behind the eyes—and so could surely imagine the breath-holding steadiness of

hand and body required to materialize Krinitz's visions.[9] Continual endurance of these tiny stresses and injuries, to say nothing of the emotional
effort required to recall these scenes and render them precisely, is a lavish-
ly colored crafting, or reenactment, of survival itself.[10] As Owen observes
about most labor-intensive crafting, the "process is inextricable from the
final result" (2011, 83). While the form of Krinitz's work replicates the demands of survival, the larger process records the temporal characteristics
of the trauma from which it originated.

Although the thirty-six panels can be arranged into a roughly linear
narrative, Krinitz did not create them in that order. The first two panels,
made in 1977 and 1978, depict nostalgic prewar scenes of her childhood
in Mniszek. Krinitz then took a ten-year hiatus, and upon resuming her
work, created panel twenty-six, which depicts a nightmare that she had in
November 1942. She created the thirty-fifth and thirty-sixth panels last,
in 1999, portraits of her husband (as she recalled him in 1949) and her
granddaughter. While the beginning and the end of her story are chrono-
logically sequential, the traumatic middle is heedless of the demands of an
orderly, linear, and progressive time. October 15, 1942, for instance, the
day that Esther and Mania fled the Gestapo, occupies five separate panels.[11] Just as nonlinearity resonates with the chaotic psychic experiences
of trauma, Krinitz's extended temporal process—often taking months to
create panels that depict single moments—mimics the temporality and
durability of traumatic memories (Felman and Laub 1992; Caruth 1996).

In creatively inhabiting trauma, Krinitz refuses the authority of its
founding violence to dictate the terms of its representation. Her artistic
production, which spanned two decades and included seven years (1991–
1998) of intense generativity, continually reiterates the fact of her aliveness, a stealing of vital time away from orchestrated killing engineered to
deprive it.[12] And then there is the reparative work of the process itself. Ann
Cvetkovich posits that comforting practices and routines, like crafting,
function as life-affirming antidotes to depression. Immersive and inventive,
the work of crafting constructs a "utopia of ordinary habit" (2012, 191).
Craftwork unfolds incrementally, demanding (and eventually rewarding)
a substantial—and potentially limitless—investment of time. Cvetkovich
theorizes this as a productive refusal of the "slow death" wrought by systems designed to grind out human life (167). The regularity of the stitches,
made one by one in a disciplined practice that required months of steady
work and patience, claims aliveness through the ordinary activity of craft-

FIG 1. Esther Nisenthal Krinitz, *Stefan's House*. Embroidery and fabric collage, 1993. © Art and Remembrance. Caption reads: "October 15 1942. My sister and I arrived in the village of Dombrowa and went to the house of Stefan our fathers friend, we begged him to help us, he embraced us and promised to help, but after two days, he sent us out into the rain, with no place to go but the forest."

ing. But against the redemptive fantasy that creative practice can fully and finally eradicate trauma, the duration of Krinitz's painstaking engagement with the Holocaust signals the recurrence and persistence of suffering, as well as the daily recommitment to engage it.

Stefan's House—panel twenty-one, created in 1993—is especially evocative of this process of flourishing in catastrophic conditions (fig. 1). The panel, among the largest in Krinitz's oeuvre, condenses four separate events into a single rectangle, roughly 56" x 40": arrival at Stefan's house, hiding in his attic and stringing tobacco leaves, expulsion from his house into the rain, and hiding in the forest. In the diegesis of the panel, these events are not logically arranged (another echo of traumatic temporal confusion), and the hand-stitched caption at the bottom is essential for interpreting the scenes and the sequence that links them. Krinitz's luminous needlepoint skills in this panel display her characteristic cleverness in representing elements that might not lend themselves to expression in this medium. A detailed resplendence of color and texture ranges from the gray stitches that indicate drops of rain falling on Esther and Mania, to the mushrooms growing in the forest, leaves on the ground, berries on the bushes, and the paisley pattern of the girls' dresses. The quadrupling of Esther and her sister heightens this sensory intensity and serves as a profuse assertion of their mobility, presence, and aliveness, both past and present.

This scene, moreover, both rebuffs a voyeuristic gaze at the girls during this period of mortal vulnerability, and refuses to perform abjection. In two of the four moments, Esther and Mania seem to be smiling, as the red stitches for their mouths are gently curved and upturned. Elsewhere, their mouths are grimly set, barely frowning behind the diagonal spray of raindrops. The sharpest revelation of their desperation is also completely masked; they greet Stefan with their arms wide, but while his expression is beatific, viewers see Esther and Mania from the back, deprived of whatever secret confession their faces might make. We are not suggesting that survival is a simple matter of stoicism, but rather highlighting the intervention that Krinitz's aesthetic choices make in dominant modes of representing the Holocaust, which generally depend upon a narrowly conceived ideal of female victimization (Young 2009, 1778).[13] Krinitz's needlework panels also deviate from more familiar Holocaust imagery in their relative lack of carnage; for example, even the bodies of dead Nazi soldiers in panel thirty-two, *The Way to Berlin*, are covered with branches. When familiar symbols of the Holocaust do appear—like the pile of confiscated shoes in panel thirty-one, *Maidanek*—they are altered to be outsized, almost fanciful: instantly recognizable but also stripped of their visual authority to over-determine the meaning of the image and constrain spectator responses to it.

Krinitz renders survival in an impressionistic visual language, which is hyperreal in its level of detail and its vibrant coloration. Manipulation of scale and dimension amplify this effect. In order to reconstruct her story in this medium, Krinitz disproportionately enlarges small things like the bees that chase the Nazi soldiers away in panel twenty-eight, *The Bees Save Me*. Additionally, the form of the wall-hanging panel largely refuses three-point perspective, a collapse of dimension that simultaneously lends a storybook quality to the images and forces viewers to confront the entire scene at once. These aesthetic strategies magnify the affective disjunction between the luscious materiality of the embroidery and collage and the horrors portrayed. The seamlessness of this combination is profoundly disorienting but speaks reparatively to the power of the everyday to organize and sustain lifeworlds in hostile environments. One of the hallmarks of Krinitz's work is the ubiquity of nature, particularly plant and animal life, which often vibrates fecundity even in scenes of extreme violence. In Nina Shapiro-Perl's documentary about Krinitz, *Through the Eye of the Needle*, commentators interpret this motif as hopefulness, comfort, and regeneration. We want to keep this interpretation in critical tension with the rather involuntary quality of plant and animal survival, which cannot be accurately explained in human terms of resistance, agency, and struggle. This tension hovers over the moment of survival. It reminds us to trouble reassuring narratives of empowerment and politicized agency in response to trauma, favoring instead attention to the quotidian work of routine activities that ensure survival, which are often so necessary that they seem unwilled.

Equally important, if survival complicates the picture of what it means to flourish, it also challenges ideas about what it means to fail—at life or at living. Queer theorists in particular have lately reconceptualized failure as an eschewal of various imperatives to succeed: the biopolitical demand to reproduce and regenerate (Edelman 2004; Halberstam 2011), and the neoliberal insistence on self-sufficient prosperity. Most notably, in *The Queer Art of Failure*, Judith Halberstam argues that failure can be understood not as an inability to be successful, but as a refusal to participate in the political economy. "Under certain circumstances," Halberstam writes, "failing, losing, forgetting, unmaking, undoing, unbecoming, not knowing may in fact offer more creative, more cooperative, more surprising ways of being in the world" (2011, 3). Failure, in other words, can be an intentional embrace of a subjectivity that rejects inscription as a disciplined subject of neoliberal capitalism. Yet the notion of failing deliberately implies a preceding privilege, a relinquished chance to succeed. In the context of militarized violence, such possibilities are foreclosed, sometimes mortally. Survival is another unexpected way of being in the world, a form of existence that stands outside strictures and imperatives of neoliberal ideals of human productivity: not so much a refusal, as an inability to flourish in these terms, while also succeeding, wildly, in the simple act of continuing to live. Simultaneously, it is a mode of living that challenges fantasies of resistance that value lives marked by volitional expressions of agency against structures of oppression. Militarized violence, in other words, changes the capacities through which agency can be expressed and subsequently, represented.

Unexpected Being

Examining the affective, material, and political characteristics of Krinitz's textiles, we have argued that her aesthetic strategies generate reparative visualities by capturing dimensions of survival obscured by a redemptive paradigm (in which outside forces intervene or history is magically overcome). The materiality and tour-de-force qualities of Krinitz's needlepoint insist upon the *presentness* of survival: the perpetual here-and-now of living through military conflict, rather than a progressive narrative that moves toward resolution. Colors that reverberate with the energies of living, of being alive, contrast with narrative evidence of catastrophe. Krinitz uses vibrant colors and manipulates detail and dimension to amplify connections between sensations and storytelling; haptic and visual expressions give rise to narratives in which violent impositions never quite succeed in extinguishing the sisters' material existence. Survival, though, does not necessarily have a teleological vision. Instead, as this needlepoint project foregrounds, to survive is to live constantly in the moment as one navigates the ubiquitous violence that pervades a war zone. The dazzling needlework positions the viewer as much as the artist back in a "present" time or tense of surviving the Nazi occupation. This reparative project provides no political alternative or redemptive savior—Krinitz demands we stay focused on the immersive and all-consuming process of survival.

To return to our initial query about spectatorship, what insights can be gleaned from traumas visualized through aesthetically compelling representations? Why, in other words, use a kaleidoscopic color palette or enchant the viewer with impressive needlework? Notably, Krinitz's visual strategies for contesting the death-dealing machinery of militarized violence do not conform to visualizations of intentional, politicized resistance. The spectatorial challenge of this project lies in both embracing and resisting the seductive pleasures of the marvelous needlework in order to gaze persistently at the genocidal violence depicted through the perspective of everyday survival. This necessitates abandoning the quest for images that gratify idealized visions of oppositional living and heroic dying, and thereby contesting the violent imposition of normativity that inheres in such representations. Instead, the sensual beauty of Krinitz's work illuminates the paradoxes of survival in a context of militarized violence, as she renders her mother's shawl and her sister's braids with the same level of intricacy as the mushrooms, cows, pinecones, Nazi uniforms, and barbed wire. Painstakingly embroidered, these ornamental representations challenge viewers to recalculate both the horror and the loveliness of the ordinary in grimly extraordinary times.

Rebecca A. Adelman is associate professor of media and communication studies at the University of Maryland, Baltimore County. Her first book, *Beyond the Checkpoint: Visual Practices in America's Global War on Terror* (2014), maps the circuits of visual practices that link the United States, its citizens, and its enemies.

Wendy Kozol is professor of comparative American studies at Oberlin College. Her recent book, *Distant Wars Visible: The Ambivalence of Witnessing* (2014), examines visual cultures that depict twenty-first-century U.S. military conflicts to consider the politics of spectatorship and empathy shaping visual witnessing practices.

Notes

1. A 2015 estimate identified ten wars and five serious armed conflicts in progress worldwide (Goldstein 2015). Feminist critics of just war theory raise concerns that conventional attention to the battlefield, such as air power or combat conditions, disregards the long-term effects that militarism has on vulnerable civilian populations, especially women, children, and the elderly (Sjoberg 2006, 52).
2. See Boltanski's (1999) landmark discussion of distant suffering. For recent perspectives, see Blocker 2009 and Frosh and Pinchevski 2009. Sontag's (2003) last work also addresses this debate.
3. For a sustained engagement with the idea that events like the Holocaust cannot (or should not) be represented, see Mandel 2007. See also Didi-Huberman's piercing meditation on this debate (2008).
4. This has proven to be a compelling strategy for many critics of Western media's relentless promotion of a self/other narrative in which the "other" is always only a victim or an enemy. Alternative sites of expressive culture hold out the promise of more complex and critical perspectives. For a powerful example of this, see Al-Ali and Al-Najjar 2012.
5. In addition to traveling exhibitions, the panels can be viewed online. See Art and Remembrance 2013.
6. Krinitz originally intended the panels to be mementos for her daughters; after her death, her daughters founded the Art and Remembrance foundation to disseminate her work to a broader audience (Shapiro-Perl 2012, 236).

7. Adelman first encountered her work in an exhibit on storytelling at the American Visionary Art Museum in Baltimore.

8. For a consideration of the status of "craft" in art practice and criticism, see Buszek 2011.

9. Watching a visionary artist at work, Wojcik said his creative process appeared entirely immersive, as a "suspension of time and space" (2008, 193).

10. Shapiro-Perl writes, "We can imagine that through the meditative art of stitching, moving and being still at once, in and out, out and in, over many hours and days and months and years that Esther was able to come to grips with her life and her loss. She was able to mend herself and her heart and *externalize* the pain" (2012, 235, italics in the original).

11. These panels were created in 1991, 1998, 1994, and 1993.

12. For more detailed considerations of the relationships between time, power, and bodily autonomy, see Freeman 2010 and Sharma 2014.

13. On the need to move beyond canonical atrocity photographs of the Holocaust and for a consideration of the philosophical, ethical, and aesthetic possibilities foreclosed by such images, see Hartouni 2012.

Works Cited

Abbas, Asma. 2010. "Voice Lessons: Suffering and the Liberal Sensorium." *Theory & Event* 13 (2).

Al-Ali, Nadje, and Deborah Al-Najjar, eds. 2012. *We Are Iraqis: Aesthetics and Politics in the Time of War.* Syracuse, NY: Syracuse University Press.

Art and Remembrance. 2013. "Fabric of Survival: The Art of Esther Nisenthal Krinitz." Accessed December 15, 2015. http://artandremembrance.org/galleries/fabric-of-survival/.

Berlant, Lauren. 2004. *Cruel Optimism.* Durham, NC: Duke University Press.

Blocker, Jane. 2009. *Seeing Witness: Visuality and the Ethics of Testimony.* Minneapolis, MN: University of Minnesota Press.

Boltanski, Luc. 1999. *Distant Suffering: Morality, Media, and Politics.* Translated by Graham Burchell. Cambridge: Cambridge University Press.

Buszek, Maria Elena. 2011. "Introduction: The Ordinary Made Extra/Ordinary." In *Extra/Ordinary: Craft and Contemporary Art,* edited by Maria Elena Buszek, 1–19. Durham, NC: Duke University Press.

Butler, Judith. 2004. *Precarious Life.* London: Verso.

———. 2009. *Frames of War.* London: Verso.

Caruth, Cathy. 1996. *Unclaimed Experience: Trauma, Narrative, History.* Baltimore, MD: Johns Hopkins University Press.

Chow, Rey. 1996. "Where Have All the Natives Gone?" In *Contemporary Postcolonial Theory: A Reader*, edited by Padmini Mongia, 122–47. New York: St. Martin's Press.

Cvetkovich, Ann. 2012. *Depression: A Public Feeling.* Durham, NC: Duke University Press.

Didi-Huberman, Georges. 2008. *Images in Spite of All: Four Photographs from Auschwitz.*Translated by Shane B. Lillis. Chicago: University of Chicago Press.

Edelman, Lee. 2004. *No Future: Queer Theory and the Death Drive.* Durham, NC: Duke University Press.

Felman, Shoshana, and Dori Laub. 1992. *Testimony: Crises of Witnessing in Literature, Psychoanalysis, and History.* New York: Routledge.

Freeman, Elizabeth. 2010. *Time Binds: Queer Temporalities, Queer Histories.* Durham, NC: Duke University Press.

Frosh, Paul, and Amit Pinchevski, eds. 2009. *Media Witnessing: Testimony in the Age of Mass Communication.* New York: Palgrave Macmillan.

Goldstein, Joshua S. 2015. "Wars in Progress." *Internationalrelations.com* (blog). July 31. http://www.internationalrelations.com/wars-in-progress.

Grewal, Inderpal. 2005. *Transnational America: Feminisms, Diasporas, Neoliberalisms.* Durham, NC: Duke University Press.

Halberstam, Judith. 2011. *The Queer Art of Failure.* Durham, NC: Duke University Press.

Hartouni, Valerie. 2012. *Visualizing Atrocity: Arendt, Evil, and the Optics of Thoughtlessness.* New York: New York University Press.

Hesford, Wendy. 2011. *Spectacular Rhetorics: Human Rights Visions, Recognitions, Feminisms.* Durham, NC: Duke University Press.

History and Memory. 1991. Directed by Rea Tajiri. New York: Women Make Movies.

Krinitz, Esther Nisenthal, and Bernice Steinhardt. 2005. *Memories of Survival.* New York: Art and Remembrance.

Langford, Barry. 2013. "Globalizing the Holocaust: Fantasies of Annihilation in Contemporary Media Culture." In *Holocaust Intersections: Genocide and Visual Culture at the New Millennium*, edited by Axel Bangert, Robert S.C. Gordon, and Libby Saxton, 112–29. Oxford: Legenda Books.

Mandel, Naomi. 2007. *Against the Unspeakable: Complicity, the Holocaust, and Slavery in America.* Richmond, VA: University of Virginia Press.

okay bye-bye. 1998. Directed by Rebecca Baron.

Owen, Paula. 2011. "Fabrication and Encounter: When Content Is a Verb." In *Extra/Ordinary: Craft and Contemporary Art*, edited by Maria Elena Buszek, 83–96. Durham, NC: Duke University Press.

Rancière, Jacques. 2007. *The Future of the Image.* Translated by Gregory Elliott. London: Verso.

Reinhardt, Mark. 2007. "Picturing Violence: Aesthetics and the Anxiety of Critique." In *Beautiful Suffering: Photography and the Traffic in Pain,* edited by Mark Reinhardt, Holly Edwards, and Erina Duganne, 13–36. Chicago: Williams College Museum of Art and University of Chicago Press.

Sedgwick, Eve Kosofsky. 2003. *Touching Feeling: Affect, Pedagogy, Performativity.* Durham, NC: Duke University Press.

Shapiro-Perl, Nina. 2012. "*Through the Eye of the Needle: The Art of Esther Nisenthal Krinitz:* Witnessing the Witness through Filmmaking." In *The Power of Witnessing: Reflections, Reverberations, and Traces of the Holocaust,* edited by Nancy R. Goodman and Marilyn B. Meyers, 235–38. New York: Routledge.

Sharma, Sarah. 2014. *In the Meantime: Temporality and Cultural Politics.* Durham, NC: Duke University Press.

Sjoberg, Laura. 2006. *Gender Justice and the Wars in Iraq: A Feminist Reformulation of Just War Theory.* Lanham, MD: Lexington Books.

Sontag, Susan. 2003. *Regarding the Pain of Others.* New York: Farrar, Straus and Giroux.

Taylor, John. 1998. *Body Horror: Photojournalism, Catastrophe, and War.* New York: New York University Press.

Through the Eye of the Needle: The Art of Esther Nisenthal Krinitz. 2014. Directed by Nina Shapiro-Perl. Washington, DC: Art and Remembrance. Accessed March 9, 2016. https://www.youtube.com/watch?v=HCvlhYCKruQ.

Wojcik, Daniel. 2008. "Outsider Art, Vernacular Traditions, Trauma, and Creativity." *Western Folklore* 67 (2/3): 179–98.

Young, James E. 2009. "Regarding the Pain of Women: Questions of Gender and the Arts of Holocaust Memory." *PMLA* 124 (5): 1778–86.

Zarzycka, Marta. 2014. "Outside the Frame: Reexamining Photographic Representations of Mourning." *Photography and Culture* 7 (1): 63–78.

Zimmermann, Patricia. 2000. *States of Emergency: Documentaries, Wars, Democracies.* Minneapolis, MN: University of Minnesota Press.

Special Affects: Mermaids, Prosthetics, and the Disabling of Feminine Futurity

Cynthia Barounis

> *I'll tell you about the mermaid*
> *Sheds swimmable tail   Gets legs for dancing*
> *Sings like the sea with a choked throat*
> *Knives straight up her spine*
> *Lancing every step*
> *There is a price*
> *There is a price*
> *For every gift*
> *And all advice*

> —Adrienne Rich,
> "Quarto"

In February 2009, the world was introduced to Nadya Vessey, an Australian double amputee with a seemingly spectacular narrative of personal transformation. Television New Zealand's (TVNZ) *Close Up*, the news program that first covered the story, introduced their segment "A Mermaid's Tale" on Vessey with the following lines:

> It's a fantasy isn't it, for many little girls, to be a beautiful mermaid, gracefully swimming through the water, splashing her tail. But when an Auckland woman sent a casual email to the film producers of the Weta Workshop, she never dreamed she'd one day be doing just that. In what's thought to be a world first, the double amputee now has a mermaid tail to help her swim. (2009)

WSQ: Women's Studies Quarterly 44: 1 & 2 (Spring/Summer 2016) © 2016 by Cynthia Barounis.
All rights reserved.

The story, in brief, goes something like this: after being questioned on a beach by a curious child who had observed her removing her prosthetic legs, Vessey playfully fibbed that she was a mermaid. A competitive swimmer, Vessey subsequently became taken with the idea of having a functional mermaid tail and submitted her request to the Weta Workshop, a special effects company whose film projects have included *The Lord of the Rings* and *The Chronicles of Narnia*. Viewing the project as an interesting challenge, the Weta Workshop accepted Vessey's request and a team of designers immediately set to work assembling the complicated prosthetic. Describing the process on their website, the team explains that "[e]very aspect of the tail has been custom made to Vessey's body using a blend of 3D modeling and milling technology, combined with Vi Vac vacforming, and a polycarbonate spine and tail fin" (3-Fins 2015). The result was a visually stunning and mechanically impressive piece of wearable technology, which Vessey modeled in several photo shoots.

The story soon became a minor news sensation, with pictures, videos, and descriptions of Vessey-as-Mermaid circulating on various websites and blogs—each with their own colorfully exaggerated headline. One website, for example, declared: "Mermaid dream comes true thanks to Weta" (Calman 2009). Another hyperbolically reflected: "From Double Amputee to Mermaid? Famed movie director gives woman new life" ("Agreyson" 2011). Inspirational language like this is, of course, standard fare in human-interest stories involving disability, and many of the online comments posted in response to TVNZ's *Close Up* segment extended this logic of charitable rescue or courageous overcoming. Scripting Vessey into a familiar "pity" narrative, the public understands her to be dependent on the charity and benevolence of others, lacking the physical adaptations necessary for her own continued survival.

And yet there is something undeniably queer and crip in the incongruous narratives of feminine and disabled futurity that converge uneasily around Vessey's adult mermaid embodiment. Following the work of Robert McRuer and Alison Kafer, I intend the term "crip" to signify in this context both as a defiant refusal of the able-bodied norm and as a recognition of the performative nature of compulsory able-bodiedness as it inspires an endless series of failed repetitions. In what follows, I argue that Vessey's own playful relationship to her mermaid prosthetic makes the usual inspirational narratives and the affects they are meant to generate impossible to sustain. The result is the production of two related but distinct versions of

camp sensibility. While Vessey's own clear commitment to artifice, styliza-
tion, and novelty makes her readable as a crip-femme dandy with a keen
camp eye, the stubbornness with which many commentators persisted in
equating Vessey's story with inspirational narratives of overcoming adversity makes the news coverage itself readable as naive camp. By considering
the news media's staging of the Weta Workshop's gift to Vessey alongside
queer theorizations of "temporal drag" and crip critiques of children's
charities, I suggest that the media's anachronistic mapping of sentimentalized girlhood onto Vessey's adult body produces a series of performative
effects/affects that destabilize conventional narratives of womanhood,
compulsory heterosexuality, and able-bodied futures. Performing the role
of the terminally ill telethon child from the space of adult vitality, Vessey
flaunts the fact of her own biological persistence. In doing so, she crucially
reframes the crip art of survival, not as the spectacle of cure or the revitaliz-
ing power of charitable acts—but as the mundane afterlives of that which
has been consigned to premature death or extinction.[1]

Vessey's performances of biological persistence emerge in dialectical
relation to the genealogical persistence of the "mermaid" itself as an overdetermined cultural signifier. As mythological sirens, mermaids are understood to be premodern femme fatales whose feminine allure is fraught
with heterosexual peril. As subjects of the modernist imagination, they
emblematize the pain of female heterosexual indifference.[2] As sideshow
spectacles during the nineteenth century, they became natural wonders,
items of capitalist exchange, and scientific specimens. Indeed, far from J.
Alfred Prufrock's idealized visions of "sea-girls wreathed with seaweed red
and brown" (1991, 7), these mermaids were bearers of physical monstros-
ity, clumsily fabricated to embody an unsettling hybrid between species.[3]
Recall, for example, P. T. Barnum's infamous Feejee Mermaid, composed
of the stitched together remains of a monkey and a fish. Bearing out emerging scientific narratives that understood racial others, gender deviants, and
disabled individuals to be "missing links" and evolutionary throwbacks,
Barnum's mummified "mermaid" confused categories of gender, race, ability, and species.[4]

Against these "nightmare" embodiments, contemporary mermaids
play starring cinematic roles in Disney dreamscapes as the culturally
cleansed heroines of childhood fairy tales. Consider Ariel, from *The Little
Mermaid* (1989), who longed to walk among humans—even as thousands
of young girls longed for Ariel's enchanting mermaid existence "under the

sea." Five years earlier, Daryl Hannah had already glamorized the figure of the mermaid in Ron Howard's *Splash* (1984), in which Hannah plays a lovestruck mermaid struggling to keep her tail a secret as she courts the affection of a human man (Tom Hanks) living in New York City. Choosing the name "Madison" for herself, after seeing a sign for Madison Avenue, she subtly gestures toward the mermaid's dual commercial histories, both as a profitable freak show specimen (Madison Square Garden is the site at which P. T. Barnum debuted his "Greatest Show on Earth") and as a marketing tool in the advertisement of feminine beauty products.

The narrative confusion that results from these multiple histories is partially reflected in the YouTube comments that follow the *Close Up* segment. Evenly split between envy and pity, some articulate a gendered longing for a mermaid tail of one's own, while others lament the misfortune of disability as the occasion for prosthesis. In this context, conventional desires for feminine glamour and allure connect with new narratives of disabled futurity. Like a siren's song itself, Vessey's mermaid tail/tale is both seductive and deceptive, foreclosing the very cultural frames that it appears to invite. The resulting hermeneutic failures are left scattered like so many sailors' bones on the rocks.

Feminine Futurity

In media coverage of Vessey's mermaid prosthetic, the desire for mermaid embodiment is presented as desire for a particular form of feminine glamour. As "A Mermaid's Tale" reminds us, it is nearly every girl's "fantasy" to be a "beautiful mermaid, gracefully swimming through the water, splashing her tail." Though Vessey's custom-made tail is framed here as a rare or even extraordinary opportunity to enact this apparently universal girlhood fantasy, it's worth noting that similar (though much less expensive) mermaid-tail swimsuits are available for purchase from various websites that market their product to adolescent girls. A company called 3-Fins, for example, advertises "tailor-made, custom mermaid-tails" with the following copy:

> These stunningly realistic looking Mermaid Tails were inspired by my 3 daughters and their love of all things Mermaid! . . . They are made to SWIM IN as the material used is top of the line swimsuit fabric. Colors currently available are: green, red, blue, orange and fuchsia-pink. Each

of the fabrics are very sparkly and reflective, and look beautiful, when worn in and out of the water. Make a girl's Mermaid dreams a reality with a gorgeous custom made tail. (2015)

This contains several obvious echoes of *Close Up*'s rhetorical framing for Vessey's prosthetic. Both tails are presented as the product of technological and aesthetic innovation, both are "tailor-made" at great cost, and both are introduced as the culmination of a "mermaid dream come true." In this context, the "mermaid dream" is readable as a coming-of-age fantasy in which the awkwardness of female adolescence is replaced with the elegance and sexual allure of imagined mermaid adulthood. Unsurprisingly, many cosmetics companies have capitalized on this glamorized image of the mermaid, with products including Deborah Lippmann's "Mermaid Dream" nail polish and Kevin Murphy's "Mermaid Hair Kit," which one fashion blogger describes precisely as the realization of a childhood dream: "Basically, my whole life, I've wanted Mermaid hair—that kind of Ariel-slash-beachy-wavy 'do that only supermodels seem to be able to achieve" (Lo 2011). In examples like these, mermaid embodiment—and the aspirational womanhood that it allegorizes—circulates as a commodity for adolescent and teenage consumption.

Is it is no surprise, then, to find Vessey's own transformation couched in the language of glamorized femininity. In "A Mermaid's Tale," one female costumer from the Weta Workshop explains: "I didn't want her to be wearing a black neoprene sock, I mean, she's a mermaid, I want her to be beautiful and sexy" (2009). We are similarly informed by the voiceover narration that "their challenge was to make it functional as well as beautiful." In the accompanying video, the viewer is provided with glimpses of the tail's skeletal mechanics as well as the "digitally printed scales" that adorn its gold Lycra sock. There is a "behind the scenes" feel to this progression, which concludes, appropriately, with an emphasis on costuming—"a makeover," we are told, "befitting a mermaid." In the accompanying sequence, Vessey is shown wearing an elaborate blue bathing cap resembling sea flowers. Like an actress being prepped for a role, she is flanked by two makeup artists, who apply a dramatic blue shadow to her eyelids and attach an eccentric pattern of pearly white sequins to her skin.

It is important to note that Vessey's mermaid makeover is overlaid with a set of assumptions about the inherent undesirability of the disabled woman. As one designer explains, "We have, over the years, done a number of things like this for people who have disabilities—specialist prosthesis, makeup to cover up bad injuries, or issues around cancer and such, and we thought we could assist in some way" (2009). This emphasis on charitable "assistance" weds a set of aspirational narratives about conventional womanhood to a set of inspirational narratives about disabled dependency. Thus, while the emphasis is on both "fashion" and "function," the logic of the coverage ultimately collapses into the latter, with fashion functioning instrumentally as a tool of rehabilitation. While Vessey's mermaid makeover is explicitly framed by this narrative of compulsory glamorized femininity, it is also overlaid with the assumption that the disabled woman is an "ugly duckling" whose rehabilitation requires aesthetic as well as practical interventions. Presented as that which masks the unsightly stigma of disability, the mermaid tail is designed not only to propel Vessey through the water but also into a newly available feminine futurity.

More than simply figuratively philanthropic, the Weta's ability to "donate" the tail to Vessey relied on the *literal* contribution of a high profile philanthropic organization.[5] In this way, her tail echoes—at least superficially—the outmoded trope of the "poster child." Originating in the representational practices of the charity telethon, the image of the poster child was designed to open hearts and wallets. With their impairments (and recoveries) paraded in front of a national viewership, poster children were used by telethon organizers to inspire pity, sadness, and ultimately, financial contributions. While Vessey is not framed by the rhetoric of the telethon in a literal sense, the writers covering the Weta Workshop's incredible "gift" to Vessey continue to make use of its outdated tropes. We are continually reminded, for example, that Vessey lost both of her legs as a child—a pitiable circumstance now remedied through the benevolent goodwill of her nondisabled counterparts' charitable donation.

But what makes this framework campy, rather than merely problematic, is the extent to which Vessey undercuts such narratives at every turn. As Sontag explains in her classic 1964 essay, "Notes on Camp," there are two main elements that constitute the naive camp artifact—failed ambition and the passage of time:

> When the theme is important and contemporary, the failure of a work may make us indignant. Time can change that. Time liberates the work of art from moral relevance, delivering it over to the camp sensibility. . . . Thus, things are campy . . . when we become less involved in them, and can enjoy, instead of being frustrated by, the failure of the attempt. (1999, 60)

Outmoded and passé, the camp object transparently reveals (so that we can revel in) its own anachronistic fantasies. The naive camp that saturates the discourse around Vessey's mermaid prosthetic has to do not only with historical anachronism (the outmoded logic of the telethon) but with personal and corporeal anachronism—the failed projection of a set of narratives usually reserved for young girls and disabled children onto Vessey's fifty-year-old body. The resulting incongruities "liberate" the news coverage "from moral relevance" transforming it from a merely problematic instance of disability representation to a gratifyingly naive case of gender and disability camp.

We are presented with this temporal incongruity almost immediately in "A Mermaid's Tail." As the announcer finishes proclaiming the near universal fantasy among young girls to be a "beautiful mermaid," the film cuts to Vessey herself, who tells her interviewer, "It seems to have been every girl's fantasy except mine. I never had that fantasy. I never had a fantasy to be a mermaid." The only connection that this fantasy seems to have with childhood for Vessey is the four-year-old boy who walked up to her on the beach as she was removing her prosthetic legs. Relating this anecdote, Vessey explains: "He started with all the 'why' questions, you know, 'Why haven't you got any legs,' etc. And so I said, 'Have you heard of *The Little Mermaid*?' and he said, 'Yes' and I said, 'I'm a mermaid' and he got this look on his face and he said, 'Wow that's cool' and ran off to tell his dad." While one website frames her response as an act of reverence for the innocence of childhood—an attempt, in other words, to protect the child from a frightening and potentially damaging knowledge about the disabled body—I think it makes more sense to understand her reply as a crip form of "camp wit." As Esther Newton explains, "Camp has got to be flip. A camp queen's got to think faster than other queens. This makes her camp. She's got to have an answer to anything that's put to her" (1972, 110). Thus, rather than protecting the child, Vessey is making him the audience to a camp performance—one that eventually culminates in the drag performance of mermaid transformation, staged in clips that follow.

Vessey also refuses to validate the media's insistence on the rehabilitative function of her tail. One headline in the *Telegraph*, for example, proclaims: "Disabled woman given mermaid tail to help her swim" (2009). Another article explains that "in almost no time she was able to wisp around the water . . . inspired by her newfound freedom" ("Agreyson" 2011). These frames willfully ignore the fact that Vessey was a competitive swimmer long before she ever made the request for a mermaid tail. Such acts of selective forgetting are even more astonishing given that Vessey's athletic history is explicitly referenced within the *Telegraph* article itself. We are told that "Miss Vessey began swimming after she had her first leg amputated at seven. Despite having her other leg amputated at 16, she swam competitively in high school and now swims as often as she can" (2009). Elsewhere in the same piece, we learn that Vessey is "thinking of using the tail to help her complete the swimming section of a triathlon. She said: 'I thought rather than just having it as a plaything, I would take it further.'" While the first the sentence privileges the tail's prosthetic functionality—the tail is something that will "help her compete"—the following sentence reveals Vessey's orientation to the tail to be one of fashion-over-function. The mermaid tail is neither a life-saving intervention nor a lifelong dream come true but merely a "plaything," an aesthetic novelty that might be repurposed as an athletic tool. Vessey goes on to discusses the process of adjusting to the mermaid tail *as* a prosthetic, a process that is neither easy nor seamless. Just as the drag queen's fabulous five-inch heels—while certainly "functioning" as shoes—may nonetheless require practice, adjustment, and even discomfort, the tail emerges here as a cumbersome, if gratifying, fashion accessory.

Crip-Femme Anachronism

I would like to turn to the peculiar paradox of mermaid futurity that is laid bare by Vessey's performance. Though the "mermaid dream" may on the one hand allegorize a fantasy of feminine maturation, it simultaneously signals a certain immaturity—a girlhood dream that must be relinquished upon entrance into womanhood. It looks to the future, in other words, but it belongs to the past. In her mermaid drag, then, the fifty-year-old Vessey enacts multiple queer refusals of feminine futurity. She refuses to be the little girl who dreams of becoming a mermaid, but she also refuses to be the adult who has grown out of that fantasy. If the proper time and place of mermaid fantasy is childhood, then Vessey's performance of mermaid adulthood represents not the fulfillment of girlhood dream but a casually irreverent form of camp novelty.

Vessey's mermaid embodiment thus enacts what Elizabeth Freeman has called "temporal drag" (2010, 62). A mode of queer performativity that shakes up normative chronologies of gendered selfhood, temporal drag carries "all the associations that the word 'drag' has with retrogression, delay, and the pull of the past on the present" (62). For Freeman, one of the most provocative dimensions of temporal drag is the way that it stages questions of feminist generationality by "point[ing] us toward the identities and desires that are foreclosed within social movements" and "illuminating the often unexpected effects of such deferred identifications" (85). Extending the "wave" metaphor that is often invoked to name the successive phases of the feminist movement, Freeman reflects on how present feminist articulations might be inflected by the gravitational "undertow" of previous feminist movements, which "pull backward even as they seem to follow on one another. . . . [T]he undertow is a constitutive part of the wave; its forward movement is also a drag back" (63). We might, therefore, read Vessey's mermaid drag as not only a "drag" back to the anachronistic narratives of girlhood, but also to the "anachronistic" first and second wave feminisms of Simone de Beauvoir and Dorothy Dinnerstein, whose classic texts were deeply informed by a reading of Hans Christian Andersen's fairy tale "The Little Mermaid."

For Dinnerstein and de Beauvoir, however, the coming-of-age allegory implicit in Andersen's fairy tale has less to do with a mermaid dream come true than with the gendered nightmare of female adulthood. After all, in Andersen's fairy tale, the magical transformation that occurs is not from human to mermaid, but from mermaid to human. Noting that the little mermaid leaves behind a carefree adolescence in the water for the discomfort of a bipedal adulthood, both authors replace the desire for maturity with nostalgia for the lost freedoms of girlhood. If the mermaid commodities discussed earlier promised to exchange the awkwardness of adolescence with glamorized "mermaid" adulthood, then Dinnerstein (1967) and de Beauvoir (1949) present a crucial feminist counter-reading that emphasizes the past, rather than the future, as the site of female agency. In *The Second Sex*, de Beauvoir observes that "the day Andersen's little mermaid becomes a woman, she experiences the yoke of love and suffering that is her lot" (303). For Dinnerstein, the pain of the mermaid's new feet, like "sharp knives and piercing needles" can be understood as the "special female pain of traditional sexual initiation" (1967, 107). Thus, in becoming a woman, the little mermaid exchanges her voice and tail (the source of her mobility and agency) for the sexual vulnerability that comes with having a pair of female legs. Through this lens, we can understand Vessey's mermaid makeover, despite its strongly heterosexualized framing, as a powerful *refusal* of compulsory heterofuturity.

Disability scholars have also mined the fairy tale's crip subtexts, understanding it as an allegory related to mobility impairment and the pressures of physical rehabilitation.[6] Here, the physical pain the mermaid feels when she walks signifies not only the gendered pain of sexual initiation, but also the pain and discomfort some disabled people experience as they attempt to mold their bodies to fit the contours of an inaccessible environment. To become human, in this context, is to overcome one's disability, passing as "normal" among nondisabled (in this case, land dwelling) society. Through this lens, an additional counter-reading of Vessey's mermaid tail emerges. If, as I argued earlier, news coverage attempted to frame the mermaid transformation as a form of both physical and aesthetic rehabilitation, then here the desire to be a mermaid becomes, to the contrary, a form of willful crip dis-identification with the structures of compulsory able-bodiedness—a sly refusal to become "part of your world" (Menken and Ashman, 1989).

Vessey thus asserts a crip futurity in the face of those rhetorics that would keep disability confined to the body of the child. The poster child's relationship to adulthood and to sentimental futurity is, after all, a paradoxical one. While Lee Edelman (2004) has famously identified the future as the province of the Child and, as such, the horizon of reproductive futurity, disability theorists have been careful to point out that, within the popular imagination, the future is neither the "time" nor the "place" of the disabled poster child. As Alison Kafer (2013) has recently and powerfully demonstrated in her meditation on crip temporality, the "better" future that is often imagined on behalf of the disabled child (the future that the telethon's charitable donations are understood as a down payment on), is a future that she or he will never actually come to inhabit. The disabled adult, in other words, cannot exist because the disabled child is always already dying.

This foreclosed futurity is perhaps best allegorized in the rhetoric of the Make-A-Wish Foundation, a "wish-granting organization" that exclusively serves children. As their website explains, to be "eligible for a wish," the child must have a "life-threatening medical condition" and be between the ages of two-and-a-half and eighteen. Among the "wish categories" on the foundation's website is the wish to "be" something for a day—a "fireman," a "police officer," a "cowboy," a "princess," or even a "mermaid," to name a few recent examples (2015). There is a strange temporal collapse at work here, a slippage between being and becoming in which fantasies of an always already foreclosed adulthood futurity are enacted and performed melancholically within the present. Through this lens, Vessey's "mermaid dream come true" becomes readable as an anachronistic camp subversion of the ubiquitous Make-A-Wish Foundation narrative. Treating Vessey like a terminally ill child whose last wish was to be a "mermaid for a day," one costumer sentimentally explains to the camera: "It was absolutely amazing. It's beautiful to watch Nadya swim and to see that dream come true and to be a part of it. I feel quite blessed" (*Close Up* 2009). But here, the "dying" body of the Make-A-Wish child is anachronistically mapped onto the body of the very much alive and thriving middle-aged Vessey.

This temporal incongruity is intensified by the accompanying montage, which features Vessey-as-mermaid reclining serenely on a set of rocks and taking an awkward dip in the ocean waves. During her swim in the ocean, her head peeks above the water, gaze turned back toward the camera, which is positioned on shore. The soundtrack playing during this sequence—"Song to the Siren" by Tim Buckley—provides a mournful and poignant accompaniment as Vessey drifts farther and farther out to sea, presumably to disappear into the loving arms of her Maker as "Heaven's Special Child."[7] As if anticipating the news segment's maudlin framing of this moment, Vessey delivers one final—if barely discernable—camp line. Though her voice is quite literally "drowned out" by the song's mournful lyrics, Vessey appears to be shouting to the camera "Goodbye, cruel world!" a joke that wryly undercuts the news story's sentimentalized narrative from within. Thus, in temporal drag, Vessey irreverently performs the foreclosed futurity of the disabled child from the very site of its negation—the pleasures of crip adulthood. It is in this way that Vessey both resurrects and disregards vocabularies of pity, calling out to inspirational tropes while leaving them, ultimately, to sink in the undertow.

Posthuman Disinterest and Camp Recovery

I have suggested that the flurry of media attention that resulted from Vessey's mermaid prosthetic allows her to stage a camp spectacle that unmasks the "special affects" of inspiration and pity as little more than a series of cinematically manipulated "special effects."[8] In this process, the familiar contours of the "human-interest" story collapse into what might more accurately be called "posthuman disinterest." I am using the term "posthuman disinterest" here to suggest a uniquely crip variation on the queer dandy's aesthetic boredom, and his related proficiency in resurrecting and repurposing discarded objects.[9] Camp is, after all, an aesthetic form that thrives on the survival of objects that have either outlasted their usefulness or been disconnected from their appropriate temporal or spatial contexts. "Outliving" the human-interest frameworks that would consign her to premature death, Vessey's adult embodiment exceeds both the "human" and the mainstream media's necropolitical "interest" in disability.[10] At the same time, Vessey's "posthuman disinterest" is ahead of its time, looking forward to a future in which the human-interest story has outlived its own usefulness as a cultural form. Indeed, part of the irony of Vessey's camp performance is that it is not widely readable as such. The illegibility (or semi-legibility) of her camp appropriations can be traced to the persistent vitality of tropes that should, by all accounts, be long dead.

To grasp the contours of "posthuman disinterest," we might finally turn to the Disney adaptation of *The Little Mermaid*, setting our sights on Ariel's carefully curated collection of human discardables, recovered from shipwrecks and seashores, and proudly displayed to her aquatic friends in the film's iconic "Part of Your World" number (Menken and Ashman, 1989). Ariel's "whozits," "whatsits," and "thingamabobs" produce novel delight to the extent that they have been creatively divested of their former function on land. Under the sea, they lose their integrity as symbols, becoming merely a "trove / of treasures untold." Detached from their original locations in time and space, and liberated from their original use-value, they are free to be appropriated and repurposed through the mermaid's camp eye ("Look at this stuff," she asks, "isn't it neat?"). But, of course, Ariel's acts of camp resignification do not constitute an untroubled rejection of human culture. On the contrary, this is also the moment that Ariel declares her assimilationist desires, directing the audience to understand her as one of the many "[b]right young women, sick of swimming / Ready to stand." In his crip appropriation of Judith Butler, Robert McRuer notes that the "failure to approximate the [able-bodied] norm" is not the same thing as "subversion of the norm" (2006, 30). When Ariel combs her hair with a kitchen fork, she may not be intentionally engaging in an act of camp subversion. But her failed attempts at "imitating" the (able-bodied) human world nonetheless reveal the "imitative structure of [able-bodiedness] itself."

Thus, we might read the fetish objects in Ariel's collection as talismans of recovery, in both senses of the word. Literally speaking, she has recovered these items in an ongoing salvage operation that is at the heart of the camp enterprise—what Andrew Ross has referred to as "the rediscovery of history's waste" (1989, 320). But Ariel also invests in practices of medicalized recovery by making use of sorceress Ursula's rehabilitative magic, trading her voice for a functional pair of legs. Ursula is readable here as a campy amplification of charity culture's coercive underside. Claiming benevolence while turning a profit, Ursula's insincere performance of pity for the "poor unfortunate souls" under her care echoes the discursive operation of the telethons. Meanwhile, her status as a "wish-granter" for the mermaid who dreams of being human playfully inverts the Make-A-Wish narrative. Rather than becoming a "mermaid for a day," Ariel is offered the opportunity to become human for a limited duration (three days, to be exact), but in neither instance is crip (or mermaid) futurity truly envisioned as a possible, or even desirable, outcome.[11]

I'd like to conclude by turning to one final instance of mermaid drag. In 1978 Bette Midler debuted her mermaid cabaret persona, Delores DeLago. A fish out of water, Midler's mermaid used a wheelchair for mobility (preceding Lady Gaga's wheelchair-using mermaid alter ego Yuyi by over three decades [Perpetua 2011]). In one particularly memorable number, Midler performed Gloria Gaynor's legendary "I Will Survive," thronged by a troupe of wheelchair-using mermaid backup singers. Pausing briefly after the lines, "At first I was afraid / I was petrified," Midler asks her audience to consider "petrified" not simply as a matter of fear but of fossilization. Midler, however, refuses to remain a passive object of excavation. Flaunting her tail from her motorized wheelchair, she assures us that she is "not dead yet."[12]

On the one hand, the mermaid would seem to embody an evolutionary terminus, troubling linear narratives of historical time, individual maturation, and species progression. As with Barnum's half-ape, half-fish hybrid, we understand her as a "throwback" who has failed to adapt—and therefore failed to survive. Yet she nonetheless persists within the present, and continues to animate fantasies of the future. She belongs not only to a fantastical elsewhere but also (to borrow a term from Kafer) to an ideologically saturated "elsewhen." It should be acknowledged that Kafer's "elsewhen" does not refer to the retrograde fantasies of the past, but rather to the horizontal promise of a future that is finally welcoming to feminist, queer, and crip bodies. I appropriate it here to suggest it is precisely the intractability of those retrograde fantasies—their stubborn survival into the present—that make them available as resources for articulating eccentric new visions of feminine and crip futurity.

Cynthia Barounis teaches in the Department of Women, Gender, and Sexuality Studies at Washington University in St. Louis. Her current book project is titled *Vulnerable Constitutions: A Queer-Crip Genealogy of American Masculinity*. Recent work can be found in *Criticism* and the *Journal of Modern Literature*.

Notes

1. In referencing the "crip art of survival," I am playing on Jack Halberstam's discussion of the "queer art of failure" (2011). For Halberstam, failure is queer to the extent that it refuses compulsory futures of success and achievement. But as Alison Kafer notes, disability is most often seen as the "sign of no future" (2013, 3). Against compulsory narratives that cast disabled people as "better off dead," or not having been born at all, flaunting one's continued survival is a crip art, indeed.
2. "I do not think that they will sing to me" (1991, 7), says J. Alfred Prufrock of the "mermaids singing" in the closing lines of T. S. Eliot's famous poem. It is not the danger of death that is invoked here, but the lamentable absence of female attention.
3. For Susun Sontag, the freak show spectacle is not easily readable through the logic of camp. "[N]atural odditites" or the "products of immense labor," she notes, "lack the visual reward—the glamor, the theatricality—that mark certain extravagances of camp" (1999, 60). Though such a discussion is beyond the scope of this essay, I believe Vessey's mermaid drag may serve as a provocative counterexample.
4. For more on P. T. Barnum and the Feejee Mermaid, see Rogers 2010.
5. As Weta's website reports, Vessey was able to fund the materials for the prosthetic through a grant that she received from the Kerr-Taylor Foundation Trust.
6. See, for example, Yenika-Agbaw 2011.
7. See Longmore 2013.
8. In using the term "special affects," I am referencing charity discourse's instrumental manipulation of affect (pity, sadness, inspiration) as well as the euphemistic connotations of "special" as one of the patronizing vocabularies of mainstream discourse on disability.
9. For more on crip dandyism, see Kuppers 2002.
10. It is notable that Vessey deconstructs the "human" not only through her relation to technologies and objects, but also in her performative enactment of interspecies corporeality.
11. Ursula herself has a striking camp lineage. *The Little Mermaid*'s directing animator has acknowledged that the iconic drag queen Divine provided one source of inspiration for the character's staging, while Pat Carroll, who

voiced the role, "envisioned Ursula as an aging Shakespearean actress" (Sells 2008, 182). A more explicit source of inspiration came from the character of Norma Desmond from *Sunset Blvd.*, the aging actress who responded to the line "You used to be in silent pictures. You used to be big!" with the iconic camp retort "I am big. It's the pictures that got small." Thus Ursula, too, is overlaid with a feminine temporality that designates that one can outgrow or "outlive" one's usefulness as an object of the masculine and/or able-bodied gaze. For more on this, see White 1993.

12. Here I am referencing the disability activist group Not Dead Yet, which has worked to oppose assisted suicide for disabled people.

Works Cited

3-Fins. 2015. "3-Fins: Tailor Made, Custom, Mermaid Tails." Accessed September 12. http://3-fins.com/.

"Agreyson." 2011. "From Double Amputee to Mermaid? Famed Movie Director Gives Woman New Life." Beliefnet. Accessed September 12. http://www.beliefnet.com/columnists/goodnews/2011/05/from-double-amputee-to-mermaid-famed-movie-director-gives-woman-new-life.html.

Beauvoir, Simone de. 2011. *The Second Sex.* New York: Vintage.

Calman, Matt. 2009. "Mermaid Dream Comes True Thanks to Weta." Stuff.co.nz, February 3. http://www.stuff.co.nz/national/1756623/Mermaid-dream-comes-true-thanks-to-Weta.

Close Up. 2009. "A Mermaid's Tale." Television New Zealand, February 24. https://www.youtube.com/watch?v=hUIhBoD1RfE.

Dinnerstein, Dorothy. 1967. "The Little Mermaid and the Situation of the Girl." *Contemporary Psychoanalysis* 3: 104–12.

Edelman, Lee. 2004. *No Future: Queer Theory and the Death Drive.* Durham, NC: Duke University Press.

Eliot, T. S. 1991. "The Love Song of J. Alfred Prufrock." In *Collected Poems, 1902–1969,* 3–7. New York: Harcourt Brace Jovanovich.

Freeman, Elizabeth. 2010. *Time Binds: Queer Temporalities, Queer Histories.* Durham, NC: Duke University Press.

Halberstam, Judith. 2005. *In a Queer Time and Place: Transgender Bodies, Subcultural Lives.* New York: New York University Press.

———. 2011. *The Queer Art of Failure.* Durham, NC: Duke University Press.

Kafer, Alison. 2013. *Feminist, Queer, Crip.* Bloomington, IN: Indiana University Press.

Kuppers, Petra. 2002. "Image Politics without the Real: Simulacra, Dandyism and Disability Fashion." In *Disability and Postmodernity,* edited by Mairian Corker and Tom Shakespeare, 184–97. London: Continuum.

Lo, Danica. 2011."Medicine Cabinet Confidential: How to Get Mermaid Hair, Affordable Palettes, and Limited-Edition Fragrances." *Glamour*, December 15. http://www.glamour.com/lipstick/blogs/ girls-in-the-beautydepartment/2011/12/medicine-cabinet-confidential-2.

Longmore, Paul. 2013. "'Heaven's Special Child': The Making of Poster Children." In *The Disability Studies Reader*, edited by Lennard Davis, 34–41, 4th ed. New York: Routledge.

Make-A-Wish. 2015. Accessed September 12. http://wish.org/.

McRuer, Robert. 2006. *Crip Theory: Cultural Signs of Queerness and Disability.* New York: New York University Press.

Menken, Alan and Howard Ashman. 1989. "Part of Your World." Los Angeles: Walt Disney Pictures.

Newton, Esther. 1972. *Mother Camp: Female Impersonators in America*. Chicago: University of Chicago Press.

Perpetua, Matthew. 2011."Bette Midler Says Lady Gaga Ripped Off Her Mermaid Character." *Rolling Stone*, July 18. http://www.rollingstone.com/ music/news/bette-midler-says-lady-gaga-ripped-off-her-mermaid-character-20110718.

Rich, Adrienne. 2009. "Quarto." *The Nation*, May 20. http://www.thenation. com/article/quarto/

Rogers, Molly. 2010. *Delia's Tears: Race, Science, and Photography in Nineteenth-Century America*. New Haven, CT: Yale University Press.

Ross, Andrew. 1989. *No Respect: Intellectuals and Popular Culture*. London: Routledge.

Sells, Laura. 2008. "Where Does the Mermaid Stand?" In *From Mouse to Mermaid: The Politics of Film, Gender, and Culture*, edited by Elizabeth Bell, Lynda Haas, and Laura Sells, 175–92. Bloomington, IN: Indiana University Press.

Sontag, Susan. 1999. "Notes on Camp." *Camp: Queer Aesthetics and the Performing Subject—A Reader*, edited by Fabio Cleto, 53–65. Ann Arbor, MI: University of Michigan Press. First published in *The Partisan Review* (Fall 1964): 515–30.

Splash. 1984. Directed by Ron Howard. Los Angeles: Touchstone Pictures.

Telegraph. 2009. "Disabled Woman Given Mermaid Tail to Help her Swim." February 26, http://www.telegraph.co.uk/news/newstopics/ howaboutthat/4839818/Disabled-woman-given-mermaid-tail-to-help-her-swim.html.

The Little Mermaid. 1989. Directed by Ron Clements and John Musker. Los Angeles: Walt Disney Pictures.

Weta Workshop. 2009. "A Mermaid's Tale." Accessed September 12, 2015. http://www.wetanz.com/a-mermaid-s-tale/.

White, Susan. 1993. "Split Skins: Female Agency and Bodily Mutilation in *The Little Mermaid.*" In *Film Theory Goes to the Movies*, edited by Jim Collins, Hilary Radner, and Ava Collins, 182–95. New York: Routledge.

Yenika-Agbaw, Vivian. 2011. "Reading Disability in Children's Literature: Hans Christian Andersen's Tales." *Journal of Literary & Cultural Disability Studies* 5 (1): 91–107.

Surviving Codespace: Tracing Lived Space through Digital Literary Writing

Laura Shackelford

As theorists, activists, artists, and writers begin to speculatively—if also wishfully—anticipate what comes "after biopolitics" or lies "beyond biopolitics,"[1] it is worth considering whether the very topographies of survival have not already shifted significantly. Computational processes and architectures, as I will suggest, unwittingly open new perspectives on spatial practices and the performativity of space, prompting our appreciation of a range of *spatiotemporal* material practices that corealize complex, multileveled knowledges and experiences of lived space. These most recent spatiotemporal shifts, and the predominance of social arenas and everyday practices reliant on computational processes and digital technologies—what critical geographers term "code/space" (Kitchin and Dodge 2011, 16) or "movement-spaces" (Thrift 2008, 89)—catalyze alternate perspectives on "life," "lived space," and other terms of survival. These computational processes and technologies coordinate the spatiotemporal dimensions of everyday physical life so pervasively that Kitchin and Dodge reconceive the spaces we inhabit every day as complexly coproductive, interwoven "code/spaces"—social domains and practices realized to differing degrees via computational technologies and infrastructure (2011, 16). Instead of being confined to computers or software or operating as self-contained technical objects that create their own virtual spaces, computational processes and products are now "everyware" (Greenfield, 2006) even at the micro-, atomic-, and nanoscales of biological research and medical practices.

The very challenges introduced by codespace—and its ubiquitous interweaving of computational architectures and abilities into the lived spac-

WSQ: Women's Studies Quarterly 44: 1 & 2 (Spring/Summer 2016) © 2016 by Laura Shackelford.

es of everyday life—may also open onto distinct possibilities for thinking survival beyond the present oppositional, thanatological discourses. In the current biopolitical discourses and practices, the survival of a social body—conceived of in organic terms of health, well-being, and integrity—is premised on immunological operations that relentlessly trade on certain people's and life forms' deaths or quarantining to accomplish this social body's "negative production of life" (Esposito 2011, xvii). If it is not currently possible or imaginable to unhinge "life" and the politics of survival from this biopolitical terrain, is it, nonetheless, possible to comparatively register fortuitous problematics, rifts, or drift that these spatiotemporal shifts may be introducing into a modern biopolitics of "life"?

Feminist digital literary writing and "locative narrative" practices[2]—such as Teri Rueb's 2004 GPS-based locative narrative sound installation *Drift*—creatively engage with mobile location technologies, computational architectures, and the material practices on which contemporary codespaces rely to understand the kinds of spatial experiences, knowledges, and mobilities they seem to, and might otherwise, corealize. Their experimental digital practices undercut earlier assumptions that codespaces would comprise a secondary, abstract, or virtual "cyberspace" that is over and against—or above and beyond—geographical place, its racialized and gendered colonialist territorializations, or the lived space of embodied life. Through their digital literary writing, these feminist authors explore how prior modes of inhabiting, affectively experiencing, and navigating lived space and material lifeworlds remain primary even as computational processes and technologies are ubiquitously interwoven with everyday life on multiple biological, geographic, social, cultural, and phenomenological scales.

Drift explores how prior dimensions of lived space and material space-making practices *survive* the transformations introduced by computational processes, infrastructures, and their late capitalist political economies. Re-approaching emergent codespaces as an opportunity to (re) understand material space-making practices as they corealize, inform, and exceed social action, culturally distinct experiences, and knowledges of space, *Drift* and other feminist digital literary practices reveal how tracing lived space through codespace and reorienting its transformative technics and spacetimes is key to survival. Finding ways to register and appreciate the "drift" within—as well as between—distinct modalities and metrics of life and the lived space they open onto and foreclose, serves as a crucial means of survival as "life" is reconceived in computationally legible and manipulable terms. *Drift* creatively pursues the dynamic, unfolding, *indeterminate* senses of place and point of view enabled, quite paradoxically, by *location* technologies. Retracing these emergent orientations to lived, intersubjective space, this installation engages with "drift" at another level, in the potential it finds for *reorienting* mobile technologies by understanding lived space and mobility in alternate ways. It intimates that resonant movements of "drift" are not, in fact, opposed to the calculative digital metrics of location technologies and codespace, but, to some extent, are inherent to these technics, the very outgrowth of degrees of indeterminacy and randomness introduced (however paradoxically) through computation. An apprehension of "drift" is also pursued through the installation's efforts to move between and amidst distinct, coexisting—though perhaps equally calculative—metrics of life-informing lived space today. From this vantage, *survival* is not a spatial or temporal "living beyond" the technical transformations and introversions of codespace. Instead, it comes to be premised on, and understood as, the tactical engagement and apprehension of: shifting, multileveled, material space-making practices; the various human and nonhuman agencies that continually, discrepantly corealize these lived spaces today; and the indeterminacy, or "drift," reintroduced through mobile location technologies and their (in)calculably calculable codespace.

Tracing Lived Space through Codespace

Critical geographers studying the emergence of information-based social spaces and communication networks since the late 1970s have noted several crucial dimensions to contemporary social space and circulatory practices that are revealed by these latest, emergent topographies (though not necessarily unique to them). Following Henri Lefebvre (1991), they stress that space-making is a productive material process, rather than conceiving of either space or place as static, preexisting, neutral backdrops to late-capitalist modes of production and their global political economies.[3] These material infrastructures and practices subtend specific modes and systems of social, economic, cultural, and geographic circulation. Extending these inquiries into the performative power of space beyond the technological transformations and political economies so central to postmodern space-making, theorists such as Doreen Massey, John May, and Nigel Thrift insightfully underscore the persistent, multilayered experiences of contemporary "timespaces" (May and Thrift 2001, 3). May and Thrift stress that "the nature and experience of social time is multiple and heterogeneous" as is "its manner of construction" (2001, 3). They go on to identify at least four interrelated ways in which our sense of space and time is differently shaped: 1) the material world's bodily, tidal, and seasonal rhythms; 2) the social—through disciplines of clock, calendar, domestic arrangements, religious and cultural practices, and economic practices; 3) our relationships to a variety of instruments and devices; and 4) through texts that give meaning to new conceptualizations of space and time (3–5). Whereas technological, economic, and sociopolitical forces are frequently identified as the primary, if not sole, agents of spatiotemporal transformations today, these critical geographers remind us that a range of material practices, more and less complex, continue to inform spatial experience and social life today, surviving the most recent spatiotemporal transformations.

Importantly, space-making as a series of processes *precedes* and in multiple material, biological, and technological respects, *exceeds* human agencies and efforts, according to May and Thrift's and Massey's formulations. Massey insightfully describes the "emergent powers of the spatial," noting that material spaces are not mere "outcomes" of social relations with "no material effect" because the social is also spatially constructed, which means that material spaces have "unexpected consequences," and "effects on subsequent events that alter the future course of the very histories which have produced" them (1994, 266, 288). More recently, new materialist and posthumanist theorists, such as Elizabeth Grosz, have reconsidered the dynamic temporal force of physical and biological life of many kinds as an ontological impetus to variation, unpredictability, and change. Recognizing the temporal dynamism of biological and other material life, more frequently understood in passive, unchanging, inert terms, Grosz develops her concept of the "untimely" as a way to understand the "virtual" or potential "microagencies" that catalyze life, opening it to the "accidental, the random, the unexpected" (2004, 7). She argues that biological life unfolds through the "surprising, unpredictable, and mobile force of time," as Darwinian theory effectively illustrates (7). Grosz suggests that cultural processes reciprocate in turn, devising and introducing equally "untimely," unpredictable, ruptures and nicks into material and biological processes of becoming.

Through this concept of the "untimely," Grosz suggests that we might understand and appreciate the surprising temporal impact of biological life as a catalyzing force inducing (though not directing or determining) transformation, change, and difference in cultural processes. In turn, we can begin to understand how such cultural processes themselves devise and introduce untimely, unpredictable ruptures and nicks to biological and other material processes of becoming. In this way, Grosz advocates re-understanding cultural, political, economic, and artistic life in complex, nondeterministic, yet transformative relation to these material forces of biological time. This approach emphasizes the nonrepresentational, catalyzing relays between this "untimely" indeterminacy of biological life, and our cultural efforts at sociotemporal organization, which attempt to engage these forces to other ends. From this perspective, it is precisely "because we act in a world whose complexity we cannot fully perceive or comprehend, which we cannot fully anticipate or control, that we invent, we make more of ourselves than life makes of us" through untimely "leap[s] outside ourselves" (Grosz 2004, 12). This embrace of the surprising, unexpected force of discrepant temporal agencies, introducing "nicks," "ruptures," or other "virtual" spaces *between* is of central concern in *Drift*. As I suggest below, *Drift*'s experimental practices both explore and extend the "virtual," "untimely" potential of codespaces and mobile technologies, and encourage participants to recognize the equally untimely pull of biological processes and microagencies. They join forces in actively pursuing such "drift," within, as well as beyond, the present terrain.

Mobile Repositioning

A remarkable genealogy of feminist engagement with digital spaces and writing predates and elaborates on critical geographers' and cultural theorists' most recent insights into the interweaving and entanglement of computational technologies, embodiment, intersubjective relations, and other parameters of lived space.[4] These feminist inquiries, aware of how the very differentiation of space and time has effectively aligned women and colonized subjects with the material world and positioned them outside the time of modernity, understand the reanimation of space as a significant feminist and postcolonialist project. Directly experimenting with digital media practices to encounter, unfold, and explore the potentialities and oversights of twenty-first-century mobile technologies and codespace, digital literary works such as *Drift* are especially cognizant of the process-es through which experiences and knowledges of lived space are coreal-ized through distinct material practices, technologies, modes of address, physical actions, intersubjective relations, and—as importantly—through written, visual, and aural representational texts, practices, and cultural his-tories. They situate interwoven, virtual, and physical codespaces amidst a longstanding, much wider range of both analog and digital practices of space-making and their technically enabled processes of augmenting re-ality to both materially and symbolically orient different bodies to each other and to the world in historically, culturally, and technologically dis-tinct ways.

Drift and other recent feminist digital writing practices are fully aware of the Euro-American gendering of space (feminine, passive, organic) and time (masculine, active, cultural), as well as the more complex ways in which contemporary lived space is further differentiated and "orient-ed" toward certain bodies, sexual orientations, and gendered, racialized, and spatialized relations.[5] Drawing on this awareness, feminist digital writing practices tactically re-approach predominant material practic-es of space-making, frequently using strategies of spatiotemporal "dis-orientation" and "reorientation"—to extend Sara Ahmed's concepts to the terrain of digital writing and codespace (2010, 254). Their practices comparatively unfold digital technics and reflect back on how these and other computational practices currently reshape, without fully replacing, existing embedded social, cultural, and technological topographies and experiences of lived space and the intersubjective relations and self-under-standings these social spaces facilitate and foreclose. Such digital literary practices are, for this reason, a crucial site from which to reconsider the problems, risks, and alternate possibilities codespace and its topographies introduce to survival. They might identify ways to circumvent its current thanatological, differential production of "life" and "death" through the quantification, qualification, and management of populations and sustain-ing bioinformatic circulations, and the supposed maintenance of a highly systematized social "body," especially now that the lived space of "pop-ulations" and social bodies are conceived and re-realized in organic and computational terms, at once.

Rueb's *Drift* is an explicit outgrowth of mobile communications tech-nologies (personal digital assistants, cellphones, iPads, global positioning and information systems, Wi-Fi, and Bluetooth capabilities) and their emergent cultures. Installed along the Watten seashore, where the Elbe river feeds into the North Sea at Cuxhaven, Germany, *Drift* invites visitors to wander along the beach with headphones and a small pocket PC and— as their movements trigger a series of unseen motion sensors—to listen to a range of what Rueb describes as "ambient sound textures" (2004), including the sounds of footsteps and spoken passages from Joyce, Mann, Woolf, Rousseau, Dante, and others addressing themes of spatial disloca- tion and wandering. Recordings of the same passage in several additional languages follow these literary passages read in their original languages. These are scattered amidst additional, atmospheric sounds and intermin- gled with the actual soundscape of the sea. Inviting participants to wander through its ubiquitous virtual and physical sea and soundscape, *Drift* ex- ploits the locative, site-specific character of mobile, personal media to re- visit some of the most longstanding, aural, physical, embodied parameters and experiences of lived space.

Implicitly posing the question of how such mobile, location-sensitive media change our experiences of relating to and navigating material en- vironments and also influence more complex, cultural understandings of the meaning of space (often differentiated as place), *Drift* intently situates these latest digital space-making practices within the context of multiple preceding and coexisting modes of spatiotemporally co-orienting physical embodiment and perception to lived spaces in geographic, national, lit- erary, and phenomenological terms. Whereas the technological elements of networked codespaces and their infrastructures are frequently privi- leged and, at times, figured as the only, or most important, agent of spa- tial transformations today, *Drift* situates these complexly coordinated and coordinating mobile communications technologies, pocket PCs, sensors, and sound capabilities amidst other (oceanic and technological) material practices of space-making that are simultaneous contributors to contem- porary lived codespace.

Drift contextualizes the influences of these latest GPS-based space-mak- ing technics on lived experience and social space, reminding participants that walking, listening, spoken language, and even literary and other rep- resentational practices equally, if differently, serve as phenomenological and material practices that shape spatial experience at multiple levels and in multiple registers. Such cultural practices position subjects, both ma- terially and symbolically, in distinct relations to a more complex environ- ment, thus helping to selectively corealize lived space and repertoires of embodied interaction. Approaching "'place' as a highly indeterminate cho- reography and 'point-of-view' as radically multiple, fragmented, fluid, and unstable" rather than as a noun, (Rueb 2008, 130), *Drift* engages mobile technologies in the service of re-approaching and re-apprehending spatial- ization as a verb—as a dynamic, ongoing, spatial and temporal practice, at once. Similarly to new materialist and posthumanist efforts to complicate a Cartesian understandings of matter as static, uniform, and homogenous and the Euclidean geometry and Newtonian physics that follow from that understanding,[6] *Drift* encourages participants to experience and appreci- ate spatial practices as an ongoing, unfolding, unpredictable, emergent, "untimely" activity to which multiple human, nonhuman, and technolog- ical agents co-contribute.

At one level, the work can be read as a fully oppositional, critical com- mentary on Global Positioning Systems, Global Information Systems, and Google Earth, among other location technologies, which are geo-refer- enced to "absolute space" on a Cartesian grid provided by U.S. Geological survey maps and appear to inhabit a static present-tense. It is the shared reference points provided by "absolute space" that allow for these tech- nologies to coordinate and map space and spatial movements according to this uniform, neutral grid. The goal of Rueb's work might seem, from this vantage, to introduce "drift" and experiences of flux, wandering, and movements of disorientation at multiple levels (environmental, physical, affective, linguistic, cultural, historical, technological) back into codespac- es that are premised on the calculability of uniform, "absolute" space. As Rueb states in her description of *Drift* on her website: "simply knowing one's geographical location as expressed in longitude and latitude coor- dinates has little bearing on one's personal sense of place or direction" (2004). Without question, the installation somewhat tactically reori- ents these mobile, site-specific digital technologies so as to better appre- hend, not override the complexities, specificity, and indeterminacies of lived space. Its location at the seaside may even index and counter nine- teenth-century dreams of a "chronometrical sea" that "behaved like a clock, a sky-like entity which would yield to metrical and mathematical analysis," a stabilization of the sea's movements now accomplished with the help of satellites, computers, and lasers as orientation devices (Thrift 2008, 95). Relocating mobile communication technologies amidst other material space-making processes, including the physical drift of the ocean's tides, this locative narrative seemingly reintroduces the random and incalculable into locative technologies and related biopolitical efforts to map and control matter premised on the calculability and uniformity of standardized metrics of space. Following the spatiotemporal drift of the ocean's tide, *Drift*'s motion-activated sensors shift forward and backward through the course of the day and night, emphasizing that even codespace is informed by the force of this material environment.

Reintroducing this untimely agency of the material world, aural perception, and embodied physical movement to our understandings of "mobility," furthered and enabled by mobile communications and GPS technologies that typically privilege abstract, static, visual modes explicitly gendered masculine, *Drift* is clearly aware of the ways in which masculinist understandings of material space, matter, and human agency have worked to cast women (historically aligned with the material world in Euro-American traditions) in similarly passive, neutral, unchanging, and homogenous terms and as a result have devalued these modes of perception, spatial experience, and knowledge. In this reading, then, the concept and understanding of "drift" that the installation opens onto can be unambiguously located within—and aligned with—the contingency and indeterminacy of the material world and its spacetimes in contradistinction to the locatability and calculability of codespace and mobile communication technologies. It seems to encourage longing for a time when it was still possible to get lost, to wander, to dislocate oneself or imagine oneself unlocatable. And it seems to recommend that within the vastly intensifying rate, scale, and scope of location technologies and other biopolitical methods of numerically identifying, documenting, and standardizing subjects and intersubjective experience and lifeworlds according to the imperatives of a hegemonic, global political economy, the best solution is to resist calculation, position, and location, as a whole—at least on this quantifying, masculinist register. This reading appears to reinforce the title's reference to a prior, situationist practice of the *dérive*, which literally means "drifting." *Drift*, in other words, seems to promote a longing for some excess or outside to these computationally thick, systematized, biopolitical registers and modes of circulation, to their modes and metrics of quantifying "life" in the name of "life" and death.

Lived Spaces of/and "Numerical Flow"

Drift's engagement with and understanding of lived space as it is coordinated with codespace and computational infrastructures today is, fittingly, a bit more complex. While it is thoroughly invested in the kinds of indeterminacy mobile location technologies somewhat paradoxically open onto and foreclose—and the spatial awareness and alternate mobilities these might, if creatively engaged, afford—the dynamic spacetimes it encourages participants to appreciate and help to unfold are premised on and entwined with the very architectures of calculability they might, at first, appear to counter. These spatiotemporal experiences of dynamic, highly contingent, and variable flows are one notable outgrowth of the thoroughgoing systematization and numerical standardization of space and time now being realized at unprecedented scales through codespace. Describing codespace as new kinds of "background time-spaces that are making their way into the world," or "movement-spaces" (2008, 89), Thrift stresses their status as the latest realization of an extensive cultural history of co-realizing the world numerically through mathematics, spatiotemporal metrics, listing, and logistics. The codespace *Drift* references and relies on is the latest outgrowth of a "tightly constrained and ordered world of calculation in which potentially every thing and every location (the two becoming increasingly interchangeable) could be given a number and become the subject of calculation, and in which each calculation could potentially be redone several times a minute" (Thrift 2008, 96).

In light of its latest, computationally based, rapid, recursive calculative manifestations, spatiotemporal navigation and orientation devices, such as GPS and other location technologies, are increasingly characterized by "numerical flux" (Thrift 2008, 96). They are giving rise to what are described as "flow architectures," according to K. Knorr Cetina, which are based on continuous calculations in which static representation becomes subordinated to flow:

> In a timeworld or flow-world . . . the content itself is processual—a "melt" of material that is continuously in flux, and that exists only as it is being projected forward and calls forth participants' reactions to the flux. Only "frames," it would seem, for example, the frames that computer screens represent in a financial market, are pre-supposed in this flow-world. The content, the entire constellation of things that pass as the referential context wherein some action takes place, is not separate from the totality of ongoing activities. (2003, 4)

As Knorr Cetina's description of the architectures of flow in dynamic codespaces suggests, the uniform, static, abstract, Cartesian grid on which GPS and other location technologies rely today is not at all incompatible with the dynamic practices and experiences of unfolding spacetimes as ongoing, emergent "flows" or with understandings of "place" as a verb that *Drift* both registers and works aesthetically and perceptually to cultivate. In fact, these understandings of place are premised on precisely such processes of "shaping numerical flow," through which a "nomadologic of movement becomes the natural order of thought" (Thrift 2008, 97). Returning to Rueb's characterization of an emerging genre of locative narrative reliant on mobile communications technologies that approaches "'place' as a highly indeterminate choreography and 'point-of-view' as radically multiple, fragmented, fluid, and unstable," it is worth underscoring that the dynamism, indeterminacy, and fluidity of "place" and a "point-of-view" characterized by "multiple frames" is, in fact, significantly, if not radically, enhanced rather than elided or repressed by twenty-first-century location and communication technologies and their late-capitalist codespaces.

According to this somewhat altered reading, *Drift* can be understood to register degrees of indeterminacy and randomness introduced precisely by locative technologies and their current realizations of a dynamic, highly contingent, yet no less calculative codespace. It is a dynamic codespace produced through the recursive informational relays or "flows" between the participants' physical movements, their pocket PCs, the sensors, and the global positioning satellites and networks continuously registering and coordinating this data and sending it back to these material devices, multiple media framings, and the participants' perceptual experience.

Indeterminate Orientations to Codespace

Crucially, this reading enhances, rather than undermines, *Drift*'s critical engagement with these understandings and technologies of codespace and the kinds of survival they might open onto. In addition to registering the increasing flux of codespace, *Drift* engages with the productive indeterminacy of lived space at several other levels as well, suggesting and even reintroducing and reapprehending their legibility and agency within these techno-economic relays. Visitors' movements are largely unpredictable, introducing another level of drift into this narrative practice and its processes of material and symbolic, intersubjective, and affective space-making. Their wanderings may not trigger the same sensors and will not likely follow the same order as other participants. The number of visitors and the time of day are also largely indeterminate and, as mentioned above, the placement of the sensors shifts according to the movements of the tides and the relative fluctuation of the material environment that particular day. Further, depending on participants' linguistic abilities and literary familiarity with these texts and authors, their experience of the seascape and of wandering may vary significantly. Language and literary practices, not to mention cultural histories, are all collated and co-imbricated in this site-specific installation, re-approached as nonrepresentational yet co-productive "interface relations" that inform the way we understand and inhabit—and interact in—affective, physical, geographic, national, networked, intersubjective, and environmental lived spaces. In this way, *Drift* reintroduces multiple (and multiply) indeterminate orientations to this lived space, and catalyzes viewers' discrepant experiences of its site-specific narrativization. Quite importantly, lived space is corealized in terms that can no longer be meaningfully parsed or divided according to prior binaries of digital/analog, virtual/physical, abstract/embodied, technological/organic, temporal/spatial, or masculine/feminine.

Similarly to the situationist practice of the *dérive*, *Drift* can be understood to catalyze and carry out an alternate mode of reorienting participants, of navigating and mapping this lived codespace through a "calculation of their possibilities" (Debord 1956), which attends to both their determinate and indeterminate parameters. It is worth noting the difference between drifting as a distinct kind of "playful-constructive behavior and awareness of psychogeographical effects," in Debord's terms, as opposed to a more romantic embrace of randomness, chance, or indeterminacy, which might cast it as the "other" to the structuring of urban space and other social space or, in this case, codespace.[7] Debord's conceit of "calculating the possibilities" resonates in interesting ways with Luciana Parisi's recent research. Parisi's work suggests that "randomness has become the condition of programming culture due to the tendencies of algorithms to be overshadowed by infinite volumes of data" (2013, ix), once again pointing toward the centrality of indeterminacy, incompleteness, and drift to computation itself, its architectures, and even its aesthetics.

Drift's reorientation of lived space and its exploration of the unregistered potentialities of mobile codespace is, admittedly, significantly complicated by the primacy of just such a "nomadologic of movement" to codespace, as well as the processual nature of content as a performative, recursive "bringing forth" of the world through a series of enframing media, modes, and metrics. If codespaces, as "movement-spaces," are now premised on precisely such time and place sensitive flows, what does *Drift* contribute to a critical awareness of contemporary experiences and practices of lived space to the ends of biopolitical calculation, not to mention to the realization of alternate, feminist practices of space-making and intersubjective relation?

In contextualizing the dynamics of emergent codespace alongside a series of predigital, multimodal processes through which discrepant metrics and modes of lived space and shared spacetimes are realized, *Drift* encourages its participants and remote readers to more self-reflexively co-orchestrate these relays linking "place, time, narrative, and the mobile body of the participant" today. Rueb's *Drift* juxtaposes and intermingles these locative technics and knowledges, encouraging participants' symbolic reflection on and literal navigation of lived space as a dynamic relation between these physical, biological, cognitive, affective, cultural, literary-symbolic, linguistic, and technologically realized experiences of space. Further, *Drift*'s narrative practices strategically reside *between* and encourage participants to accommodate the dynamic, recursive technological, cultural, linguistic, proprioceptive, and affective circuits regularly linking its visitors to its geography and to its multivalent, open-ended material practices and understandings of lived codespace. Its radically multiplied, emergent narrative point of view—though not fully unique from the increasingly frame-specific informational flows characterizing computational architectures today—registers distinct dimensions to lived space. *Drift* stresses how spatial practices, while regularly and complexly coarticulated, are not reducible or translatable to the same information. In fact, gaps remain between each modality of space-making and its coencounter with material life, and each modality of lived space is, itself, comprised of select informational parameters and content, rather than providing a comprehensive field or one-to-one representation.

Drift's privileging of geographic flux, auditory experience, and physical navigation through a material environment reapproaches mobile codespaces and cultures that are more frequently explored as/through visual perception, media, and masculine modes of intersubjective relating. In creatively realizing these unfamiliar, haptic dimensions to lived space through codespace and hegemonic mobile and locative technologies, *Drift* unsettles the predominant sensorial and perceptual hierarchies that typically shape and define our encounters with and orientations to codespace, revealing their blind spots and limitations.

Lastly, *Drift* positions participants as one of many agencies in its spatiotemporal co-orchestration of a multivalent, multilayered, lived space. These coagencies include locative technologies, material environments, embedded cultural histories of seascapes, prior literary and narrative practices of orientation, gendered, racialized, and sexualized social repertoires informing embodiment, movements, and mobilities within lived social space, and nonhuman life in the differential, ongoing emergence of this multileveled lived space. In the context of the latest bioinformatic, techno-economic transformations of space, *Drift* stages a reencounter with the material, historical, medial, social, and intrapersonal embedding and *embeddedness* of lived space. From its vantage, space-making practices are always already methods of (re)orientation, which, I'd stress, encourages participants' perceptual attunement to this multiplicity of processes through which lived space is engaged and repurposed, not replaced. *Drift* implicitly poses the question: How might registering the "drift" between, as well as within, distinct modalities and metrics of "life" and the lived space these open onto and foreclose, itself, serve as a means of survival in promoting the apprehension of lived space as a thick, multivalent, multiagential, embedded historical practice in which neither humans nor technological forces are the only, or even unequivocally, the primary agents? It recommends a sense of agency might emerge from a more self-reflexive, multiplicit co-orchestration, as well as co-ordination of these dimensions, modes, media, and metrics of lived space. Survival amidst codespace— and surviving codespace—initially suggests a "living beyond" in either or both spatial and temporal terms, living to inhabit another world or a better time and presumably one outside or beyond codespace. Yet *Drift* and other digital literary practices recommend re-approaching these contemporary politics and poetics of lived space and their multivalent topographies with an ear to their (in)calculable potentialities.

Laura Shackelford is associate professor of English at the Rochester Institute of Technology and chair of the Women's and Gender Studies program. The author of *Tactics of the Human: Experimental Technics in American Fiction* (2015), her research explores comparative literary and media studies, digital literary practices, bioinformatics, and feminist science studies.

Notes

1. The title of Patricia Ticineto Clough and Craig Willse's 2011 collection and the theme for the November 2015 annual Society for Literature, Science, and the Arts conference at Rice University, respectively.

2. I use the term *digital literary* to stress how these works creatively juxtapose and recombine prior print-based media, modes, and genres of writing with emergent, multimodal digital practices. In the case of *Drift*, this site-specific soundscape is explicitly characterized by Rueb as a "place-based" or "locative narrative" and its spoken literary narratives play a central role in juxtaposing how prior print-based writings inform spatial experience with the kinds of narrative practices digital location and mobile technologies might enable.

3. In choosing to use the term social space, I intend to complicate and rethink the opposition between place and space on which so many theories of postmodern space have relied, and to suggest ways that we might resist the assumptions reinforced by the opposition of (material) place from (social) space without invalidating the usefulness of explorations of "place."

4. This list would be quite extensive, though a forthcoming collection of essays by prominent contemporary women digital artists and writers, edited by María Mencía and titled *#WomenTechLit* is an important recent reference point. For another analysis of feminist spatial queries carried out in another digital literary work, see the experimental tablet game, *Luxuria Superbia*. Also see Shackelford 2015.

5. See Massey 1994 for a thoroughgoing analysis of the gendering of space and time and its impact well beyond the field of critical geography. More recently, Sara Ahmed (2006) combines these lines of inquiry with postcolonial theory, phenomenology, and queer theory to address the processes through which spatiotemporal "orientations" are, at once, gendered, racialized and sexually and geopolitically informed.

6. For an introduction to recent feminist science studies and new materialist rethinkings of this Cartesian legacy, see Coole and Frost 2010, where they describe how Descartes's definition of matter as "corporeal substance constituted of length, breadth, thickness; as extended, uniform, and inert . . . provided the basis for modern ideas of nature as quantifiable and measurable" and facilitated the absolute space of Euclidean geometry and mechanical, linear causality of Newtonian physics (7).

7. Importantly, as Debord stresses in *Les Lèvres Nues #9*, "The *dérive* includes both this letting-go and its necessary contradiction: the domination of psychogeographical variations by the knowledge and *calculation of their possibilities*. In this latter regard, ecological science—despite the narrow social space

to which it limits itself—provides psychogeography with abundant data"
(1956; emphasis mine).

Works Cited

Ahmed, Sara. 2006. *Queer Phenomenology: Orientations, Objects, Others*. Durham,
   NC: Duke University Press.
———. 2010. "Orientations Matter." In *New Materialisms: Ontology, Agency, and
   Politics*, edited by Diana Coole and Samantha Frost, 234–57. Durham, NC:
   Duke University Press.
Clough, Patricia Ticineto, and Craig Willse, eds. 2011. *Beyond Biopolitics: Essays
   on the Governance of Life and Death*. Durham, NC: Duke University Press.
Coole, Diana, and Samantha Frost, eds. 2010. *New Materialisms: Ontology,
   Agency, and Politics*. Durham, NC: Duke University Press.
Debord, Guy. 1956. "Theory of the Dérive." *Les Lèvres Nues* #9, November.
   Situationist International Online. http://www.cddc.vt.edu/sionline/si/
   theory.html.
Esposito, Roberto. 2011. *Immunitas: The Protection and Negation of Life*.
   Cambridge: Polity Press.
Greenfield, Adam. 2006. *Everyware: The Dawning Age of Ubiquitous Computing*.
   Berkeley, CA: New Riders.
Grosz, Elizabeth. 2004. *The Nick of Time: Politics, Evolution, and the Untimely*.
   Durham, NC: Duke University Press.
Kitchin, Rob, and Martin Dodge. 2011. *Code/Space: Software and Everyday Life*.
   Cambridge, MA: MIT Press.
Knorr Cetina, K. 2003. "How Are Global Markets Global? The Architecture of a
   Flow World." Paper presented at the Economies at Large Conference, New
   York, November.
Lefebvre, Henri. 1991. *The Production of Space*. Translated by Donald Nicholson-
   Smith. Oxford: Blackwell Press.
Massey, Doreen. 1994. *Space, Place, and Gender*. Cambridge: Polity Press.
May, Jon, and Nigel Thrift, eds. 2001. *Timespace: Geographies of Temporality*.
   London and New York: Routledge Press.
Mencía, María, ed. Forthcoming. *#WomenTechLit*. Morgantown, WV: West
   Virginia University Press.
Parisi, Luciana. 2013. *Contagious Architecture: Computation, Aesthetics, Space*.
   Cambridge, MA: MIT Press.
Rueb, Teri. 2004. *Drift*. Terirueb.net. http://www.terirueb.net/drift/.
———. 2008. "Shifting Subjects in Locative Media." In *Small Tech: The Culture
   of Digital Tools*, edited by Byron Hawk, David M. Rieder, and Ollie Oviedo,
   129–33. Minneapolis, MN: University of Minnesota Press.

Shackelford, Laura. 2015. "Writing and/as Touch at the Interface: *Luxuria Superbia*'s Exploratory Play with Self-Writing." *Frame: Journal of Literary Studies* 28 (1): 71–94.

Thrift, Nigel. 2008. *Non-representational Theory: Space, Theory, Affect*. New York: Routledge Press.

The Story of Oil

Abigail Simon

When I was a child, I had a book—a book that was already old, a relic—
The Story Of Oil. In the book was a drawing—it must have been a drawing,
although in my memory it is as vivid as a photograph: the landscape is rendered in the soothing, alien palette of Pleistocene dioramas—ocher skies
and yellow grasses. In the center is a vast lake of tar in which Strange Beasts
of the Past (another book—another story) are trapped, struggling against
an inescapable destiny—which is to become the engine and essence of this
inevitable present. A gentle giant of some sort (a mastodon? a giant sloth?)
whose only crime was mistaking death for drinking water, struggles to lift
her feet, her eyes filling with a deep pooling sadness as relentless as the tar
itself. Riding her back is a tigerbeast, as opportunistic as pickpocket, angry
and snarling, trapped by her own greed. The image is a parable, a gazing
ball through which the entirety of evolution is revealed, not only pointing
to "us" but to the combustion engine. Decoded correctly, any child can see
that the reason these prehistoric beings lived and died (and suffered) was
to lubricate and propel the future perfect present in which we live.

I am stuck in this image, as surely as the animals depicted in it. I think
of it often, as it is a vision of horror, like a lake in hell. This image is a Trojan
horse, carrying many agents and messengers. Through this image I am ini-
tiated into many "truths"; encoded in the DNA of this image is evidence of
the cruel suffering caused by the processes of the natural world. This idea
of the Cruel Natural World preempts any discomfort one might feel at the
evidence of cruel suffering caused by human intervention in the Natural
Order . . . All beings live, starve, suffer, and die—we are not a disruption
but simply a flavor. In fact, look at this image long enough, and swallow it

WSQ: Women's Studies Quarterly 44: 1 & 2 (Spring/Summer 2016) © 2016 by Abigail Simon. All rights reserved.

deeply enough, and it is clear that our appropriation of their animal bodies is a form of redemption. These wooly mammoths, like Christ, died so that we might live.

But symbolic orders are unreliable and have a tendency to shift, leaving us stranded and floating. Now I am an adult, and I know we do not get our oil from wooly mammoths but from phytoplankton (so much more difficult to depict microorganisms struggling in lakes of tar—I get that). I also know the bottom is really the top: Perhaps we are the ones who live, whose combustible engines fire, so that the phytoplankton (who, let's face it, had dominion orders of magnitude longer than it has taken us to evolve from shrew-like peons) can purge the earth? Perhaps we are only the mechanism to bring to fruition the version of the universe that became locked and trapped in these cells, slumbering like a genie in a lamp until our catalytic converters set it free?

The thing about immortality is that you have to take the long view: to give up your attachment to notions of stasis/normality and accept the eternal constant of change that eternity means . . . Perhaps these ancient animals are simply time bombs, correcting for a planet that has become overrun with mammals—particular mammals: pants-wearing, gun-toting, phanstasmaphilic bipeds full of sentiment and overly sensitive to change.

Seen from far enough away, one has to ask: Why all this sentimental attachment to a blue planet? Thought of as a process of corruption, the translation of molecules in the atmosphere disturbs . . . but if you think of it as liberation, from the tyranny of chlorophyll and sunlight, what then? Is it possible to imagine an illustration in which we (and by "we" I don't just mean humans, but polar bears, hippos, frogs, and bees) are suffering/surrendering so that an unimaginable future can struggle into being?

Immortality means there is always time for another roll of the dice—perhaps there are many ways to be consumed by the inevitable, and being stuck in a lake of tar is only one.

CHORUS

There is a dark force in the universe of material things, and it is Anxiety . . . It is the fascia of history and thought. It is the unseen coefficient of Time . . . Anxiety splits Now (the eternal pleasant) from Then (the atoms of everything from the atoms of everything else).

SECOND VERSE

I will tell you a story, and I want you to imagine yourself inside of it.

This story itself is (as always) a body, the language I excrete around it, a skin.

I am a wormhole through which the universe spins itself around us both. You are a wormhole through which I am hoping to catch a ride. Language is the only available mode of cosmic transport. It is the only way we can imagine things as other than they are. It is both virus and cure—let's not forget it is how we created this world too. It passes like a fever, creating wormholes and mutations in the structure of things as they are, or were. The virus of language turns paper to plastic. Toxic to cosmic. Yes to know.

These molecules of thought are stronger than atoms, but there is a flaw in this system—they require atoms to transmit. As the signal travels (from me to you, now to then) it decays. But if it did not decay, it would be obsolete. These truths, like so many others, often hurt.

EPILOGUE

Behind all technical equations, underneath all formulas and schemes and plans, the cipher behind the mask of numbers and images is the unseen hand of the desire to live without pain and death. I understand this—and I sympathize. I also understand that while this is possible, there is a catch: in order to be beautiful forever, I need to become something other than myself. In order to feel no pain, I need to feel nothing. For some of us this is not a simple binary. Some of us would rather bleed than float. Some of us would rather scream than sleep.

At the bottom of every ocean is a world of ghosts.

Body objects transpose from the bottom of the ocean until they are the sea itself.

This is both upside and downside: we are floating in a fine mist of other bodies, breathing and burning the cellular structures of the universe as it was into the universe as it will be. Seen from far enough away, this is an elegant solution. Seen from close up, there is a lot of loss involved. Seen from far enough away, there is breathing room and possibility. But you will never ever step in that same river ever never again. Or maybe the problem is you will never step out of it.

Somewhere in this tsunami of possible outcomes, the algorithm for carbon-based living lost its panache. Death is the enemy, so what better solution than to make Death the cure? Is it easier to imagine feeling than to feel? I look at myself in the mirror and I am looking for someone else.

OPTION B

I can fix myself in an eternal half-life, volunteer for transmutation in the tar pits of the future. In payment for my cells and software, I will never be anything but the idea of myself as I never was. Silicon breasts, silicon skin, imprinted with a 3D printer on a silicon heart.

We tend to worry more about preserving the evidence of our being than whether or not there will be someone to receive our transmission. Anxiety is eternal and immortal. Anxiety and

Abigail Simon's work as a writer and photographer can be found in the *New York Times*, the *New Musical Express*, and *SPIN* magazine, as well as in the books *SHIFT: 2006*, *Naval Gazing*, and *Petroleum Manga*. Simon has taught at Pratt Institute, NYU, the School of Visual Arts, and the International Center of Photography, where she is currently a seminar leader in the General Studies program. She received an MFA from Bard College in 2006.

Visual Marginalia: Marina Zurkow's Immortal Trash

Marina Zurkow

WSQ: Women's Studies Quarterly 44: 1 & 2 (Spring/Summer 2016) © 2016 by Marina Zurkow and Elena Glasberg. All rights reserved.

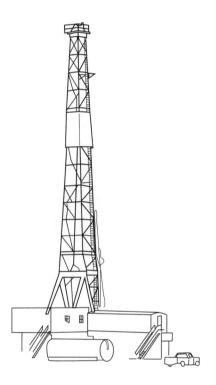

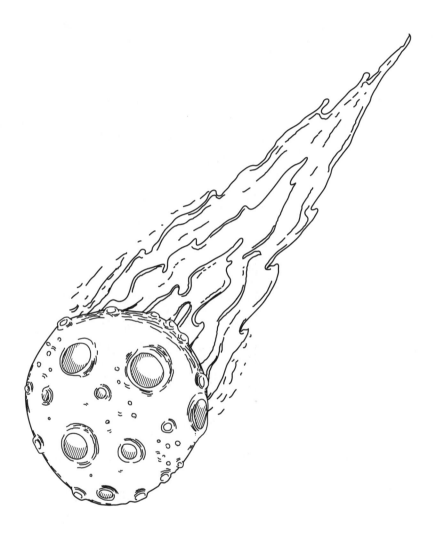

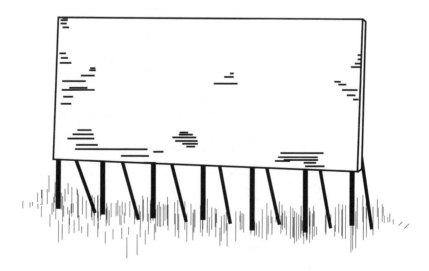

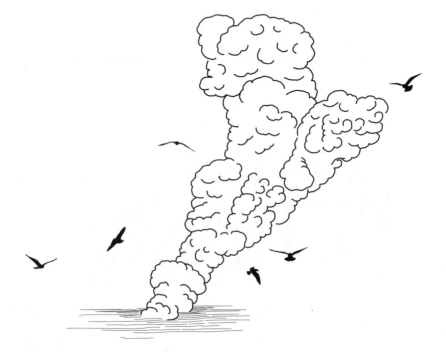

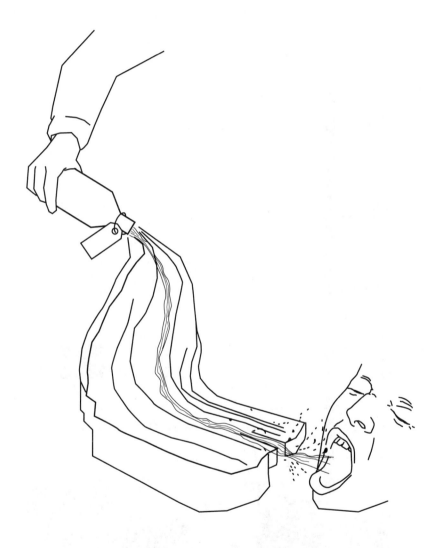

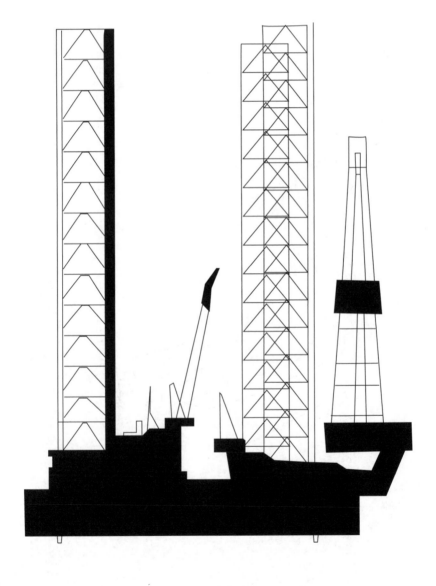

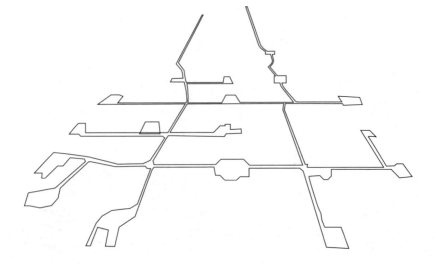

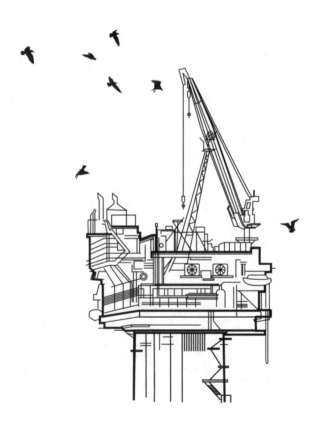

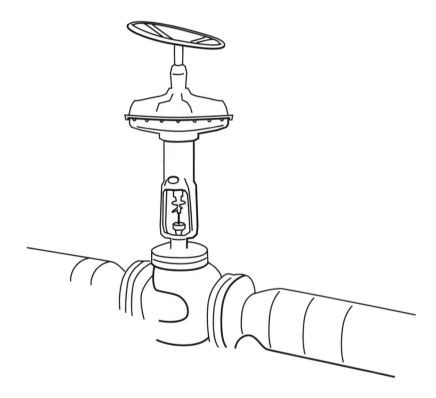

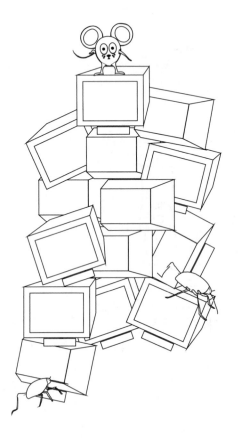

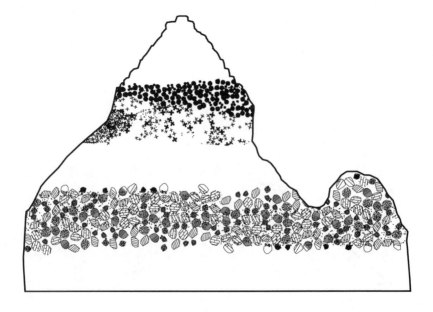

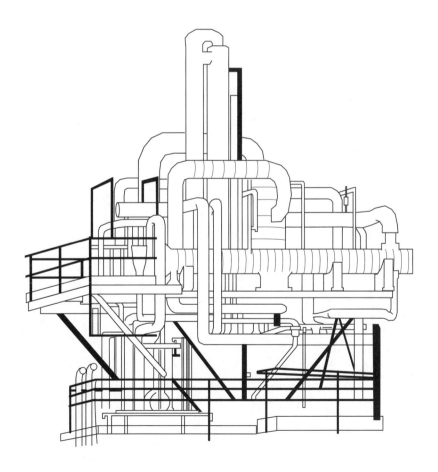

Artist Statement

Elena Glasberg

Marina Zurkow is a media artist who works with and within systems to build new systems. Beginning her career as a digital animator, Zurkow has flowed through and colonized sculptural, video, conceptual, linguistic, solo-installation, collectivist-activist, and bio forms of art practice. Visiting her studio, one is struck by the vivacious and tenacious objects that comprise her manufactory: books, computer screens and storage equipment, video displays, printed images tacked up, models, plastic figurines, moldering painted canvases, and shaped mycelium spores. From her earliest digital image-sound animations, Zurkow was drawn to create abstract patterns both beautiful and purposefully annoying enough to drill into your senses, while her abject-heroic biomorphic figures clung impossibly to the edges of propriety, and of life proper. Zurkow's universe of perverse cartoons eventually began to meld with the strange parts and cast-offs of the global ecosystem as it continually shreds and dies off and remakes itself under the pressures of irreversible anthropogenic change. Over the years, as her installations and vision have expanded in ambition and reach, the once-abject cartoons and sketches (as in sketchy, not to be totally trusted) were squirreled away in files and forgotten. Now they are gathered and dispersed—parts of no part—as a wordless visual essay.

The visuals were selected by Zurkow and the editors of *Survival*, and further selected by the editors of *WSQ*. Their placement on the page is a result of random processes and layers of selection that include the Feminist Press art department. The appearance of these parts of parts, digital ghosts, and leftovers of a coding and assembling process have been collectively dis/organized.

The *Visual Marginalia* comes together through the shared concerns of those involved in *Survival* and in feminist publishing practices in general. And yet an ineluctable force emanates from the visuals themselves—perhaps they placed themselves to a certain extent, landed where they willed, working their cute, exaggerated, and strange appearance to hook the human eye or to clump together, as dandelion seeds adhere lightly to each other before they disperse to other adherences, not the least of which may be the retinas of yet-unknown readers.

Marina Zurkow is a media artist focused on near-impossible nature and culture intersections, researching "wicked problems" like invasive species, superfund sites, and
petroleum interdependence. She has used life science, bio materials, animation, din-
ners, and software technologies to foster intimate connections between people and
nonhuman agents. Her work spans gallery installations and unconventional public
participatory projects. Currently, she is working on connecting toxic urban waterways
to oceans, and researching the tensions between maritime ecology and the ocean's
primary human use as a capitalist Pangaea. She is a full-time faculty member at ITP,
Tisch School of the Arts, New York University, and is represented by bitforms gallery.

PART IV. **CLASSICS REVISITED:**
VALERIE SOLANAS'S *SCUM MANIFESTO*

Spitfire and Sass: Valerie Solanas's "A Young Girl's Primer" and the Creative Possibilities of a Survival Self

Breanne Fahs

In July 1966, Valerie Solanas had just finished her play, *Up Your Ass*, and would soon begin to pen her famed indictment of men, masculinity, and "Daddy's girls," *SCUM Manifesto* (self-published in 1967, published with Olympia Press in 1968, self-published again in 1977 as the "CORRECT" version). While scholars have taken the intellectual contribution of the *SCUM Manifesto* and its relevance to contemporary (radical) feminism seriously (Deem 1996; Fahs 2008; Harding 2001; Harrison 2013; Haut 2007; Heller 2001; Ronell 2004; Third 2006; Warner and Watts 2014; Winkiel 1999), and a few have analyzed the histories of *Up Your Ass* (Harding 2001; Rosenberg 2010)—particularly its role in inspiring Solanas to shoot Andy Warhol (Rowe 2013; Warner 2012)—most work on Solanas has grossly ignored the savvy, subversive, and wildly funny essay Solanas wrote for *Cavalier* magazine, "A Young Girl's Primer, or How to Attain the Leisure Class" (1966). As Solanas's biographer, I have contextualized her life in relation to the times and places she inhabited, just as I have worked to frame her writing in relation to her various (and changing) constructions of herself (Fahs 2014). As her third piece of published writing, the "Primer" most directly speaks to the conditions of her embodied, lived experiences as a homeless prostitute on the streets of New York and, as such, serves as a commentary not only about Solanas herself but also about survival more broadly.

Deploying rhetorical and affective strategies of nihilism, anger, and callousness, Solanas reveals how survival can paradoxically require contradictions and tensions like optimism/pessimism, humor/outrage, and grandiosity/self-effacement. This essay explores these contradictions and

WSQ: Women's Studies Quarterly 44: 1 & 2 (Spring/Summer 2016)

255

tensions, revealing the ways that Solanas carefully constructs different selves in her text and in her life that play up these alter egos and caricatures, all while actually struggling to survive on a daily basis. Barely getting by, starting to unravel with various symptoms of her emerging paranoid schizophrenia, and struggling as a writer who had to carry her typewriter from one crash pad to the next (Fahs 2014), Solanas wrote the "Primer" as a textual counterpart, an effortful meditation on how she could (and did) survive in a context that degraded and dismissed her.

While most people may imagine "survival" to mean meeting one's basic needs for food, shelter, and safety, Solanas's needs presented a much more complicated set of priorities. As a fringe character on the margins of Greenwich Village bohemia and Warhol's "Stupid Stars," and as a brilliant writer and thinker (she scored in the ninety-eighth percentile on her IQ test), Solanas's survival ambitions extended far beyond mere physicality. Solanas's need to survive differently, embodied in her decision to craft an alternative self who could withstand the stressors of her daily life, shines through in the "Primer." Whatever deterioration she experienced in her actual self/body, she could resist these indignities and intrusions by honing her skills as a writer and satirist. Vivid in its startling contradictions with her actual self, brash and bold in its depiction of the shamelessly downtrodden, funky, low-down counterpart who emerges unscathed from life in the "Primer," Solanas cultivates a revolutionary self who thrives on the chaos of New York City panhandling and S&M sex.

This essay considers this "survival self" as a viable strategy for (struggling) feminist artists, writers, and thinkers—particularly those whose conditions of daily life require an "alter ego" to endure the various taxations, trivializations, violences, and mockeries directed toward women within a patriarchal culture. Building on previous work on constructions of the self (Smith and Sparkes 2008), I first trace the particular textual assertions of Solanas's alter ego in the "Primer," and then analyze how it contradicted Solanas's lived conditions in 1966. Following this, I return to Solanas's philosophy of the gutter, where knowledge, revolution, and self are produced within conditions of trash, waste, and excess, and I make connections to Solanas's politics of the visceral, "guttural," and trashy/trasher. Finally, I analyze Solanas's playful construction of her "survival self" and its relationship to the various tensions, contradictions, and paradoxes she inhabits and embraces.

"A Young Girl's Primer, or How to Attain the Leisure Class"

In the late 1960s, *Cavalier* published articles, photos, and commentaries similar to *Playboy*, including tastefully nude photos of celebrities and models alongside articles that targeted middle-aged men's interests and preferences. How Solanas came to publish in this particular magazine—known for its trivializations of women's lives, frankly sexist depictions of women, and mockeries of any sort of gendered rebellion (this was *prior* to the start of the women's movement)—is unknown. That said, Solanas typically pressured a wide swath of publishers and producers to consider her work, often without regard to their audience, reputation, or stylistic choices. (Certainly, Solanas never shied away from "smutty" or "sleazy" types.) In July 1966, her "Primer" appeared as the sixth article in the magazine, titled "For 2c: Pain: The Survival Game Gets Pretty Ugly." The table of contents listed her article with a line by the *Cavalier* editors that said, in a mocking fashion, "How a nice young lady can survive in the city: The easiest way to be comfortable is flat on your back."

Audacious, confident, brash, and funny, the "Primer" details the sexual pursuits of a no-nonsense city girl in New York, who casually makes money selling conversation and sex in order to free up time to do what she truly wants to do: write and pursue her own interests (including time with "secure, free-wheeling, independent groovy female females"). "Flat on her back" or not, Solanas's writing packs a punch, with its nonchalant mix of full-blown snark, wit, and vengeance. As Mary Harron, director and writer of the 1996 film *I Shot Andy Warhol*, wrote of the "Primer," "The persona Valerie adopts here—confident, cool, swinging, in charge—is an idealized self, the version of herself she most wanted to be" (1996, xvii). The self that Solanas depicts in the "Primer" panhandles for fun rather than necessity, takes advantage of men as dupes, and chides middle- and upper-class women as fools.

Solanas's quick pace and rapid-fire speech take center stage in the "Primer," as she moves through the circuits of Manhattan on a "fast-paced day of miniature rejections and small triumphs, idle time and outright hustling, with biting humor thrown in for good measure" (Fahs 2014, 45). A master of humorous reversals of language, she begins the "Primer" by mocking the lack of job opportunities for single, educated women: "Being fresh out of college, I found myself in the typically feminine dilemma of carving out for myself in a male world a way of life appropriate to a young woman of taste, cultivation and sensitivity. There must be nothing crass—like work" (Solanas 1966, 38). Poking fun at well-heeled housewives, investment bankers, and the New York elite, Solanas chooses a survival self that cackles her way through the city while teasing and taunting affluent and middle-class people, asserting herself and her time as being of ultimate importance. Writing of a fellow panhandler, she says: "Here comes that old derelict: 'Say, Miss, could you help me out? All I need's another seven cents and I can get me a drink.' 'You lying mother, you don't want a drink; you're collecting money for mutual funds'" (39).

Much like she did as an undergraduate newspaper columnist for *The Diamondback* at the University of Maryland, Solanas takes pleasure in wordplay, double entendre, trickery, mockery, and straightforward power-tripping. Outsmarting supposedly intelligent men on the streets, she confidently tricks them into giving her money, duping them and framing them as worthless and stupid. For example, she outwits one man who is trying to solicit information from her about prostitutes in the area: "'Tell me where there's some girls and I'll give you a dollar.' 'Okay, give me the dollar.' 'Here.' 'There's girls all over the street. See ya.'" (40). Her love of revenge, of poking fun at men's stupidity while in pursuit of her own libidinous and creative pursuits, is splashed all over this text. She jokes, heckles, sasses, interjects, intervenes, and insists that her valuable time as a writer trying to get by in New York City matters most to her ("No elaborate stories; it goes faster . . . the preciousness of my time demands brevity," 40). She tells a man who wanted to chitchat: "Look my time's valuable. Standing here talking to you'll cost me four-fifty an hour" or, later, "That's conversation. I charge six bucks an hour for that" (76).

The alter ego that Solanas constructs in the "Primer" amuses herself above all else, cracking herself up while pulling a fast one on passersby (especially if they fetishize lesbian sex). Whizzing from restaurant to restaurant, from Feenjon's to Jack Delaney's (both don't serve panhandlers) to Blue Mill Tavern and Lindy's, Solanas purposefully plans her days as a mix of duping others and writing: "Won't take tomorrow off, despite a good night tonight. Can't—I need winter clothes. But it'll be short and sweet, no dillydallying. I pan my way home, planning the next night's agenda: pan around, six bucks for the opportunity to try, chomp a fast snatch, then home" (76). She pokes fun at socialists, constructs shoplifting as patriotic, and quips: "I'll grab a listen. A Socialist. I listen a while, then leave, continuing to do my bit toward bringing about socialism by remaining off the labor market. But first a few little acquisitions from the 5&10, since it's right there. I enter, considering what more I, as a woman, can do for my country—shoplift" (40).

Evidence of Solanas's hard life, of actual days spent struggling for food and shelter, putting up with sleazy johns, trying to find comfort and time to write despite mounting evidence of mental illness, all seems to dissolve in the "Primer," replaced by a personal life filled with self-confidence, brains, and spitfire. (She does, after all, ask men to pay her for dirty words.) Solanas's self in the "Primer" is uncharacteristically optimistic about her prospects of amusing herself, even while she recognizes the nihilistic sentiments later showcased in *SCUM Manifesto*. After convincing one man to pay her six dollars for an hour's worth of conversation about sex over dinner, she adds, "For an additional four bucks I do the illustrations on the napkin" (76). Enduring men who ignore and chide her, or who request that she step on them with golf shoes, stilettos, and cowboy boots, she never reveals a persona who sinks into shame and depression or embraces her lot in life passively. Instead, Solanas distances herself from emotional and physical degradation by treating prostitution like an amusing game:

> "'Are you a lesbian?' 'Yeah.' 'Tell me. What do you lesbians do?' 'Well, first we . . . ' 'Yeah?' 'Then we . . . ' 'Yeeaahh?' 'And then . . . ' His eyes are glassy: *'Yeeaaahhh?* Hey, that I'd like to see.' 'For twenty-five bucks apiece I think I could arrange it.' Wheel over to Sixth Avenue and Eighth Street. 'Hey, Gwen . . .' Room for three at Hotel Earle. This one's a cheapie—watches and beats his meat; saves an additional twenty-five. Three days off, then back to work." (40)

She later jokes, "I pass a magazine stand and sneak a free skim through a table of contents: *How to Meet Men*" (77).

Much like her disdain for "Daddy's Girls" in the *SCUM Manifesto*, Solanas reserves her most vicious and biting jokes for the "Nice, middle-class lady, one of Betty Friedan's 'privileged, educated girls'" she so despised (77), writing of her choice of panhandling as a lucrative career, "This job offers broad opportunity for travel—around and around and around the block. And to think—some girls settle for Europe" (76). When she meets a woman handing out intellectual fliers only to men, Solanas fires back, "She's been programmed beautifully" (76). With a revolutionary spirit and haughty attitude, Solanas ponders her goals in life: "A few days off, then back to work. I pan around, wondering how I can help rid the world of war, money and girls who hand pamphlets to men only. Salvation won't stem from nice, middle-class ladies pushing for Mr. Cole" (77).

1966: Greenwich Village

In stark contrast to the "survival self" Solanas creates in the "Primer," her actual life during these years, particularly when she circulated through Greenwich Village in 1966, was certainly not as airy, carefree, or whimsical. Solanas had a persistent desire to write, which led her to carry around her heavy, old manual typewriter as she moved from hotel to hotel: "From one temporary crash pad to the next, from the Hotel Earle to the Chelsea Hotel, she always carted it along, and when she had no home, she kept it in a storage locker" (Harron, quoted in Fahs 2014, 43). When she had a home, Solanas spent her days just off Washington Square Park at the Hotel Earle, a small, dumpy hotel that offered a separate wing for drag queens and lesbians. Eating cheap meals at the Twenty-Third Street Automat, she struck up random conversations with people, drifted, bummed cigarettes, panhandled on corners, drifted some more, and passed her time with too little food and too little fun. (Later, when she was admitted to various prisons and mental hospitals during the late 1960s and early 1970s, she wrote to her family that she felt relieved to have consistent food, implying that prison and mental hospitals were a step up from her previous existence.)

The portrait of Solanas's actual self in 1966, struggling and desperate, lonely and without allies, is haunting in its stark contrast to the "Primer" self. Solanas's existence on the margins is reasonably well-documented, as she often asked friends, strangers, and even those she hated (like Maurice Girodias, her sleazy publisher) if she could live with them for a while. She often missed rent and got evicted from her residence, moving from Hotel Earle to the scummy welfare hotel, the Village Plaza Hotel (79 Washington Place) in late 1965, and then on to room 606 at the famed Chelsea Hotel (222 West Twenty-Third Street) (Fahs 2014). Never staying anywhere long (both by her choice and the choices of others), she had a life of constant struggle, of enduring year after year of the "shit we have to go through in this world just to survive" (Marmorstein 1968, 11). As Mary Harron wrote in her personal notes from around 1992:

A picture of her life in cheap hotels, days spent drifting . . . I see her lying on the bed in a room filled with old newspapers and piles of manuscripts, panhandling on street corners, cheap restaurants, automats. She liked to hang out, to 'shoot the shit.' In those days there was such a thing as bohemia—a true division between hip and straight, between downtown and uptown—but Valerie's world was on the far margins, isolated even from bohemia. (as quoted in Fahs 2014, 43)

There was weariness to Solanas's existence then, a pressure, a tension, a sense of imploding possibilities and foreclosed futures. Solanas heightened these foreclosures by nurturing a voice in her writing that bordered on grandiose, often mimicked the styles of satire, and, at times, sailed into full-blown mania. Solanas fought back in the only way available to her, the only way she knew how: through her wickedly funny, satirical, serious, audacious writings like *Up Your Ass*, *SCUM Manifesto*, and the "Primer."

"Whores, Dykes, Criminals, Homicidal Maniacs"

Though Solanas never overtly framed her work as having a particular "philosophy," she seemed to prize knowledge that arose from the gutter, from scum, from the downtrodden, worn out, washed away, and trashy. Using SCUM, scum, and *SCUM* interchangeably in her letters, one gets the sense that Solanas had slippery boundaries between the text of *SCUM Manifesto* and the philosophy of "SCUM girls" and "scummy things" (as she once called her performance/meeting of SCUM). SCUM was, at once, a manifesto, a state of mind, a sort of performance art, and a revolutionary underworld force. The mistaken claim that Solanas meant for *SCUM Manifesto* (no punctuation) to be called *S.C.U.M. Manifesto (Society for Cutting Up Men)*—a ploy used by her publisher Girodias to sell more books but never endorsed by Solanas—worked to reduce the important philosophical implications of her work. Valerie continuously believed her ideas were being ripped off; in response to radical feminist Jo Freeman arguing that she had not taken her title of *Bitch Manifesto* from *SCUM Manifesto* but rather, from the *Communist Manifesto*, Valerie retorted, "By this logic a title consisting of any noun at all in front of the word Manifesto would qualify the title as a take-off on the CM. Then why the word bitch? Why not spaghetti?" (quoted in Fahs 2014, 288). The "Primer," too, put forth a witty and satirical title, one that strikes a blow to middle-class sensibilities and "proper" femininity, and yet was altered in *Cavalier* to reflect a less witty, less provocative title (and one that managed to mock and trivialize the piece rather than preserve its cutting satire). Solanas intentionally operates from a scummy position of the underclass, poking fun at wealthy Daddy's girls and the New York leisure class; SCUM is her philosophy as much as her creative brainchild.

When radical feminist Jane Caputi dined with Solanas in the mid-1970s, Solanas clarified her position about the intentions of *SCUM*, shedding light on her philosophy of SCUM: "She reiterated that she never meant for *SCUM* to refer to the Society for Cutting Up Men, that Maurice had made it up against her will." Caputi continued, "I do think it's an important philosophical distinction. She really meant the lowest, most abject being that has the most power to provide knowledge. I think that's a great philosophical claim. She talked about scum coming from the gutter, scum coming from everything objectified and thrown away. This is a brilliant philosophical position" (quoted in Fahs 2014, 278). Indeed, in a June 16, 1968, letter to radical feminist Ti-Grace Atkinson, Solanas reiterates that SCUM (the organization that she characterizes as a group of women with a "SCUM state of mind") is for "whores, dykes, criminals, homicidal maniacs" (Solanas 1968a). Here she purposefully reclaims those discarded from society, cast out, shipped off, denigrated, degraded, and forgotten. Solanas has declared her audience and her camaraderie as clearly designated within the spaces of scum.

Fascinating overlaps between Solanas and trash—somehow signaling her philosophical investment in the gutter—exist throughout her story as well. She asserted her love of "garbage mouth dykes" when advertising auditions for *Up Your Ass*. While in Bellevue mental hospital in 1969, notice of her sentencing after the Warhol shootings appeared buried in the *New York Times*, deep in the back pages of an article which appeared adjacent to a notice to Manhattan residents about a change in the summer garbage collection schedule (Fahs 2014). Even in her last published piece of writing, Solanas expressed an obsession with thinking about garbage, saying of Robin Morgan's *Going Too Far* (1978), "The book's garbage. I didn't read it yet, but I don't have to to know it's garbage. Then why do I want the book? Because I'm a garbage collector. My next book's gonna be about garbage—the cause, nature of and cure for garbage" (Solanas, quoted in Dunn 1977).

Gutter/Guttural, or, Sprouting a Survival Self

For Solanas, several questions swirl around this striking juxtaposition between her "Primer" self (survival self), her actual self, and her philosophies
of SCUM: What kind of self (selves) can emerge from the gutter? Can she
understand herself differently by embracing her gutter/guttural self, the
self that refuses to be distanced from the scummy and scuzzy conditions of
her life? What sort of "survival self" can she create *from* and *within* the gutter, and how does this serve her needs and support her well-being? Why
and how does she seemingly occupy such stark contradictions (optimism/
pessimism; humor/outrage; grandiosity/self-effacement)? Certainly, she
was far ahead of her time in championing the abject, visceral, scummy,
and trashy; only in recent years has the gutter become a productive and
recognized space for art (Kino 2010), queer theory (Holland, Ochoa,
and Tompkins 2014), and writing (Carr 2008). Solanas thrived on trash
(trashy words, trashy people, trashy diners, trashy parts of town) and excess, particularly as she moved within spaces that prized conspicuous consumption, vapid markers of fame, and the shallow/hollow sensibilities of
Warhol's Factory.

The "Primer" presents an amusing alter ego survival self that refuses to
feel destroyed by conditions of poverty and homelessness; this textual self
also implies that writing, for Solanas, allowed her to reimagine the conditions of her gutter-self. The separation between art and life has always
been slippery for Solanas (Does her shooting Warhol invalidate the satirical sensibilities of *SCUM Manifesto*? Can we imagine Solanas as both completely serious and completely funny?) (Fahs 2008). Her writing in the
"Primer," in essence, *stands in* for the actual self, *becomes* the real self while
the real self becomes the "Primer" persona; she *is* the survival self. Much
like other feminist writers who have constructed fictive selves to survive
their actual lives (Allison 2013; Gilmore 1994), or studies that suggest
that creative writing helps women cope with sexual aggression and poverty (Booth-Butterfield et al. 2007; Sloan and Marx 2004), Solanas used
her writing to blur the line between her fictive and actual identity. Hers
was not a dissociative self, a self that *forgets* the "real self," but rather, one
that created a new lens for seeing and surviving terrible living conditions
and harsh realities. It defiantly laughs, feels amused, outsmarts, and out-

wits the "real self." The "Primer" version of Solanas has abundant energy, optimism, funkiness, and possibility. This textual alter ego is unscathed, moving constantly, never stuck or weighed down, never burdened with fatigue, hunger, or trauma. This self cashes in subway tokens for cash, engages men in verbal sparring and wordplay, asserts that she *deserves* to earn money for conversing with them, giggles at her johns, and opportunistically "chomp[s] a fast snatch." It's the "self she most wanted to be."

Creative Possibilities

When writing my biography of Solanas—an undertaking of over a decade and one that exhausted and inspired me in equal measure—I have often been asked to situate the relevance of Valerie Solanas to contemporary feminist politics and writings. After answering questions about whether she *meant* the SCUM Manifesto as serious (my answer: she fused satire and seriousness together as one), I often diverge into claims about what we can learn from Solanas's defiant spirit and her extraordinary story of survival. Solanas did, in the 1960s, what many (young) contemporary feminists, particularly feminist writers, must do today, particularly within a culture of hypervigilant surveillance, social media frenzies, slut shaming, and the ever-more-sophisticated fusions between patriarchy and capitalism: she sprouted an alternative survival self through her writing. This self, emerging from her creative work, did not *split* her persona into different parts but instead held them together. Much like the SCUM Manifesto, the "Primer" showcases the voice of someone on the edge of her sanity, on the verge of madness, teetering. The "Primer" self is clear and funny and witty, but also wholly and deeply tragic, imbued with trauma at its edges, born of the layers and sediments of years that Solanas spent on the margins.

This textual, creative resistance to unlivable conditions (maybe even to *being* a woman in a patriarchal culture at all, particularly during the 1960s) presents an admirable and compelling alternative to being smashed under the crushing weight of poverty, homelessness, prostitution, patriarchy, and lifelong abuse. The "Primer" self held together the loose ends of Solanas's life for at least a decade, clear in its intention to champion the persona full of spitfire. When tracing the patterns and resonances of Solanas's life, I found that when Solanas was actively writing, whether in college for *The Diamondback*, in Greenwich Village for *SCUM Manifesto*, *Up Your Ass*, and the "Primer," or in the late 1970s for *Majority Report*, she could survive (Fahs 2014). Conversely, when she stopped writing (in 1971 when she refused to communicate while at Matteawan and after 1977 when she roamed through New York, Phoenix, and San Francisco), her mental health rapidly worsened and, in her later years, she seemed to forget about the self she once called Valerie Solanas (Fahs 2014). Solanas's writing not only defined her, shaped her, put her on the map, it served as a way for her to create a self with an abundant number of unresolved contradictions, tensions, and paradoxes. Through her writing, she could grip on to the last bits of a coherent identity; when she stopped writing, schizophrenia swallowed her up.

What, then, can Valerie Solanas—her words and her life—teach us about survival? For all of her nihilism and tragedy, Solanas understood the survival self as inherently joyous and full of possibilities (even if it contradicted the so-called "real self"). She played up these incongruities in all of her work, imploring her readers to laugh but also to feel startled and even disturbed. Solanas linked radicalism, humor, feminism (though she would deny an identity as a "feminist"), and violence, possibility and foreclosure of possibility. As her critics and fans have duly noted, Valerie Solanas is, at once, feminism's worst nightmare and one of its great heroes. She is vividly present and in the world, and forever disappearing, surviving as an idea of herself as she withers away. Picture this: Solanas, alone (Avital Ronell called this Solanas's "autistic spheres of solitude" [2004, 31]), largely without consistent companionship and friendship, writing as a historian of an imaginary future: "A 'male artist' is a contradiction in terms. A degenerate can only produce degenerate 'art.' The true artist is every self-confident, healthy female, and in a female society, the only Art, the only Culture, will be conceited, kookie, funkie females grooving on each other, cracking each other up, while cracking open the universe" (Solanas 1977, 4).

Breanne Fahs is an associate professor of women and gender studies at Arizona State University. She recently published the first ever biography of Valerie Solanas, entitled *Valerie Solanas: The Defiant Life of the Woman Who Wrote SCUM (and Shot Andy Warhol)*. Her other books include: *Performing Sex*, *The Moral Panics of Sexuality*, and *Out for Blood*.

Works Cited

Allison, Dorothy. 2013. *Skin: Talking about Sex, Class, and Literature*. New York: Open Road Media.

Booth-Butterfield, Melanie, Steven Booth-Butterfield, and Melissa Wanzer. 2007. "Funny Students Cope Better: Patterns of Humor Enactment and Coping Effectiveness." *Communication Quarterly* 55 (3): 299–315.

Carr, David. 2008. *The Night of the Gun*. New York: Simon and Schuster.

Deem, Melissa D. 1996. "From Bobbitt to SCUM: Re-memberment, Scatological Rhetorics, and Feminist Strategies in the Contemporary United States." *Public Culture* 8 (3): 511–37.

Dunn, Gregory. 1977. "Valerie Charges Back." *New York Daily Planet*, June 28– July 4.

Fahs, Breanne. 2008. "The Radical Possibilities of Valerie Solanas." *Feminist Studies* 34 (3): 591–617.

———. 2014. *Valerie Solanas: The Defiant Life of the Woman Who Wrote SCUM (and Shot Andy Warhol)*. New York: The Feminist Press.

Gilmore, Leigh. 1994. *Autobiographies: A Feminist Theory of Women's Self-Representation*. Ithaca, NY: Cornell University Press.

Harding, James M. 2001. "The Simplest Surrealist Act: Valerie Solanas and the (Re)Assertion of Avantgarde Priorities." *TDR/The Drama Review* 45 (4): 142–62.

Harrison, Katherine. 2013. "'Sometimes the Meaning of the Text is Unclear': Making 'Sense' of the *SCUM Manifesto* in a Contemporary Swedish Context." *Journal of International Women's Studies* 10 (3): 33–45.

Harron, Mary. 1996. "Introduction: On Valerie Solanas." In *I Shot Andy Warhol*, by Mary Harron and Daniel Minahan, vii-xxxi. New York: Grove Press.

Haut, Mavis. 2007. "A Salty Tongue at the Margins of Satire, Comedy, and Polemic in the Writing of Valerie Solanas." *Feminist Theory* 8 (1): 27–41.

Heller, Dana. 2001. "Shooting Solanas: Radical Feminist History and the Technology of Failure." *Feminist Studies* 27 (1): 167–89.

Holland, Sharon P., Marcia Ochoa, and Kyla Wazana Tompkins. 2014. "On the Visceral." *GLQ* 20 (4): 391–406.

Kino, Carol. 2010. "Where Art Meets Trash and Transforms Life." *New York Times*, October 21. http://www.nytimes.com/2010/10/24/arts/design/24muniz.html?pagewanted=all&_r=0.

Marmorstein, Richard. 1968. "SCUM Goddess: A Winter Memory of Valerie Solanis [*sic*]." *Village Voice*, June 13.

Morgan, Robin. 1978. *Going Too Far: The Personal Chronicle of a Feminist*. New York: Random House.

Ronell, Avital. 2004. "The Deviant Payback: The Aims of Valerie Solanas." In *SCUM Manifesto*, edited by Amy Scholder, 1–34. New York: Verso.

Rosenberg, Tina. 2010. "Still Angry after All These Years, or Valerie Solanas under Your Skin." *Theatre Journal* 62 (4): 529–34.

Rowe, Desireé D. 2013. "The (Dis)Appearance of *Up Your Ass*: Valerie Solanas as Abject Revolutionary." *Rethinking History* 17 (1): 74–81.

Sloan, Denise M., and Brian P. Marx. 2004. "A Closer Examination of the Written Disclosure Paradigm." *Journal of Consulting and Clinical Psychology* 72 (2): 165–75.

Smith, Brett, and Andrew C. Sparkes. 2008. "Contrasting Perspectives on Narrating Selves and Identities: An Invitation to Dialogue." *Qualitative Research* 8 (1): 5–35.

Solanas, Valerie. 1965. *Up Your Ass, or From the Cradle to the Boat, or The Big Suck, or Up from the Slime.* Unpublished manuscript. Pittsburgh, PA: Andy Warhol Museum Archives.

———. 1966. "For 2c: Pain: The Survival Game Gets Pretty Ugly" (also known as) "A Young Girl's Primer, or How to Attain the Leisure Class." *Cavalier*, July, 38–40 and 76–77.

———. 1968a. Letter to Ti-Grace Atkinson. June 16. Cambridge, MA: Ti-Grace Atkinson Personal Collection.

———. 1968b. *SCUM Manifesto*. New York: Olympia Press.

———. 1977. *SCUM Manifesto*. New York: Self-published.

Third, Amanda. 2006. "'Shooting from the Hip': Valerie Solanas, SCUM, and the Apocalyptic Politics of Radical Feminism." *Hecate* 32 (2): 104–32.

Warner, Sara. 2012. *Acts of Gaiety: LGBT Performance and the Politics of Pleasure.* Ann Arbor, MI: University of Michigan Press.

Warner, Sara, and Mary Jo Watts. 2014. "Hide and Go Seek: Child's Play as Archival Act in Valerie Solanas's *SCUM Manifesto*." *TDR/The Drama Review* 58 (4): 80–93.

Winkiel, Laura. 1999. "The 'Sweet Assassin' and the Performative Politics of *SCUM Manifesto*." In *The Queer Sixties*, edited by Patricia Juliana Smith, 62–85. New York: Routledge.

Kill Daddy: Reproduction, Futurity, and the Survival of the Radical Feminist

Mairead Sullivan

A curious thing always happens on the first day of my Introduction to Women's, Gender, and Sexuality Studies courses. During my opening notes, I ask students to define two terms: feminist and feminism. We begin with feminist. I ask the class to describe a feminist, giving them permission to draw on cultural stereotypes as well as their own understandings of the term. Without fail, the following responses end up on the board: lesbian, man hating, radical, extreme, opinionated, does not shave. Leaving these descriptors on the board, I then ask them to define feminism. Again, the answers are nearly always the same: a commitment to women's rights; the belief that men and women should be equal. As a pedagogical exercise, I ask my students to explain how column one relates to column two and, not surprisingly, they are quick to come to the defense of feminism's insistence on equality and reprimand the negativity associated with the definition of a feminist. The joy and intrigue of the exercise, for me, is how readily it highlights this persistent bifurcation of the figure of the feminist and feminism as ideology, with the clear distinction that the former is bad and the latter is good. What is even more apparent in this bifurcation is how the image of virulent radical feminist as the embodiment of feminism persists so vehemently, even in the face of a seemingly more palatable juridico-political definition of feminism as tethered to civil equality.

How does this figure of the radical feminist persist, indeed, survive, in our current cultural moment? Furthermore, how has the radical feminist's survival as a malevolent extremist enacted her effacement as a critical figure for contemporary queer and feminist theory? Building on these questions, how does the figure of the radical feminist further push a critique

WSQ: Women's Studies Quarterly 44: 1 & 2 (Spring/Summer 2016) © 2016 by Mairead Sullivan.

of reproductive futurity, as recently argued by Lee Edelman in *No Future: Queer Theory and the Death Drive* (2004)?[1]

In her recent book *Feeling Women's Liberation*, Victoria Hesford presents the figure of the "feminist-as-lesbian"—a figure explicitly connected to radical feminism—as a spectral trope that has served to both define and discredit the women's liberation movement (2013, 1). This figure, which emerged in the early 1970s, served not only to demarcate the boundary between proper and improper (read: heterosexual) femininity, but was also a catalyst for certain schisms and shifts within the burgeoning women's liberation movement. The lesbian, Hesford argues, "becomes the figure through which the emotive force of the attack on women's liberation is generated. . . . As a consequence, women's liberationists are marked as anterior to normal women, with the lesbian the boundary figure through which that separation is made" (2013, 27–28). Interestingly, in *No Future*, Edelman proposes a very similar figure—albeit one coded strictly as male—in the "sinthomosexual." Like the "feminist-as-lesbian," Edelman's sinthomosexual identifies the cultural fantasy of queerness as simultaneously the *abject other* and *defining border* of the normative political subject. Following this similarity between the feminist-as-lesbian and the sinthomosexual, this essay reads the two figures together in order to argue that the figure of the radical feminist, as the heir of the lesbian-as-feminist position, persists as a sinthomosexual figure. Pushing Edelman's argument further, I aim to demonstrate that the radical feminist reads more violently than his sinthomosexual, and thus, is more closely aligned with the destructive forces of the death drive, which Edelman highlights.

Edelman's polemic takes to task an affirmative, humanistic political regime that grounds itself in an ever-deferred future staked on the symbolic logic of the Child. Edelman dubs this "structuring optimism of politics" as *reproductive futurism* (2004, 5). The queer, Edelman argues, figures in this logic as a negativity that "names the side of those *not* 'fighting for the children,' the side outside the consensus by which all politics confirms the absolute value of reproductive futurism" (3). The central argument of Edelman's polemic is that those who find themselves marked by this stain of queerness, rather than disavowing this position, should claim this abjection precisely for its rejection of a politics structured on sentimentalized futurity.

In order to make this argument, Edelman offers the neologism "sinthomosexual," drawing together the Lacanian concept of the *sinthome* with the figure of the homosexual. The sinthome, according to Edelman, is "the template of a given subject's distinctive access to *jouissance* . . . as the knot that holds the subject together, that ties or binds the subject to its constitutive libidinal career . . . " (35–36). Extrapolating from the subject, the sinthomosexual points to this constitutive site in the fabric of the social. While not meant to be literal, the sinthomosexual might be understood as follows: much of what we do and claim in politics and in our social structuring is based on the premise of improvement and forward movement. The Child is most frequently interpellated as the benefactor of this future oriented do-gooding. The sinthomosexual, by contrast, is imagined to evade this commitment, insisting instead on present pleasures. By refusing the normative logic of futurity, the sinthomosexual opens other avenues of investment and thereby threatens the cohesion of this singular structure. In this way, Edelman positions the figure of the queer—as sinthomosexual—in "the place of the social order's death drive"(3). The sinthomosexual names the threat of dissolution that the queer represents in the heteronormative mandates that put genetic reproduction at the center of the social.

Feminist response to Edelman's text has been primarily critical. Jack Halberstam, for example, identifies "the excessively small archive that represents queer negativity," offering instead an "antisocial feminism" drawn from the work of Valerie Solanas, Saidiya Hartman, and Jamaica Kincaid, among others (2011, 109). Similarly, Jennifer Doyle challenges Edelman's reliance on antiabortion rhetoric. Doyle critiques Edelman for his failure to recognize both the place of the maternal body in the logic of the Child, and those women for whom such kinship claims are never possible (2009). Questioning the success of Edelman's challenge to sexual difference, Chris Coffman demonstrates that the sinthomosexual serves to maintain the symbolic structuring of sexual difference (2012). Others have critiqued the nihilism evoked by Edelman's call for the queer to assume this figural position of negativity. Most famously, Jose Muñoz has countered Edelman's negation of futurity by figuring queer in the utopic space of "the yet to come" (2009).

I share in both the challenges and seductions that have made Edelman's text such a ubiquitous interlocutor for recent feminist and queer theory. I want to resist the dual impulses to either argue against Edelman, or to simply add to the archive of the sinthomosexual. Rather, this essay builds on that tension. I do not add the radical feminist to the archive of the sinthomosexual solely to highlight Edelman's blind spots. I intend to push the figure of the sinthomosexual, and with it the myriad debates surrounding social negativity, further. My task here, then, is threefold. First, building on Hesford's "lesbian-as-feminist," I demonstrate that the radical feminist occupies a sinthomosexual structural position. Second, I argue that feminism's threat to futurity figures more violently than Edelman's sinthomosexual. I connect this violence not only to the "destructive politics" of radical feminism, but also to the material effects of some women's refusal of biological reproduction. I conclude by rethinking the place of the sinthomosexual in the wake of feminism's radical history.

In order to make this argument, I draw from two seminal radical feminist texts. The first is Valerie Solanas's iconic *SCUM Manifesto*, and the second is the more obscure "C.L.I.T. Papers," published anonymously as several essays in *off our backs* in 1974. The "C.L.I.T. Papers" have all but disappeared, available mostly in the archives of feminist media projects. What little is available in the secondary sources on the "C.L.I.T. Papers" makes it clear that they were highly controversial, precisely for their arguments—via the politics of lesbian separatism—in favor of full scale rejection of the social. Both of these works anticipate the sinthomosexual logic that Edelman proposes, and it is for this reason that I bring these two texts together. Furthermore, the survival of *SCUM* in the canon of feminist theory speaks to feminist identification with a politics of destruction, even if only on the level of the figural. "C.L.I.T."'s failure to survive follows the post early-seventies bifurcation of feminism away from the vitriolic tone of *SCUM* and the controversial claims of radical feminism. Considering the murderousness implied in the sinthomosexual's relation to the death drive, I invoke the figure of the radical feminist to demonstrate how the threat of feminist separatism as a destructive politics survives, even in occlusion, in our contemporary theoretical moment.

The Feminist-as-Lesbian and Radical Feminism

In *Feeling Women's Liberation*, Victoria Hesford names the event of women's liberation as a turning point in the U.S. imaginary of feminist politics. Returning to the archive of 1970, and, most specifically, to the widespread media attention given to women's liberation following the publication of Kate Millet's *Sexual Politics*, Hesford demonstrates that the emergence of the figure of the feminist-as-lesbian had a "defining effect on the way in which women's liberation in particular and feminism in general has been remembered and represented, in both the supracultural domain of the mass media and in the subcultural domains of popular and academic feminism and queer theory" (2013, 4). The figure of the feminist-as-lesbian, Hesford argues, operates "as a ghost rather than an icon or symbol" due to "such overfamiliarity and hypervisibility" (15). The ghostliness that Hesford names in this figure is exemplified in my students' quick moves to disavow the relation between feminism and the lesbian. That may have once been true, they seem to say, but the persistence of this association is meant to spook rather than name. Beginning with Solanas and the *SCUM Manifesto*, as well as the "C.L.I.T. Papers"—a derivative manifesto of radical feminism—I turn here to consider the *spookiness*, indeed the terror, of what I will demonstrate is the specter of destruction that the figure of the radical feminist contains.

The mark of radical feminism in the early 1970s was the refusal of femininity as conscripted by heterosexuality and full-scale rejection of the nuclear family (Echols 1989). Although mainstream feminist politics sought to cast off the confines of the feminine social position through a liberal politics of assimilation, a radical approach advocated a more destructive form of feminism—often articulated in a politics of lesbian separatism. Beyond practice, such feminism was enacted largely through manifestos, political writings, and direct actions (1989). The association between feminism and destruction begins with allegations of bra burning at the 1968 Miss America Pageant.[2] The image of the burning bra has persisted as a metaphor for the violence of feminists; this image is posed in distinction to the good liberalism of feminism as an ideology of equality. Published around the same time as the infamous bra burning, Valerie Solanas's *SCUM Manifesto* has become, perhaps, the most read example of a feminist politics of destruction. Though most remembered for advocating a homicidal cutting up of men, Solanas's true target was the gender system at the center of a capitalist, bourgeois state. Solanas's weapon was her words and the vitriol of her writing became a rallying point for a radical feminist movement.

Many scholars have connected Solanas to an antisocial politics similar to the one characteristic of the sinthomosexual. In responding to Edelman's limited archive, for example, Halberstam offers Solanas as "an antisocial feminist extraordinaire" (2011, 108). Similarly, Avital Ronell highlight's the manifesto's "antisocial edge," and connects Solanas to "nonplace . . . the *non* bound by the *nom*, as Lacan would say" (Solanas and Ronell 2004, 2, 5, 23). In describing Solanas's "antisocial practices" as a kind of refusal of "the burdens of social and sexual reproduction," Hesford's analysis draws Solanas most clearly into the realm of the sinthomosexual:

> The antisocial practices of *SCUM* are the actions of women "too child-ish" and too "uncivilized" to accept the burdens of social reproduction . . . Solanas's *SCUM* revolution won't happen through marches and movements—through a protest that is also an appeal to the laws of dad-dy's bourgeois society—but through the mayhem wrought by refusing to acknowledge the legitimacy of those laws. (2013, 102)

SCUM gains its critical traction through an embodiment of the structural epithet that would seek to dismantle its prerogative. Laying claim to the space on the margins, in "the gutter," *SCUM* refuses bourgeois politics in-vested in class ascendancy, in the political promise of social capital. The gutter serves not only as a rejection of the prescriptions of heterofemi-ninity but also as militant uprising, what Hesford has labeled "a Solanas-esque politics of refusal" (299). What Solanas enacts in *SCUM* is not only a rejection of heterosexually scripted femininity, as is often ascribed to the motives of separatist feminism, but a wholesale refusal of politics bent on claiming a universal good. *SCUM* does not simply scoff at reproduc-tive futurism. Rather, it calls for a homicidal revolt whose ultimate goal is not equality, assimilation, or recognition but the destruction of the male sex and with it any vestiges of biology, culture, and capital that would tie women to reproduction.

The *SCUM Manifesto* takes radicalism as destruction to its limit. The politics of *SCUM* is a homicidal ideology. The bulk of the publication fo-cuses on men's deficiency, their animalistic inferiority to women, and their self-annihilating commitment to fucking. But riddled throughout, and most pointedly in the final pages, are Solanas's calls on *SCUM* to destroy men in the most literal sense—through men's own transition to women, through technological overtake of reproduction assuring that only females are born, or, if necessary, through murderous means. Rejecting a politics of the status quo, denying that change can happen through protest or simply opting out, Solanas calls for a kind of warfare against men, both "men" in the literal sense and all that the patriarchy has come to bolster.

The status of *SCUM* as the harbinger of this antisocial politics gained critical speed through Solanas's interpellation as a figure of radical fem-inism. Indeed, many of the most acerbic, destructive, and man-hating writings to come out of the radical movement attribute their influence to

Solanas's *SCUM*. Among them are the "C.L.I.T. Papers." The "C.L.I.T. Papers" were first released as a series in the radical feminist publication *off our backs* (*oob*) and were then quickly republished in the lesbian feminist journal *DYKE*. Written by a group of anonymous lesbian feminists calling themselves Collective Lesbian International Terrorists (C.L.I.T.), the "C.L.I.T. Papers" primarily took aim at the mainstream media, whose accusations of "lesbian" were seeking to discredit and, perhaps, dismantle the movement for women's liberation. Published as two separate statements in the May and July 1974 issues of *oob*, the "C.L.I.T. Papers" outlined the formation of the collective, its goals and intentions, and the steps to achieve its goals. Ultimately, C.L.I.T. sought the end of patriarchy through the destruction of heterosexuality. The means by which they sought this end, however, was full withdrawal from the capitalist systems that were intricately bound to patriarchy and bolstered by the class ascendant, heterosexual, nuclear family. To begin, the C.L.I.T.s called for a lesbian refusal of the straight press—as writers, readers, or publishers. In boycotting straight press, they argued, the radical feminist movement could not only control their own means of information dissemination but, even more importantly, they could thwart the cooptation of a sterilized and neutered lesbian figure pawned by the liberal-minded, humanitarian press.

Kill Daddy

The polemicizing force of sinthomosexual is grounded in what has been called a "suicidal politics," one that in refusing futurity, refuses survival. The *jouissance* that Edelman claims is embodied by queerness is associated with a kind of excessive, orgasm-driven sexuality, measured mostly through practice.[3] Yet, the figures that Edelman draws on are not marked by sexual excess in the way one might imagine but, rather, by a kind of callous and depraved disregard for an appropriate humanistic investment in the other—that itself results in a kind of perverse pleasure.[4] Edelman's tacit insistence on *jouissance* as a kind of orgasmic pleasure linked to the fantasy of queer sexuality gets displaced by the murderousness that characterizes the sinthomosexual in his readings of Hitchcock's *North by Northwest* (1959) and *The Birds* (1963). When reading these figures, we find a different relation between *jouissance* and the death drive, understood through a kind of homicidal pleasure. This alignment of the death drive with a kind of murderous, annihilative force is well captured in the stated aims of radical feminism. The push to declare feminism "no longer relevant" does not come from its overly sentimentalized emphasis on liberal equality, but rather from its relation to a violent, destructive, indeed murderous, figure. What makes the radical feminist so threatening is that she seems to take a perverse pleasure in the hating—and perhaps killing—of men. In order to consider the sinthomosexual potential of radical feminism, I want to first consider the most salient and pointed articulation of Edelman's polemic:

> Fuck the social order and the Child in whose name we're collectively terrorized; fuck Annie; fuck the waif from *Les Mis*; fuck the poor, innocent kind on the Net; fuck laws both with capital ls and small; fuck the whole network of Symbolic relations and the future that serves as its prop. (2004, 29)

It is clear here that the "fucking" imagined to define the sinthomosexual is not simply or merely *fucking* in its most banal, copulative sense, but a way of giving the proverbial finger to any demand that such fucking be made to have meaning in the "structuring optimism of politics" (5). The gesture given in the "fuck" is a dismissal, a refusal, rather than an outward or aggressive attack. In this way, the sinthomosexual sidesteps the question of children as the bearers of futurity and turns elsewhere. The sinthomosexual, thus, does not operate as an active destroyer of children or, even, the future, but rather simply as brushing such questions to the side in favor of other kinds of pleasures and indulgences. The radical feminist, by contrast, continues to figure as a destructive, terrifying, even murderous threat to the cohesion of the social, to the family, to men, and, most pointedly, to male children. In the first chapter of her book on motherhood, Adrienne Rich shares the following anecdote:

> In a living room in 1975, I spent an evening with a group of women poets, some of whom had children. . . . We talked of poetry, and also of infanticide, of the case of a local woman, the mother of eight, who had been in severe depression since the birth of her third child, and who had recently murdered and decapitated her two youngest, on her suburban front lawn. . . . Every woman in that room who had children, every poet, could identify with her. (1995, 24)

That anyone, let alone a mother, would murder a child remains unthinkable today. Unthinkable to most, Rich implies, except for mothers. Jane Gallop argues that Rich "not only speaks to the secret of common maternal anger but treats that anger as a surface eruption of an even darker, deeper violence that systematically constitutes motherhood as a patriarchal institution" (1988, 2). The Child, for radical feminists, cannot be simply rejected or refused, the child, itself, is already the figuration of a thwarted future. As Jennifer Doyle (2009) has argued, Edelman's reliance on the child—particularly as the child is figured in one of Edelman's anecdotes as the larger-than-life fetus, the target of both pro-choice and antiabortion rhetoric—elides the maternal body that is always connected to that child. It is precisely the literality of feminist refusal of reproduction—the threat to the actual, biological end of generations—that marks the feminist figure as dangerous.

The Child as the bearer of the future's potentiality is not a signifier that is available to women. Gayle Rubin's groundbreaking essay, "The Traffic in Women," makes this argument by connecting Engels's work on kinship systems and Marx's analysis of the reproduction of labor in the service of capital to Oedipal drama, via Freud and Lacan (1975). The kinship system, as reinforced through heterosexuality, Rubin argues, is structured so as to assure the persistence of wealth and social capital for the patriarchal lineage. Articulated in Lacanian parlance through the symbol of the phallus, this inheritance is given through the exchange of the phallus in the Oedipal drama. As Rubin reminds us, "The girl never gets the phallus. It passes through her, and in its passage is transformed into a child" (54). The child, then, does not promise a political or social future for all but, rather, becomes the instantiation of the father's future, via the phallus. The child is always the proto-father. We might also argue, by this Oedipal logic, that the girl is both always a child and never a child. She fails to overcome the Oedipal drama because she is never able to become other than a woman, specifically a mother, and thus is never able to be or have the phallus.

By being against children and refusing the mandates of reproduction, the sinthomosexual also refuses the Oedipal inheritance of the phallus. Without the Oedipal drama and its concomitant threat of castration, the law of the father, the motor of the symbolic, fails to inaugurate meaning. The figuring of the sinthomosexual as the excessive force of *jouissance*— reading as it does as "insisting on access to *jouissance* in the place of access to sense"—derives from the sinthomosexual's threat to the logic of the Oedipal drama that would serve to contain the sinthome (Edelman 2004, 37). The trouble here, however, is that this negation of the Oedipal does nothing to dismantle the privileged place of the phallus in the Symbolic order. Refusing the promise of the phallus, inaugurated, as Rubin argues, in its passage from father to son, does not, necessarily, collapse its value. We might find here the kind of hopeful promise of a Symbolic structured otherwise that Edelman so resolutely refuses to claim. Withholding the phallus and its promise of heterosexuality, the son-father imagines he can rescript the Symbolic otherwise. The radical feminist, however, knows that it is Daddy who must be destroyed in order to disrupt the phallic signifier.

If Edelman reads the political promise of the future in the sentimental attachment to the Child—and, we might add, with the political investment in the phallic promise of the Oedipal drama—the project of the separatist politics of radical feminism takes aim at the structural position of Daddy. Both *SCUM* and C.L.I.T. want to kill Daddy. It is Daddy that keeps women barefoot and pregnant, consigned and confined to the burdens of reproduction. By claiming lesbianism as a structural position, rather than simply a personal identity or sexual practice, radical feminism names the threat that women's refusal of reproduction poses to the patriarchal machine, inaugurated and reinforced through the law of the heterosexual nuclear family.

The destruction of Daddy as motor of the Symbolic is also the target of C.L.I.T. Tackling the Symbolic as language, C.L.I.T. called for a refusal of all cultural discourse that would seek to define and contain the lesbian. The liberal-biased attempt at social incorporation enacted by media forms invested in promotion of the avant-garde sexual deviant, they contended, renders the lesbian part of a palatable, even enviable, subculture. It is not just mainstream media that would co-opt the significatory force of the lesbian—but women's liberation and gay liberation as well. Rejecting the heterosexual "artifice" that ascribes gender difference, C.L.I.T. proclaims: "Daddy is a piece of shit who demands respect" (1974b, 11). C.L.I.T takes aim at drag culture: "Males can afford to keep on laughing at momma, having no heart, no ability to empathize with momma who is the real victim of family life" (4). The family here is the marker of the rules of both heterosexuality and patriarchy, enforced through Daddy's law. Rather than offer a refined image of the lesbian that might bring her into the confines of the familial, that might make her an identifiable subject of the properly social, C.L.I.T proclaims: "It is far more important to become unintelligible" (1974a, 16). Like the sinthomosexual, C.L.I.T. rejects "futurism's logic of intelligibility" moving instead to "insist on the unintelligible's unintelligi-

bility" (Edelman 2004, 106–7). Refusing not only the lesbian's own intelligibility, C.L.I.T.'s goal is, simultaneously, for her to become alienated
from the intelligibility of the social.

Beyond challenging the bounds of proper femininity, radical feminism
challenged the bounds of the properly political. The politics that the sinthomosexual rejects are governed by the logic of opposition that always
promises a better tomorrow. This opposition, which relies on what Wendy
Brown calls "wounded attachments," seeks legitimation through the state
via a politics of identity (1995). What is rejected in the sinthomosexual's
acquiescence is both a politics formulated on a linear narrative of progress
and one staked on empirical and tangible outcomes. If we are not fighting for rights, for the future, then what *are* we fighting for? This sense of
hopelessness in the rejection of empirical, futural politics has been labeled
by one of *No Future*'s reviewers as "political suicide" (Fontenot 2006).
Though the sinthomosexual never takes the plunge, the radical feminist
just might.

There is something nihilistic about radical feminism; it's not entirely
clear what happens to society when it has been destroyed. The queer and
feminist cultural memory of a specifically lesbian separatist radical feminism tends to align this movement with a utopic politics of elsewhere.
A recent *New York Times* article, for example, laments the loss of "lesbian
land," that was so central to certain kinds of separatist movements of the
1970s (Kershaw 2009). Although the cultural nostalgia for separatism,
perhaps mostly from within the women's movement, invokes a kind of
rural utopia, the ongoing association between feminism and nihilistic politics of destruction rests on the figure of the radical feminist. The suturing
of radical feminism to these separatist utopias serves to both redeem and
sanitize the figure of the radical feminist, thus occluding her sinthomosexual positioning. Returning to Edelman's litany of those childish figures to
whom the sinthomosexual offers a resolute "fuck you," we might imagine
the radical feminist rejoinder as follows: Kill the patriarchy and the Man
in whose name we are collectively terrorized; kill Daddy Warbucks; kill
Jean Valjean; kill the predatory rapist; kill pricks both in your pants and in
your head; kill the whole network of capitalist relations and the future that
serves as its prop.

Coda: The Child

Christina Sommers's book opens with a list of the acts of kindness, support, and grief shared by several young men in the wake of the 1999 Columbine shootings. Sommers does this in order to juxtapose these good boys with what she argues has become the "fashionable . . . pathologiz(ing) . . . of healthy male children" (2001, 14). Reading against a popular media narrative that named the actions of two male students at Columbine as symptomatic of a crisis of American boyhood, Sommers argues instead that feminism is to blame for the subsequent lapse of boys into second-class citizenship. Christy Wampole echoes feminism's disregard for men—and its ensuing effect on boys—in her opinion piece following the Sandy Hook massacre. In "Guns and the Decline of Young Men," Wampole argues that it is feminism, along with the civil rights movement, that has robbed white men of their social position and driven them to destructive excess:

> From the civil rights and feminist movements of the 1960s and onward, young men—and young white men in particular—have increasingly been asked to yield what they'd believed was securely theirs. This underlying fact, compounded by the backdrop of violent entertainment and easy access to weapons, creates the conditions for thousands of young men to consider their future prospects and decide they would rather destroy then create. (2012)

Wampole's diagnosis of the crisis of young men adds a surprising twist to Edelman's sinthomosexual. We might find a better figure for the sinthomosexual in these mass murdering young men. Their sexuality, too, contests the borders of heterosexuality and the failure of an Oedipally mature genitality. Like the figure of the effeminate boy, the hypermasculinity contained in the acts of these young men, as Michael Kimmel diagnoses it, is connected to the perils of an enduring attachment to the mother (2013). Often imagined as recluses, persistent masturbators holed up in their mother's basements, they fail to attach to the futural promise of the Child as they remain children themselves. Here, the sinthomosexual's rejection of the logic of futurity is not simply a flippant dismissal but, rather, a psychotic murderous rampage aimed to destroy— and, at its root is the wounding and castrating, indeed, the destructive effects of feminism. Feminist politics is intricately bound with questions of survival. Part of what is marked in the menace of radical feminism's commitment to destruction is the threat posed to the survival of others. The sinthomosexual's dismissal of reproductive futurism marks the possibility of sexual meaning outside of hetero-reproduction but it does not guarantee, or even suggest, its destruction. The threat of the radical feminist, on the other hand, is precisely this threat of the destruction of the future—through both an outright refusal of reproduction and a pointed disregard for the maintenance of the political field. Put another way, it is only because feminism has posed such a threat to the value of the nuclear family as the political center that our current future commitments are so thoroughly staked on the figure of the Child.

The association between feminism and the refusal of the conscriptions of heteropatriarchy has had the effect of shifting the plane in which the futural logics of liberal humanism are staked. Some might attribute the seemingly brief heyday of radical feminist politics to its inefficacy. And, yet, the cultural association between radicalism and feminism remains strong, perhaps even more so than any other radical movement. The extremism associated with radical feminism's separatist politics serves as fodder to dismiss feminism wholesale; even in many feminist or feminist-affiliated circles, radical separatism is rejected as an aberrant past. Far from being left behind, however, the figure of the radical feminist continues to inform how we maintain the logic of reproductive futurism.

The radical feminist survives as a sinthomosexual figure. Even more than the simple refusal offered in Edelman's sinthomosexual, the radical feminist as sinthomosexual marks the very real threat posed in feminist refusals of reproduction and rejections of the nuclear family. When my students read *The SCUM Manifesto*—and other radical feminist texts—I bring them back to our first-day discussion. Many are quick to ascribe these extremisms to the weariness they feel in the label "feminist." There are others, of course, who identify with the rage, the energy, and the venom of the texts. They feel called into a moment, a movement, often assumed to be past. Following this call, and in the face of our resistance to the seduction of the Child, we might do well to ask: Have we killed Daddy?

Mairead Sullivan is a doctoral candidate in the Department of Women's, Gender, and Sexuality Studies at Emory University. Archival research for this project was supported by the Mary Lily Research Grant sponsored by the Sallie Bingham Center at Duke University.

Notes

1. I use the term "radical feminist" in reference to Alice Echols's *Daring to Be Bad: Radical Feminism in America 1967–1975* (1989). Echols identifies radical feminism as a specific movement within feminism, and as part of the larger movement of 1960s radicalism. Building on Echols, I define radical feminism as a movement built largely around an ideology of separatism, specifically lesbian separatism, rather than assimilation. In doing so, I also mean to separate these terms from current instantiations of radical feminism, particularly in their essentialist and trans-exclusionary practices.
2. The allegations of bra burning at the 1968 Miss America Protest remains an apocryphal event in the history of women's liberation. For more on the debates surrounding the veracity of the bra burning claims, see Campbell 2010.
3. These practices, at least as they are taken up in queer theory, are tacitly understood as related to gay male sex. I would also argue that the implication is more readily connected to "risky" practices such as barebacking, anonymous sex, and fisting, than to anal sex.
4. I am tempted here to call these figures "assholes." And, indeed, they are, particularly following on the *anality* that is so prolific in the so-called "antisocial" strand of queer theory. We might also call these figures "dicks," and, in doing so, perhaps, shift their role in the sinthomosexual logic considered through radical feminism.

Works Cited

Brown, Wendy. 1995. *States of Injury*. Princeton, NJ: Princeton University Press.
Campbell, Joseph W. 2010. *Getting It Wrong: Ten of the Greatest Misreported Stories in American Journalism*. Berkeley, CA: University of California Press.
C.L.I.T. 1974a. "C.L.I.T. Statement #1." *off our backs* 4 (May): 16.
———. 1974b. "C.L.I.T. Statement #2." *off our backs* 8 (July): 11–13.
Coffman, Chris. 2012. "The Sinthomosexual's Failed Challenge to (Hetero)sexual Difference." *Culture, Theory and Critique* 54 (1): 56–73.
Doyle, Jennifer. 2009. "Blind Spots and Failed Performance: Abortion, Feminism, and Queer Theory." *Qui Parle: Critical Humanities and Social Sciences* 18 (1): 25–52.
Echols, Alice. 1989. *Daring to Be Bad: Radical Feminism in America, 1967–1975*. Minneapolis, MN: University of Minnesota Press.
Edelman, Lee. 2004. *No Future: Queer Theory and the Death Drive*. Durham, NC: Duke University Press.
Fontenot, Andrea. 2006. "*No Future: Queer Theory and the Death Drive* (review)." *MFS: Modern Fiction Studies* 52 (1): 252–56.

Gallop, Jane. 1988. *Thinking Through the Body*. Reprint, New York: Columbia University Press.

Halberstam, Judith. 2011. *The Queer Art of Failure*. Durham, NC: Duke University Press.

Hesford, Victoria. 2013. *Feeling Women's Liberation*. Durham, NC: Duke University Press.

Kershaw, Sarah. 2009. "My Sister's Keeper." *New York Times*, February 1. http://www.nytimes.com/2009/02/01/fashion/01womyn.html.

Kimmel, Michael. 2013. *Angry White Men: American Masculinity at the End of an Era*. New York: Nation Books.

Millet, Kate. 1970. *Sexual Politics*. New York: Columbia University Press.

Muñoz, José Esteban. 2009. *Cruising Utopia: The Then and There of Queer Futurity*. New York: New York University Press.

Rich, Adrienne. 1995. *Of Woman Born: Motherhood as Experience and Institution*. New York: W. W. Norton & Company.

Rubin, Gayle. 1975. "The Traffic in Women: Notes on the 'Political Economy' of Sex." In *Toward an Anthropology of Women*, edited by Rayna R. Reiter, 157–210. New York: Monthly Review Press.

Solanas, Valerie, and Avital Ronell. 2004. *SCUM Manifesto*. New York: Verso.

Sommers, Christina Hoff. 2001. *The WAR AGAINST BOYS: How Misguided Feminism Is Harming Our Young Men*. New York: Simon & Schuster.

Wampole, Christie. 2012. "Guns and the Decline of the Young Man." *Opinionator*, December 17. http://opinionator.blogs.nytimes.com/2012/12/17/guns-and-the-decline-of-the-young-man/.

PART V. **POETRY**

A Conversation with My Mother

Miriam Piilonen

I tell my mother hello.
My mother tells me hello, how are you?
I tell my mother I took the morning-after pill, because of an accident.
My mother tells me I should be more careful.
I tell my mother yeah, I know—I'll be more careful.
My mother tells me I'm of an age where pregnancy is an option.
I tell my mother if I were to become pregnant I'd have an abortion.
My mother tells me I don't have to make a decision about an abortion
    just yet.
I tell my mother I'm certain that if I were to become pregnant
    I'd have an abortion.
My mother tells me I can't know that for certain . . .
    unless I've already had an abortion?
I tell my mother I've never had an abortion.
My mother tells me yeah, she assumed; she's never had an abortion either.
I tell my mother I don't see the problem with an abortion.
My mother tells me she thinks women should have the right to an abortion.
I tell my mother she's the person I'd tell if I had an abortion.
My mother tells me thanks—though she's not sure she'd want to know
    about an abortion.
I tell my mother I'd want to talk about an abortion, if I were to have one.
My mother tells me thank you—she's glad I can talk to her.
I tell my mother how glad I am I can talk to her.
My mother tells me I'm the woman with whom she's closest.
I tell my mother that she's the woman with whom I'm closest.

WSQ: Women's Studies Quarterly 44: 1 & 2 (Spring/Summer 2016) © 2016 by Miriam Piilonen.

My mother tells me she wants a grandchild.
I tell my mother I don't like it when she tells me she wants a grandchild.
My mother tells me she needs to tell me she wants a grandchild.
I tell my mother I'm the wrong person to talk to about a grandchild.
My mother tells me she's the wrong person to talk to about an abortion.
I tell my mother I need to talk about an abortion.
My mother tells me she needs to talk about wanting a grandchild.
I tell my mother not to tell me she wants a grandchild.
My mother tells me I'd have a beautiful grandchild.
I tell my mother it's uncomfortable to know she wants a grandchild.
My mother tells me it's uncomfortable to talk about an abortion.
I tell my mother I need to be free not to produce a grandchild.
My mother tells me she needs to be free to want a grandchild.
I tell my mother that knowing she wants a grandchild is painful.
My mother tells me she needs to talk about wanting a grandchild,
      especially with me.
I tell my mother I need to be free to talk about an abortion,
      especially with her.
My mother tells me that talking about an abortion is too upsetting for her.
I tell my mother that talking about a grandchild is too upsetting for me.
My mother tells me that even though our conversation upsets her,
      she loves me very much.
I tell my mother that I love her very much too and that I have to go.
My mother tells me yeah, she also has to go.

Miriam Piilonen is a PhD student in music theory and cognition at Northwestern University. She blogs occasionally at putcomputer.wordpress.com.

Anecdotes, an Aphorism from Billy Bob Thornton

Amber Moore

As a child his father would take the kids to car wrecks.
Not to gawk, but to witness perhaps, and
maybe for a touch of fear—
just enough to keep you straight and
good. So you'll remember to check
all your blind spots, driving or otherwise.

Later, he'd be bothered by shows like
Cupcake Wars, because really,
how dangerous is it and should we be using the word
"war" here? Some people might not like that
very much at all.

As a final thought,
never try to pour yourself into something you shouldn't be in.
You may not like the shape it takes, or
the shadows it casts when it's all over and we're laid down.
In his case, it will be in the South, where
the air is heavier with the past,
with silences and pauses.

WSQ: *Women's Studies Quarterly* 44: 1 & 2 (Spring/Summer 2016) © 2016 by Amber Moore. All rights reserved.

Amber Moore is a Canadian high school English teacher. She holds an MA in English with a specialization in gender studies, and is currently finishing her MA in education. Her work has been printed in numerous literary publications including most recently, *FreeFall Magazine*, *Adanna Literary Journal*, and *Room Magazine*.

Sex Ed

Deirdre Daly

Lesson One

She is our sage
in black and white bondage, fresh from the convent laundry.
She preaches of gifts to the sixty eyes, thirty blank slates,
eroding and tempering their young yearnings with a voice
that whispers its sweet nothings only with Christ.
She knows all.

Intangible gifts that
are priceless, but useless, unspeakable, but virtuous,
each freckled face exudes puzzlement
with the realization that down there
is actually somewhere.

The nun softens
their blushes with the promise of redemption,
rallying the class through a call to arms through purity.
To eager ears and empty heads it sounds so easy.

That night, they dream.
Throbbing upon waking, the rubbing
of their soft and downy thighs,
births a hot shame that leeches to their core.
They dream of their damnation.

WSQ: Women's Studies Quarterly 44: 1 & 2 (Spring/Summer 2016) © 2016 by Deirdre Daly. All rights reserved.

Lesson Two

Matrimonial duty
produces and washes the charts of blood
from wedding night linen, the visceral manifestation
of their gift. They will knead it from the weave,
the hot water and soap callous their hands,
to be unfresh again for tomorrow.

This blood maps
absent histories. Wondrous in its austerity,
these stains divulge souls scrubbed clean from confession
and bodies parched by the dryness of a wafer of bread
which meant less to them than the pound note
pressed into their small hands by an old man
who insisted a girl in a white dress
sit on his lap in return.

The class wonders,
knowing so little of flesh and startled by their own warmth
that now rouses them from their slumber nightly,
how men, as though prodding cattle, could draw blood.
They check themselves, cross their legs, and discard
patent leather shoes lest they excite prying eyes.

Lesson Three

The softest night
and two girls steal to the dampness of a meadow in late March.
There is glee in the looseness of their French braids and they run breathless
with white stockings at half-mast around brazen ankles.

A solemn communion
under a haloed moon. It is too easy.
One kiss and one touch, they render their gift obsolete.
They are divine and perverse,
ecstasy and perfection in form.

Morning and no effect is seen,
but for the slightest hollow in the moss
and a trace of blood that cuts the frosts,
the christening of sacred ground,
red on white.

Deirdre Daly is a writer currently living in Dublin, Ireland. Her poetry and writing has been published, or is forthcoming, in *Word Riot*, *The Normal School*, and *The Alarmist*. In 2007 she graduated with an MA in gender and writing from University College Dublin.

Cold Pastoral

Jen DeGregorio

If John Keats had been born in the 1990s, attended
the University of Virginia, maybe on a study abroad,
he might still have written his urn ode. But I'm sure
he wouldn't have begun as he did,
feminizing the urn, that clod of stone
valued mainly for its hole, inability to do anything
but what it was made for, to store human life
burned down. Nor could he have thought
to further confine her, not just some girl
but an *unravish'd bride.* Because a bride
unravished is as rare these days
as a conflict-free diamond, and to publicly equate
woman with rock is just so politically
wrong. And even if he were fool enough
to shock us with that phrase, and marry her indeed
to *quietness, unravish'd* wouldn't be the word
but ravaged. As so many women he'd have known have been ravaged
by *eternity,* who cut out their tongues, left them lying in a grave
of broken glass in a room so far from the party raging beyond
it may as well be ancient Greece. *Lead'st thou that heifer*
through the brothers' drafty mansion, past the mantle's plastic cups
tagged with three Greek letters that address
every *maiden* who comes in heels:
Heard melodies are sweet, but those unheard
are sweeter.

WSQ: Women's Studies Quarterly 44: 1 & 2 (Spring/Summer 2016) © 2016 by Jen DeGregorio.

Nuts

Jen DeGregorio

When I read that the universe is made almost entirely of dark,
dark energy that repels, dark matter that attracts,
and none of that verifiably real, merely inferred

from effects on actual matter, slim bit
that we are, I remember the peanut I chucked once
into Lake Michigan. How what was hard in my hand

sank into ripples, radiated out. And, as I did then,
as I often do when I'm lost, I picture God
in a circus tent. Gone are the seats,

firelit hoops, high-wire for freaks
to dance across. She's sort of float-sitting there
with a paper bag, her fist inside, getting ready to make

her move. Well, not quite getting ready, not in a purposeful
way, as she's distracted by some nebulous thought, her fingers
sifting as her mind surfs distant waves,

enjoying with unconscious pleasure the way her stash
at once yields and provides pressure around her probing fingers,
not reaching for a prize at the bottom—

WSQ: Women's Studies Quarterly **44: 1 & 2 (Spring/Summer 2016)** © 2016 by Jen DeGregorio.
All rights reserved.

there is none—or even a particular nut.
Just moving for the sake of moving, the touch
of something rough on her hands.

Jen DeGregorio's work has recently appeared in *PANK*, *MadHat Lit,* and *Salon*. She teaches at Hunter College in New York (where she also received her MFA in poetry in 2013), and at Montclair State University in New Jersey.

Dear Alison

Christine Larusso

"You're very much a woman," he said
as I stole a sip of his coke. It was no use
explaining. I once loved anatomy, the bread
of musculature, the tendons. The misuse,
the sprain, the strain. When was it when that
truth became clear, that jutting hips and winks
drew I'll Remember You looks, both flat and flattering?
My bio lessons ruined by male hijinks.
And yet, my breasts. That woe. I agonized over
their size, how one would always be smaller
(I'd never say *larger*) than the other. I hover
over a petri dish in science class; the color
of the dead frog the same as LA's worst smog.
That night I would yank my unruly hair from the clog.

WSQ: Women's Studies Quarterly **44: 1 & 2 (Spring/Summer 2016)** © 2016 by Christine Larusso.
All rights reserved.

Dear Alison

Christine Larusso

I'm reading about imaginary illness.
Like the author, I have wished
for my own fever and canker, stillness
of a bloody wound I could knit into
my self-loathe. We've all been there.
I've attached unforgiving feelings
about my own thighs, height, stared
at my naked body while the ceilings
stared back, hollow roots, empty
room, image upon image, the cove.
Will the tunnel ever end? I attempt
this walking, the need that drove—
still drives—woman after woman
to walls. Seeking water from stone.

Christine Larusso recently completed her MFA at New York University. Her work has appeared or is forthcoming in *The Literary Review*, *Court Green*, *DIAGRAM*, *The Awl*, and elsewhere.

WSQ: Women's Studies Quarterly 44: 1 & 2 (Spring/Summer 2016) © 2016 by Christine Larusso.

Rana Plaza

Erin Murphy

*A building housing five factories in Savar, Bangladesh, collapsed on
April 24, 2012, killing nearly one-third of the 3,600 textile workers.*

My father was in the hospital
that day, his pulse as low as

the Bangshi during dry season.
I wanted to stay with him,

but we were warned *No time off
for illness, not even your own.*

Had he died, which, *Alhamdulillah,*
he did not, the bosses would

have said, *Nothing to be done—
if he's dead, he's dead.*

And so I left my father's side.
It was 8:10 a.m. when I arrived.

Workers gathered by the gate,
afraid. Reshma squeezed

my arm. In my mind there is
a photograph of her wearing that

WSQ: Women's Studies Quarterly 44: 1 & 2 (Spring/Summer 2016) © 2016 by Erin Murphy. All rights reserved.

purple and red salwar kameez.
Inspectors were here, she breathed

into my ear. *They say it is unsafe.*
We had all seen the cracks. Up close,

the building sounded like someone
chewing uncooked rice. And who

was surprised? Each day crews
added more floors, it seemed,

like a tower of toy blocks waiting
to topple. I am not the type

to complain. I am grateful
for work. One who cannot

read or write cannot expect
the privileges of the rich. I sew

until midnight most shifts. I sew
to feed my boys and send them

to school where I hope they learn
what they need to make

a better life. Reshma and I
hesitated. The bosses said

Don't worry, mahilaa, it's fine
and herded us through the door

like goats. *Come, come,* they said,
We have orders to fill. I turned

on my machine, a workhorse:
100 stitches per second,

so smooth it's like sewing
through ghee. If I could

afford one of my own, I would
take in jobs in our home.

It would be cramped, with all
of us in one room, but I could

roll the boys' beds during the day.
That morning, as I sat down

on my stool, I felt a shudder
and then, in a flash, the walls

were gone and the floor fell
away from my feet. I was buried

to my hips in a pile of concrete.
It took nine hours for help to come

and many more to pull me free.
But no Reshma, no Reshma,

whose name means *like silk.*
They found her two and a half

weeks later. She had survived
on rainwater and biscuits

scavenged from the rucksacks
of the dead. Even now she carries

their dust in her mouth.
Others were not as lucky.

Grandmothers, women with young
children, girls not old enough

to marry. Sweet Mita who
always bit her bottom lip

as she fed rivers of fabric
across the plate. So many lost

their lives that day. But if we
had refused to go upstairs,

we would have lost our jobs.
So we obeyed.

Erin Murphy is the author of six books of poetry, most recently *Ancilla*, a collection of poems voiced by historical figures who played ancillary roles in the lives of well-known writers, artists, musicians, scientists, and philosophers. She is coeditor of *Making Poems: Forty Poems with Commentary by the Poets*. Her works have been published in numerous journals and anthologies, and featured on Garrison Keillor's *The Writer's Almanac*. She is professor of English and creative writing at Penn State Altoona.

Next Witness

Georgia Pearle

He surged through the temple before touch
knew my touch, bowed me beneath his gray
green leagues. My want, not my want? No
one asked.

Bad myth: hair my main glory, my pronged
pulse to the sea, golden, hauling him in.
Then the jealous goddess caught me
in an eeled shriek, my head turned soft-

bellied nest. Of course I'd prayed to
maul each gaze with a hiss.
Then thought I saw gods dripping
from the oaks, mushrooms, and lichens

extending their fat shelves.
I sit in the cemetery with the monoliths
who've made shields of me.
They've tried to split me

into something they could ride:
feathered, angelic, white
with graceful haunches, or masculine,
broad-shouldered and saddled. And you—

when you look at me—Will your throat cinch?
Will you sprout into stone and erode?

WSQ: Women's Studies Quarterly 44: 1 & 2 (Spring/Summer 2016) © 2016 by Georgia Pearle. All rights reserved.

Sunset Limited

Georgia Pearle

I.

After the wreck, they drove me down
where the charred cars lay stacked
by the highway's wayside. *Look, girl.*
Seagulls bobbed and plunged at loosed
saltines. Frog calls blistered in the background.
There must have been stretchers brought,
helicopters circling in huntress swarms,
radioed calls to tote the dead away.
The train that pummels off into bayou,
that's all Momma drawn to the bogs,
no mind to her ribs, steel and bowed,
pregnant with passengers. She thinks
she's a gilled fortress. Her iron
shudders and shouts through the pines.
A woman is neither train nor wreck,
but he was the barge in fog that sent
her track akimbo? No. Not barge, not
man. A girl is neither track nor last halt.

II.

I got to drive that train once.
Sat on the conductor's lap.

WSQ: Women's Studies Quarterly **44**: 1 & 2 (Spring/Summer 2016) © 2016 by Georgia Pearle. All rights reserved.

I guess it was less driving,
more pulling a string to let
the whistle croon long-loud.
He'd pulled on his jumpsuit
that hazed September morning,
when the sky still hung pitch,
to help the bog-drenched,
the drowned, shaken bodies
from the flaming Canot. The train,
later: steel split under the weight
of its own derailment, passengers
all dispersed, the small crook
of bayou still speckled with oil.
Today you called me a train
wreck. Maybe I am more
like the girl I was, sitting
in your conductor's lap,
the view of my own sunset
limited. I have never been a train.

Georgia Pearle is a current doctoral fellow in creative writing and literature at the University of Houston as well as a VIDA Count coordinator. She lives in Texas with her two children.

my own chimera

Erica Tom

if—on a tall wheat eve
heat and rock and cricket call
                         sit down.

sweep, the vibration swells, nets
billow the rustle of mahogany bark,
of sweet thistle, worn—wear harvest
                         dust as grapes.

call me down the road.

(calla lily in the lurch) a ditch,
your simple frog pond—fertile
shadow.

      and calling me, i answer
                         let her go.

wet reeds, cattails, one
eyelash—electric.

were i the cicada
no siren song for woven branches,

rather being of the oak, bay and poplar,
      aloft, this grass leafed treehouse:

clicking, clucking, enclosing—

                  my own chimera.

WSQ: Women's Studies Quarterly **44: 1 & 2 (Spring/Summer 2016)** © 2016 by Erica Tom. All rights reserved.

Erica Tom is a scholar, artist, and educator. Currently a PhD candidate in American studies at Rutgers University, she also serves as the director of Performance Arts and Movement Research at Belos Cavalos, a nonprofit equine experiential organization in the Bay Area of California. You can see more of her work at www.ericatom.com.

PART VI. **PROSE**

Where We'll Leave This for Now

Jessica Estep

Your husband stares at your breasts as you change into the pink pajama set your mother gave you for Christmas. You quickly pull the nightshirt over your head and turn away from him, walking into the bathroom and closing the door. You cup your breasts through the cotton. They're tender from swelling, and you feel embarrassed about them, like an ex-porn star with leftover silicone implants. They aren't your husband's for enjoying. They aren't yours, either. They belong to—well. You aren't sure.

When you get in bed, your husband keeps staring at you, even more intently than he did three years ago when you chopped your hair into a pixie. He's been staring at you all evening, since you came out of the bathroom holding a pregnancy test with two pink lines. You hoped the second pink line, much paler than the first, could be stared into oblivion, the way stars can be made to disappear. Maybe your husband is staring at you with this hope, you think.

The next morning you call your doctor before you brush your teeth. Your husband goes to his job; you go to yours, and afterward, to the graduate class you're taking at night. You fall asleep at the seminar table and wake up with drool on your cheek. You've never fallen asleep in class before; you've never been lazy, not once.

You've built a good life. You can construct four walls around the reasons to have a child: your job pays fifty thousand a year; your husband's pays sixty-five thousand. You're married. You're twenty-seven, would be twenty-eight by the time the—ah, the what? What term should you pick? You try to remember the words Republicans use and the words Democrats use. Embryo? Zygote? Fetus? Virus? Life? Thing? Baby? There's a scien-

WSQ: Women's Studies Quarterly 44: 1 & 2 (Spring/Summer 2016)

tific term somewhere on the internet, but you decide on *kernel*. A kernel on the verge, kind of like you in your one-bedroom apartment. Your six-month-long marriage. Your half-completed master's degree. The fact that you don't feel ready. Those are the other walls you could build for another house, another future, but they feel more like fences that any skeptic could tear down.

When he gets home from work, your husband finds you microwaving popcorn in the kitchen. He tells you he got some advice from his cowork-er, Patrick: that the two of you should make one spreadsheet of pros and cons and another sheet to explore how having a child would impact your budget. What exceptional advice, you say. You think of Patrick, who has a two-year-old of his own, Tommy. Tommy wears his mother's hand-sewn bowties to preschool. You've seen the photos posted on social media. His mother, Olivia, wears a string of pearls and five-inch heels to every holiday party. She quit her job to stay home. You imagine Olivia tut-tutting at the news of your kernel, leaning one hand on her granite countertop, brushing the other hand through her long blond hair as chicken cordon bleu cooks in the oven.

You remind your husband of the time Patrick told everyone at the company picnic that the chili you'd labeled vegan actually had a teaspoon of Worcestershire sauce in it. You tell your husband he doesn't get to decide who knows about your pregnancy. Not Patrick, not Olivia, not your husband's entire company. His boss. Maybe he'll get a raise for the good news. Wouldn't that be nice? You're screaming at him now. Your husband tells you you're being completely crazy, that Patrick promised not to tell any-one, not even Olivia. Crazy? You, crazy? You rip open the bag of popcorn and throw it at him and tell him to get the hell out.

But your husband won't leave the apartment, and instead is squatting on the couch behind the blare of the television, so you pack a bag and drive to your friend Virginia's. She had three abortions, all of them at nineteen. Now she's thirty-two and lives alone in a studio on the twenty-second floor of a high rise. You have never known her to have a steady boyfriend, just the two cats you pet when you walk in the door. You burst into tears and tell her everything, about the pregnancy and about Olivia knowing about the pregnancy. You show her pictures of Tommy's bowties. Virginia laughs. They're stupid bowties, she says. You scroll to the Valentine's Day bowtie: hot pink with red hearts, framing Tommy's chubby face. Virginia says two-year-olds should never wear bowties; they could choke themselves. She makes tea for herself and a mug of hot lemon water and honey for you. She tells you that her coworker told her herbal tea is dangerous for, *you know*. The kernel, you say. You're calling this the kernel. She tells you that's a nice word for it. This is why you like Virginia. You fall asleep on her couch, with her stroking your hair.

The next morning you drive to work and find yourself talking aloud. Hi, kernel, you say. Are you okay with NPR, kernel? Do you want to hear an analysis of the State of the Union address? You listen carefully to *All Things Considered*, trying to stop hating your husband, hating Patrick, hating that bitch Olivia. You don't want the kernel to feel the reverberations, the flexed muscles and stress seeping into the amniotic sac. You had never even thought that you might want a kernel. You and your husband reconsidered getting married because he wanted two, maybe three. The discrepancy was tabled for a future date that is now.

You stop at a gas station halfway to work because you can't make it thirty minutes without peeing. In the bathroom, a woman changes the diaper of a newborn, its ruddy face squinting at you under the fluorescent lights. While the mother packs her diapers away, you reach across the counter to stroke the baby's pimply cheeks. You're surprised when they feel not rough but rather like the white silk purse your husband's sister let you borrow for your wedding. The mother grabs your wrist when she catches you touching her child. You explain that you just found out you're pregnant. You start to cry, and the baby starts to cry, too. The mother scoops up her child and swings through the bathroom door without a word.

After work, you're too tired to cook. Your husband asks if you want to go to your favorite Mexican place and get some tacos. At the restaurant, he says you can have a margarita if you want one. You wonder if he's joking, but he doesn't lift his eyes from the menu. You say no. It's bad enough, what with the bottle and a half of wine you split with Virginia two weeks ago to celebrate her promotion. There was a kernel then. And the three cups of coffee you drink every day—two in the morning, one for a midafternoon jolt. Your daily breakfast of toast and a fried egg with a runny yolk. The flu shot you forgot to get. And halfway through your fish taco, you remember: mercury. You read about that. You think: *fuck*! Can the kernel hear when you say *fuck*, even if it's just in your mind? Your husband asks you gently why you're crying. You look him right in the eye and say that only three months before you got married, when Dominic came in from San Francisco and you took him to Kimball House for dinner, you kissed him. You were drunk. He was drunk. But you kissed another man! And now you are pregnant!

Your husband laughs. Anything else you need to confess? he asks. You say no. The waiter pretends not to notice your sobbing as he refills your water glass. Your husband takes your hand across the table. He apologizes for telling Patrick. He says, if it makes you feel any better, Patrick told him that Olivia wants to go back to work now, but she can't find a job. A two-year gap on her resume.

See, you say, this just proves your point that men tell their wives everything.

He asks why that's a problem? What's the problem with honesty, an honest assessment?

Everything is wrong with it, you say.

He doesn't tell you you're being crazy this time. He slides into your side of the booth. Tell you what, he says, let's write down our percentages and then show each other.

What percentages? you ask.

Our percentages toward keeping it or not. Like, if you're 50/50, write that, he says.

He would have this kind of idea; he's an engineer. But you do what he says, and you write down your percentages on your tomato-stained napkin. You're 70/30, 70 percent toward not keeping it. You unfold his napkin. He's 80/20.

Really? you ask.

I just don't quite feel ready, he says. I want to camp in Denali this summer, like we talked about over Christmas. Just you and me.

Is that a reason to not have a baby? To camp in Denali? You tell him you want to want to not be selfish. It's nice, the idea of one day not being the center of your universe, of ceding all your needs and even your body to someone else.

That's what you did by marrying me, he says.

You say he hardly demands anything of you.

Well, isn't it selfish to have a baby to improve yourself? Everything is selfish. We can't escape that, he says. He wraps his arms around you and then he takes you home. You take off your clothes, and you have sex, for once without the worry of getting pregnant. You let your husband touch your breasts, but when he squeezes them, you yank away in pain. He apologizes. He starts to cry. You hold him this time. You're 10 percent stronger than he is, after all.

In the morning, you call and make a new kind of doctor's appointment. Virginia tells you she'll take you, and your husband says he'll take you, but you tell them both no. You insist several times that you'd rather go alone. Alone once more with your kernel.

On the day of your appointment, the elevator comes to fetch you from the hallway of your apartment, but you realize at that moment that you forgot your wallet in your other jacket pocket. You hear the empty elevator close and disappear as you retrieve your wallet from your coat rack. Back in the hallway, you push the elevator button again, and it returns to you, the doors opening and inviting you in. Leaning against the elevator walls, you ask: kernel, can you do like this elevator and go away and come back again soon? Can you wait just a little bit longer? You're crying again, swearing it's not a selfish thing you're asking. You promise that since this began, there's been nothing but love pulsing through your body.

Jessica Estep is an assistant professor of English at Georgia Gwinnett College. She earned an MFA in fiction from Boston University and is currently at work on her first novel.

Hearing Voices

Sokunthary Svay

Let me weep my cruel fate and sigh for my lost freedom. Let sadness shatter these chains of my suffering, if only out of mercy.

—Almirena, in Handel's *Rinaldo*

I am standing in the chapel at the Good Shepherd-Faith Presbyterian Church, which is connected to the Juilliard School of Music and part of the Lincoln Center complex in New York City. I am singing the words of the Handel opera aria "Lascia ch'io pianga" that translates to "let me weep." The character singing the aria, Almirena, has been kidnapped and held captive in solitude away from her true love. My voice teacher is telling me she doesn't believe me.

I have spent years trying to find a way to express myself. Coming from a family of Cambodian refugees relocated to New York City, meeting basic human needs like shelter, food, and clothing dominated our daily lives. My parents had survived the Khmer Rouge, a brutal and genocidal regime that ruled Cambodia from 1975 to 1979. Given their experiences, my teenage desire to pursue a path to music school was most certainly unwelcome.

Even attending the nearby high school of music and art, my parents' anxious voices followed me into the school halls. They whispered that music wouldn't take me anywhere; it would never provide a stable income. When I got to college, I played my last flute recital and accepted an English literature and classics scholarship. I developed a literary voice while analyzing dead writers and studying Latin. When I first wrote, I imagined the screams of tortured Khmers who died under the Khmer Rouge; I en-

WSQ: Women's Studies Quarterly 44: 1 & 2 (Spring/Summer 2016) © 2016 by Sokunthary Svay.

visioned mounds of skulls. When I visited Cambodia, we held prayer cer-
emonies at temples to honor ancestors. I imagined ghosts swirling around
the incense and saffron-robed monks.

These are the same ghosts who convinced my parents that life was
solely about survival. As children to my parents, we learned to silence our
wants and our needs, to keep from burdening them further—they were
already taxed in maintaining the basic needs of our family, barely afford-
ing rent, food, and our school supplies. We were perceptive enough to see
that something wasn't quite right with our family. It's clear now that many
Cambodian refugees, including our parents, had undiagnosed and untreat-
ed post-traumatic stress disorder. Being thrust into a new country, culture,
and language further complicated their attempts at healing. As Khmer
Buddhists, we not only believed in reincarnation, but that birthmarks are
signs of past lives. After she saw the birthmark on my knee, my mother was
convinced that I was her deceased son, Sothear, reborn. Although my parents and my older brother survived, they were continually haunted by the
ghosts of those who hadn't. My mother says Sothear sometimes appears
in her dreams.

It's not in the Cambodian tradition to speak about trauma. My father
has taken well to English idioms and dismissed my early inquiries with
"the past is in the past." I knew early on which battles to fight, although at
a certain point, preparing for the fight was so exhausting, I eventually gave
up. I even began to develop a defeatist attitude to most problems—it was
easier not to try than to become invested only to fail. It didn't help that my
father's household felt more like a dictatorship. I find family discussions
to be a privilege that Western societies enjoy. My father lectured us and
concluded with orders for us to follow. I vividly remember tracing my finger along the designs on our plastic covered couch as he laid out in a stern
voice his expectations of us. Did his approach come from the TV sitcoms
that taught us about American culture, which we watched daily, or from
his days in the Cambodian military, where he was a master sergeant with
twelve men under his command? Or worse, was this repressive approach
a cultural remnant of his trauma living under a genocidal regime? With a
father unwilling to speak in general, except to criticize, I knew I had to seek
answers to such questions on my own.

During my first year of college, I spent afternoons secluded in the
Southeast Asian history corner of City College's library, hoping to uncov-
er the story that my parents were unwilling to tell us. The worn cushions of

the couches in the aisles had grooves in the seat from years of sitting. I was another student joining in this communal seat, taking the place of someone else in my curiosity and ignorance. Some illuminating titles included *Cambodian Witness*, one of many autobiographies I would come to read for my thesis on Khmer American writers, and *Sideshow: Kissinger, Nixon, and the Destruction of Cambodia*, William Shawcross's investigation of Operation Breakfast, the Nixon administration's secret bombing campaign of Cambodia. Without any background or seeming interest from my parents, I began to build a picture of their Cambodia without their help. The bits and pieces I received from my parents weren't enough, and the more I learned, the more I felt compelled to inform people about my country's story. If my parents weren't even comfortable speaking about it to their own family or within their community, how much was lost to those of non-Khmer backgrounds? So I used my academic studies to pursue these questions, eventually culminating in a thesis that compared two autobiographical works, the memoir of the late Dr. Haing S. Ngor, the Academy Award–winning actor in *The Killing Fields*, and a poetry collection by U Sam Oeur. I also began writing my own poetry to address my urban upbringing as a refugee baby born in Thailand, feeling displaced and not entirely at home in Cambodia or the United States.

By creating an academic and poetic voice to fill in for my parents' silence, I foolishly thought that I was freed from their ghosts. I graduated from college and became a young professional, working at an academic research center. As an increasing number of survival memoirs and documentaries were released over the years, I started to feel more at peace. I even enrolled in an MFA program in creative writing, feeling it was time for my own experience to take precedence. In the summer of 2006, I became pregnant, and though it was unexpected, this new stage in my life gave me new focus. However easy the pregnancy itself was, there were many unpleasant surprises in store for the birth, namely the unplanned C-section and my ignorance about its arduous recovery. Coupled with adjusting to a new neighborhood and the isolation from friends and family, I slowly descended into the darkest summer of my life. The sun was stark and the oppressive heat prevented me from roaming far from home. I nearly choked on the humidity as my days became more silent, with only the raw wail of my newborn daughter.

A new, inner voice appeared alongside my worried parents' cacophonous chatter. I was in the nursery room rocking my daughter to sleep, convinced my end was near as postpartum depression set in. In spite of my poetics, I had lost the capacity to communicate my isolation, sadness, and pain. Instead, my world darkened and my Khmer ghosts were replaced with a new obsessive and ruminating self who stayed indoors and jumped at every sound as if it were a baby's beseeching.

After I attempted to put my baby in the closet to escape her cries, I sought psychotherapy. I envied her cry. They ensured she would be cared for. But I had no hope of anyone ever hearing me. My therapist was the one who implanted new words and ideas in my head. I didn't have to live with my parents' ghosts, with the burden of their responsibility to their children. I rediscovered my love for singing; I had found a new kind of voice.

Back at the church, my teacher still isn't convinced. I struggle to channel my personal pain into my voice. Throughout my childhood, I never heard my father sing a note. He whistled or tapped along to music in the car. I assumed singing embarrassed him, so I didn't feel comfortable singing at home or in front of my family. I came to associate the human voice with vulnerability. As a family we hardly exchanged words of affection already, so any form of vocal expression seemed too naked a communication. This hesitancy clearly translates into my singing of this aria. It also doesn't help that acting feels contrived to me. Yet, even in Almirena's despair, my voice teacher says there is a glimmer of hope. And I hang on to that idea, that the darkness of our journey is necessary in order for us to find release from its recesses.

The sustained notes of the aria hang in the air, exquisite in their pain. The sung voice can artfully capture the range of human emotions by accessing what is normally too difficult to articulate in everyday speech. To those who have never heard this aria, I encourage them to listen to it, particularly those who aren't accustomed to Baroque music. The word *lascia* as it is sung, with the *l* held out, sounds loving, almost as if the word were caressing the singer as it's sung. What initially sounds like weeping is much deeper if you allow yourself to hear it. When I learn a new art song or aria, I find myself unearthing a complex set of intentions and emotions. It requires compassion, patience, and, even at times, to be consumed. I reach into the voices of my past so I can connect to my current musical piece. And this is where I find my power, in declaring who I am through the vibrations of my voice, since a voice must be heard in order to have power.

The cavernous sanctuary of the church seems a safe place to allow all the real and imagined voices of my past to come together: my parents' story of regrets and tragic loss, their anxiety about my future, the singing my father never did, the words we didn't use to express love, the imagined murmurs of spirits, and lastly, my own creative voice. They haven't quieted. Instead, they are intertwined to compose my living, breathing song.

Sokunthary Svay is a Khmer writer and musician from the Bronx, New York. Her writing has been published in *Homelands: Women's Journeys Across Race, Place, and Time*; *Hyphen*; *Blue Lyra Review*; and *LONTAR*.

PART VII. **BOOK REVIEWS**

The Mothership Strikes Back

Andrew Parker's *The Theorist's Mother*, Durham, NC: Duke University Press, 2012

Ahuva Cohen

"I am your mother, Luke," said no *Star Wars* character ever. While Luke Skywalker negotiates relationships with a succession of father figures (Uncle Owen, Obi-Wan Kenobi, and Yoda) before Darth Vader declares himself to be Luke's true father and hacks off his son's hand with a castrating blow from his phallic lightsaber, Luke's mother remains obscured in his incestuous romance with Princess Leia, who is ultimately revealed to be his twin sister. Just as it would have been unthinkable for Darth Vader— much less any Jedi Knight—to have been Luke's mother in the *Star Wars* universe, when Jacques Derrida was asked, "What philosopher would you have liked to be your mother?" he responded, "It's *impossible* for me to have any philosopher as a mother . . . my mother *couldn't* be a philosopher. [*Switches to French*] A philosopher *couldn't* be my mother" (Derrida 2007). Derrida's horrified reaction is used by Andrew Parker as a launching point for his own proposal in *The Theorist's Mother*, which suggests "that what unifies the otherwise disparate traditions of critical theory and philosophy from Karl Marx to Jacques Derrida is their troubled relation to maternity" (1).

With fifty-six pages devoted to notes and a bibliography, the dense but elegant writing in the other one hundred fourteen pages of this "accidental book" provide both a challenging and pleasurable reading of Jacques Lacan and György Lukács in their roles as legitimate heirs to the traditions fathered by Freud and Marx. Preceding the three main chapters and a coda, the introduction in which Parker lays out his theoretical groundwork is the most compelling portion of the book. While claims to paternity have always been doubtful, those of maternity were assumed to be unambigu-

***WSQ: Women's Studies Quarterly* 44: 1 & 2 (Spring/Summer 2016)** © 2016 by Ahuva Cohen. All rights reserved.

ous until advances in reproductive technology made it possible for motherhood to be split along genetic, biological, and social axes. Because the identity of the mother has been revealed to be a social construction instead of a biological cornerstone, Parker concludes that such indeterminacy reveals three problems with employing the mother as a signifier: the distinction of the literal (procreating body) from the figurative (creativity), the relationship of the singular ("*my* mother") to the general ("the Mother"), and the "border between a theorist's life and writing" (22–25).

More or less corresponding to the three kinds of mother trouble identified in the introduction, the main chapters of *The Theorist's Mother* deconstruct the relationship between texts and their supplements—becoming supplements themselves, located both inside and outside of the original texts. If the work of Freud and Marx were to be compared to the *Star Wars* original trilogy, and the work of Lacan and Lukács to the *Star Wars* sequel trilogy, then Parker's book could be viewed as a highly sophisticated form of fan fiction that exposes the assumptions of canonical readings by rereading them from the perspective of a minor character. In the *Star Wars* sequel, the drama is driven by Chancellor Palpatine's tug-of-war with Obi-Wan Kenobi over Anakin's loyalty as a disciple; yet the death of Anakin's mother and his brief romance with Luke's mother function as fulcrums in the transformations of both Darth Vader's pathology and the political economy of the *Star Wars* universe. Returning to the universe of *The Theorist's Mother*, Parker's work tries to locate the role of the Queen mother as a unifying agent—both biological and social—in the reproduction of modern theory.

In the first main chapter, Parker attempts to ground this project in his own experience by describing his original exploration of the boundary between the mind and the body in a 1985 essay he wrote about his mother's hypochondria. Parker then segues into a discussion of Lacan reading his critics' responses to his earlier work while he was giving his famous seminar on female sexuality. Parker argues that Lacan's anxiety over the best method for reproducing his theoretical insights through the analytic practices of future students of psychiatry reveals a barrier between knowledge and experience inherent in Lacan's own theory of sexual difference. Resuscitating the obscure Lacanian phrase "maternal divination," Parker suggests that the exhibition of the lecturer's body might have been able to overcome the limitations of language similar to the way Lacan had once experienced the contact between his body and his child's doing. Parker leverages his own body language to conclude this chapter with the cryptic confession that rereading his essay precipitated a case of psoriasis.

Obliquely referring to the troubled relationship between singularity and generality, in the second main chapter Parker follows Lukács's reading of the eponymous hero of Sir Walter Scott's novel *Waverly*. According to Parker, Lukács understands this character as a figure whose private struggles are representative of larger historical conflicts and Scott as a novelist whose dialectical resolution of those conflicts presaged Marx's interpretation of history. Parker goes on, however, to pick apart Lukács's conclusion—that the science of Marxism is the mature product of Scott's fiction—by examining Scott's own uneasiness regarding the historical authenticity of his novels and even his claim to authorship. Although Parker himself does not make an explicit connection between Scott's anxiety over his audience's reception and Lacan's anxiety over the proper understanding of his teachings, Parker's catalog of Scott's supplements to *Waverly*—"A Postscript Which Should Have Been a Preface," introductions to new editions, footnotes, and a variety of appendixes—remind me of Lacan's obsession with "mathemes" and Borromean knots at the end of his career.

If the first chapter explores the boundaries between the mind and the body, and the second explores the boundaries between fictional and historical texts, then the third chapter attempts to explore the boundaries between the theorist's writing and his life. Although the theorist's mother disappeared in the transition from psychoanalysis to Marxism, Parker resurrects her in the third chapter on translations of the works of Freud and Marx. He begins by discussing the difficulty of determining which term is the vehicle and which is the tenor in the phrase "the mother tongue" when it is used to refer to a dialect. Following Derrida's opinion that "the mother tongue" is "the essential turn that must be taken to understand what a mother means" (2007), Parker attempts to demonstrate a connection between maternity and translation in the term "*Mameloshn*," which literally means "the mother tongue" and is used by Jewish speakers of Yiddish to refer to the language spoken in the home. He suggests that Marx's adoption of German as the language of the revolution over Mameloshn may have reflected his embarrassment over his mother's lack of education. Given the scarcity of evidence, the assertion is unconvincing, and in the larger context of the fraught relationship of Jewish intellectuals to the German language (Arendt 1968, 29–32), this connection seems particularly strained.

Parker caps *The Theorist's Mother* by putting the founders of discursiv-
ity back on the shelf, and reading from Friedrich Nietzsche's *Ecce Homo*
(2007) and Shulamith Firestone's *The Dialectic of Sex* (1970). Bringing
Firestone together with Nietzsche is a queer pairing, because the former
was a woman who bluntly declared, "Pregnancy is barbaric" (180), and
the latter was a man who claimed in his autobiography, "As my father I have
already died, as my mother I am still alive and growing" (7). How would
Parker envision a new generation of theorists, descended from a feminist
who rejected maternity in favor of artificial reproduction, and a philosopher who frequently embraced maternity as a metaphor for creativity?
Would they march out like an army of clone philosophers, or would they
appear like Darth Vader, outfitted with artificial wombs in addition to
mechanical limbs and lungs? Or perhaps Parker is suggesting we could
find models for reproducing theory that would not equate channeling the
Force with wielding the lightsaber as its privileged signifier.

Reading *The Dialectic of Sex* for the first time, I was both impressed
and dismayed by how hard Firestone worked to employ the master's
tools in her project to dismantle the master's house—in particular, her
reliance on the Oedipus complex to explain race relations in the United
States (1970, 98). If anything, Freud's and Marx's theoretical frameworks
have often been too successful in reproducing themselves—even in feminist readings such as Nancy Chodorow's *The Reproduction of Mothering*
(1978) and Mary O'Brien's *The Politics of Reproduction* (1981). Judith
Butler, however, in *Bodies That Matter*, first imagines which body part
could replace the penis as the lesbian phallus, but then concludes, "What
is needed is not a new body part, as it were, but a displacement of the
hegemonic symbolic of (heterosexist) sexual difference and the critical
release of alternative imaginary schemas for constituting sites of eroto-
genic pleasure" (1993, 57).

By rereading modern theory as troubled by its own reproduction—
because the maternal has been effaced—Parker may have provided theorists with a valuable new toolbox in which the penis could be replaced by
the womb, so to speak, as a privileged signifier. Privileging maternity over
patriarchy may not be a completely new strategy for critical analysis, but
Parker's contribution is his recognition that maternity can be untethered
from gender. By employing maternity outside of the domain of feminism,
The Theorist's Mother opens a new field for reimagining modern theory
outside the symbolic order of its founders.

Ahuva Cohen has been awarded the Paul LeClerc Prize for the best research paper, and the CLAGS Prize for the best undergraduate paper on an LGBT topic. She is currently working on a memoir about her mother's magic triangle.

Works Cited

Arendt, Hannah. 1968. "Introduction: Walter Benjamin: 1892–1940." In *Illuminations*, Walter Benjamin, edited by Hannah Arendt, 1–54. New York: Schocken Books.

Butler, Judith. 1993. *Bodies That Matter: On the Discursive Limits of "Sex."* New York: Routledge Classics.

Derrida, Jacques. 2007. *Psyche: Inventions of the Other.* Vol. 1. Edited by Peggy Kamuf and Elizabeth Rottenberg. Palo Alto, CA: Stanford University Press.

Derrida. 2002. Directed by Kirby Dick and Amy Ziering Kofman. Jane Doe Films.

Firestone, Shulamith. 1970. *The Dialectic of Sex: The Case for Feminist Revolution.* New York: Farrar, Straus and Giroux.

Nietzsche, Friedrich Wilhelm. 2007. *Ecce Homo: How to Become What You Are.* Translated by Duncan Large. Oxford: Oxford University Press.

Posthuman Fantasies

Rosi Braidotti's *The Posthuman*, Cambridge: Polity, 2013

Sarah Kessler

"Posthuman" discourse remains hotly contested within the Euro-U.S. academy, affirming that we are far from "post" the posthuman. While some of the grounding critical texts in the field of the posthumanities emerged in the eighties, the nineties and the aughts saw a swell of scholarly production around what it might—and does—mean to inhabit bodies, spaces, and spheres that can no longer be clearly defined or conceptually grasped as unproblematically "human." Crucial rejoinders to this line of inquiry have, accordingly, questioned the theoretical efficacy (not to mention the liberatory potential) of the posthuman formulation for subjects never accorded full humanity within a racist, heterosexist, and otherwise phobic and discriminatory humanistic frame. Like postmodernism, the notion of the posthuman always invokes a temporal paradox: how can one be "post" something one may never have been in the first place? Relatedly, what, and indeed who, is elided by the flash-forward into "post"-ness?

In *The Posthuman* Rosi Braidotti seeks to provide a unified and coherent assessment of the posthuman condition, one that addresses the above concerns while forcefully arguing that historical and structural elisions from the category of the human give those excluded all the more reason to embrace the radical potentiality of what she refers to as "life beyond" the human. Using her own gendered subject position to make this point, Braidotti writes, "The becoming-posthuman speaks to my feminist self, partly because my sex, historically speaking, never quite made it into full humanity, so my allegiance to that category is at best negotiable and never to be taken for granted" (81). Repeatedly championing an "affirmative" reconceptualization of posthumanity—"my favourite term: affirmative,"

WSQ: Women's Studies Quarterly 44: 1 & 2 (Spring/Summer 2016)

she quips (54)—Braidotti is unabashedly exuberant at the prospect of throwing humanity under the bus. "My deep-seated anti-humanist leanings show in the glee with which I welcome the displacement of *anthropos*," she writes (75), challenging even the most skeptical of readers not to crack a smile.

Braidotti's affirmative reading of the posthuman condition hinges on her conviction that the "horrors of our times" need not eclipse the "excitement" that accompanies the contemporary moment (186–87). Opting for a Bergsonian-Deleuzian sense of transformative "becoming"[1] rather than upholding a static notion of "being," Braidotti aims to give the reader a glimpse into the possibilities present in the expansion of our circumscribed understanding of "life" to include "Life Beyond the Self" (chapter 1), "Life Beyond the Species" (chapter 2), "Life Beyond Death" (chapter 3), and "Life Beyond Theory" (chapter 4). What happens, she provocatively asks, when we begin to conceive of life as exceeding the bounds of the now classical frames of selfhood, Man, mortality, and the academic humanities? In other words, what happens when we begin to think with *zoe*, or life itself, rather than with *bios*, or the life of the individual (and yes, neoliberal) subject? For Braidotti, *zoe* is a profoundly unifying force. *Zoe*, she writes, is "the dynamic, self-organizing structure of life itself . . . [that] stands for generative vitality. It is the transversal force that cuts across and reconnects previously segregated species, categories and domains" (60). There is a certain planarity to thinking with *zoe* in Braidotti's analysis—the hopeful fantasy of a kind of level playing field.

But before she describes the "*zoe*-egalitarianism" that for her constitutes an affirmative posthuman future (71), Braidotti begins *The Posthuman* with four vignettes that illustrate the most sinister dimensions of the posthuman predicament. These chilling slices of life chronicle the havoc wreaked by a nihilistic Finnish mass shooter brandishing the slogan "Humanity is overrated," the emergence of mad cow disease from the cannibalism forcibly engendered by biotechnology, the drone-bombing of Gaddafi's convoy before his assassination by rebel forces, and, (relatively less chillingly) an argument for the defunding of the humanities recently leveled by a Dutch cognitive science professor. Human self-annihilation, human-animal violence resulting in the threat of *mutual* annihilation, the human killing of other humans by nonhuman intermediaries, and persistent scientific justifications for the destruction of humanism, all point toward humanity's deep-seated inhumanity. The only way out of this madness, Braidotti suggests, is to accept, and cultivate the affirmative valences of our inhumanity. But how?

The answer, for Braidotti, is largely philosophical. In the book's first chapter, she lays the critical theoretical groundwork for her own particular iteration of antihumanism—critical posthumanism (45)—reviewing the Western centralization and reification of Man, from da Vinci to Marx, and rightly, railing against "the humanistic arrogance of continuing to place Man at the centre of world history" (23). She then articulates the urgent need for "elaborating alternative ways of conceptualizing the human subject" (37), a task at which the analytic posthumanism of science and technology studies falls short, due to its disinterest in the implications of human-non-human interactions for subjectivity broadly construed. Braidotti, on the other hand, wants us to follow her into thinking relationally about, say, a conversation between a robot and a person, such that this conversation becomes emblematic of an "'assemblage' of human and non-human actors" (45), charting an "affirmative bond that locates the subject in the flow of relations with multiple others" (50).

This inclination carries over into the book's second chapter, which explores, among other things, human-animal bonds as so much more than "negative" markers of the posthuman condition (as in the case of the toxic human-animal relations foregrounded by the mad cow disease predicament). For in a global context in which the commodification of life itself is par for the course, Braidotti argues, we must begin to see the "*interrelation* human/animal as constitutive of the identity of *each*" (79), not to mention the exchanges between "insects, plants and the environment, in fact the planet and the cosmos as a whole" (66) and the gleefully decentered remnants of *anthropos*. Once again, Braidotti seems to suggest that a kind of leveling has taken place; less ambiguously, she contends that a set of categorical destabilizations has occurred that allows for the productive development of trans-species relations. Holding up Dolly, the cloned sheep, as the techno-organic "icon of the posthuman condition" (74), she also proclaims, in a discomfitingly instrumentalizing gesture, that we must "trust women, gays, lesbians and other alternative forces, with their historically 'leaky bodies' (Grosz 1994) and not fully human rights, to both reassert the powers and enhance the potentiality of the posthuman organism as generative 'wetware'" (96). While Braidotti takes pains to make clear that those charged with this responsibility will likely remain subject to processes of sexualization, racialization, and naturalization under advanced capitalism, she also conjures a "beyond" to which they may lead us: "beyond gender and race, but also beyond the human" (98). We might ask, does everyone charged wish to accept this quest, to advance into the great "beyond?" And what would it mean to approach this fantasy horizon?

Another central proposition in Braidotti's text, and the subject of the third chapter of *The Posthuman*, is that we follow and probe the potentialities of the "forensic turn" taken by popular consciousness in the wake of the body's contemporary enmeshment with technology. "The inhuman forces of technology have moved into the body," she writes, "intensifying the spectral reminders of the corpse-to-come" (113). For Braidotti, this means that we must begin to think more generatively about the interrelations (another favorite word of hers) between life and death. In "think[ing] with and not against death" (129), she argues, we may arrive at a more nuanced understanding of life, one that "does not start from the assumption of the inherent, self-evident and intrinsic worth of 'life' and stresses instead the traumatic elements of this same life in their often unnoticed familiarity" (133). Of course, there are many for whom an awareness of life's "traumatic elements" need not be arrived at theoretically. The Black Lives Matter movement in this country, for instance, brings this structural inequality into sharp relief, arguing for the necessity of thinking about black life in a white supremacist national culture that persistently denies its "inherent, self-evident and intrinsic worth," upholding black death as the status quo. Refusing to permit the erasure of black deaths while simultaneously championing the flourishing of black lives, Black Lives Matter foregrounds the interrelation between the two poles.

In light of this example (and leaving aside a discussion of Braidotti's fourth and final chapter, which elaborates some directions for what she calls a "posthuman Humanities"), I want to briefly revisit the question of the "post" in the posthuman, which for Braidotti seems to coincide with the movement "beyond" she so enthusiastically promotes. Zakiyyah Iman Jackson has brilliantly critiqued the rhetoric of *beyond-ness* deployed in recent academic discourses on humanity and posthumanity, asking, "What and crucially *whose* conception of humanity are we moving beyond? Moreover, what is entailed in the very notion of a beyond?" (215). Jackson argues that prevailing calls for a movement "beyond the human" ignore, in large part, the centrality of race to Western metaphysics, and thus efface the extent to which "[w]hether machine, plant, animal, or object, the nonhuman's figuration and mattering is shaped by the gendered racialization of the field of metaphysics" (216–17). In Jackson's view, what is required is not moving beyond, or "post," the human—a phrase whose meaning remains unclear, yet which suggests circumvention—but "transvalu[ing]" the human (218): transforming the ways we conceptualize humanness. As Braidotti states in her work's conclusion, "the posthuman predicament enforces the necessity to think again and to think harder about the status of the human" (186). This seems to me not a posthuman predicament, but an all too human one.

Sarah Kessler is a PhD candidate in comparative literature at the University of California, Irvine, where she is completing a dissertation on ventriloquism in popular culture. Her article "Puppet Love," on the documentary film work of the English ventriloquist Nina Conti, is forthcoming in *Camera Obscura*.

Notes

1. For Braidotti, "becoming" describes not a consistent state but a *process* that is "not so much about determinism, inbuilt purpose or finality, but rather about . . . transformation" (91). Elsewhere, Braidotti clarifies that her "philosophy of becomings" is rooted in the notion of the intelligent, self-organizing properties of matter—including human matter (35). The boundaries of the human are thus, for Braidotti, far more permeable than they classically appear; the human does not exist separately from culture and technology but "continuous[ly] with them" (35). These assertions resonate with Elizabeth Grosz's helpful interpretation of becoming in Bergson (and later taken up by Deleuze) as "the operation of self-differentiation, the elaboration of difference within a thing, a quality or a system that emerges or actualizes only in duration" (4). See Grosz 2005; Deleuze 1988; and Bergson 1946.

Works Cited

Bergson, Henri. 1946. *The Creative Mind: An Introduction to Metaphysics.* Translated by Mabelle L. Andison. New York: Philosophical Library.

Deleuze, Gilles. 1988. *Bergsonism.* Translated by Hugh Tomlinson and Barbara Habberjam. New York: Zone.

Grosz, Elizabeth. 2005. "Berson, Deleuze, and the Becoming of Unbecoming." *Parallax* 11 (2): 4–13.

Jackson, Zakiyyah Iman. 2015. "Outer Worlds: The Persistence of Race in Movement 'Beyond the Human.'" *GLQ: A Journal of Lesbian and Gay Studies* 21 (2/3): 215–18.

Playful Paws

Brian Massumi's *What Animals Teach Us about Politics*, Durham, NC: Duke University Press, 2014

Lisa Poggiali

What do animals teach us about politics? This is the central question of Brian Massumi's brief, though complex meditation on animality, humanity, and the relational dance through which they each become themselves. Frequently opaque, though occasionally beautiful—"The story of evolution is a mad proliferation of forms so fertile as to defy the human imagination" (21), Massumi remarks in a particularly lucid moment—his text invites the reader along on an idea-journey rather than providing a straightforward analysis of what animal politics are or could be—this despite the fact that the text is formally polemical, the main essay closing, for example, with fourteen "propositions" that outline "what animals teach us about politics."

The central thesis that coils through the book, boa constrictor-like, is that the point of departure for thinking politics should not be humanity, but animality. Thus, Massumi writes against the liberalism foundational to most animal studies scholarship, the proponents of which argue that human rights should be extended to animals. The crux of Massumi's argument is radically different; namely, that to start from the perspective of "human rights" means to deny the animality that is immanent to humanity—and the humanity immanent to animality—and thus to misrecognize both. This is no space, he intuits, from which to begin political analysis or to articulate political claims. Epistemologically, Massumi decenters the human and (re)places her "on the animal continuum" (3). Contrary to what he sees as the anthropocentrism and anthropomorphism implicit in more conventional theories of animality, for Massumi, the paw engulfs the hand without replacing it; the human/animal dialectic implodes.

In order to effect this implosion rhetorically, Massumi divides his text into one main essay, "What Animals Teach Us About Politics," and three supplements: "To Write Like a Rat Flicks Its Tail" (a discussion of writing as an act through which the human becomes animal, rather than a mechanism for dividing humans from animals); "The Zoo-ology of Play" (a commentary on Gregory Bateson's work on animal play, inspired by a trip to the San Francisco zoo); and "Six Theses on the Animal to Be Avoided" (cautionary statements warning the reader against analytically disaggregating human from animal). Philosophically, Massumi merges critical theory and evolutionary biology, drawing on such thinkers as Deleuze and Guattari, Gregory Bateson, Raymond Ruyer, and Alfred North Whitehead. "Play" is his way in. It is the central concept that anchors his text, and thus the concept from which his understanding of politics unfolds. For Massumi, Bateson's notion of play as a theory of difference is instructive. A wolf cub communicates whether it is biting (engaging in combat) or nipping (engaging in play) through the style in which it performs—and enacts—the gesture. "A ludic gesture in a play fight . . . is not so much 'like' a combat move as it is *combatesque*: like in combat, but with something different, a little something more. With a surplus: an excess of energy or spirit" (9). The crucial point for Massumi—and what sets him apart from some other thinkers of animality, such as Giorgio Agamben—is that play and combat are neither distinct zones in an absolute sense, nor do they meld completely with one another, i.e., they do not produce either an "excluded middle" or a zone of undifferentiation. Rather, they operate according to the logic of the "included middle." Combat modulates the game, and play stylistically deforms combat, nudging each into a "zone of indiscernibility" where their differences are nevertheless maintained. The logic of play, for Massumi, is one of "mutual inclusion."

Mutual inclusion governs the process through which the animal continuum differentiates and reproduces itself, which is to say, the process through which humans become themselves. It is in the creativity implicit in animal play that one can be able to think (and do) human creativity. This "zone of indiscernibility" therefore "does not observe the sanctity of the separation of categories, nor respect the rigid segregation of arenas of activity" (6). While Massumi is clear that there is no foundational or normative distinction between human and animal, animal politics nevertheless cannot be understood vis-à-vis hybridity, i.e., a melding or a blurring of boundaries. Hybridity assumes undifferentiation. Animal politics, rather, is a mode of *maintaining* difference in the face of the continual creation of future copossibilities. "When we humans say 'this is play,'" says Massumi, "we are assuming our animality" and when animals play "they are preparatorily enacting human capacities" (8).

Where can one locate subjectivity in animal politics? How does human becoming—and by extension, nature itself—unfurl? On this question, Massumi is critical of both subject- and object-oriented ontologies. "There is no subject behind the creative act," Massumi cautions, "existing prior to the process. The subject is always ahead of itself, in the movement of expression" (96). In order to think the world, he tells us, we must start at events rather than objects, processes rather than substances. To capture the forward motion of animal politics, Massumi invokes Alfred North Whitehead's idea of the "superject," which he describes as "always to come, or already surpassed in a next pulse of life" (96). Agency is thus a fraught concept for conceptualizing animal/human becoming; rather, the "actor" of animal politics is a "subjectivity-without-a-subject." Nature is (re)created through self-propulsion, dynamically surpassing the given world. There is therefore also no place for Bruno Latour's "parliament of things" in animal politics,[1] as this concept denies the world its processual character. As Massumi puts it, "The world is made up of verbs and adverbs more primordially than nouns and adjectives. One sniff at the parliament of things, and the animal's expressive event is apt to snarl: smells of representation" (40).

One of the most successful sections of Massumi's book—and one that can help us think through the problem of survival—is his commentary on the zoo, entitled "The Zoo-ology of Play." Of course, zoos are spaces where animals live in a kind of suspended animation. For some, captivity quite literally shortens their life span; the day-to-day experience of life as simulacrum takes its toll. Animals cannot "survive" here. For others, the zoo is a space to regain life that would otherwise be lost. Behind the iron bars that categorically separate humans from animals, the latter can quite literally live beyond the parameters imposed by the natural world (a natural world that is, of course, always already social). But this is not the kind of survival Massumi is interested in; this is a survival that is imagined as purely utilitarian, devoid of play.

For Massumi, survival is wrapped up with the issue of instinct, which in his formulation—via Darwin and biologist Nikolaas Tinbergen—is creative and expressive, rather than functional. Play, Massumi tells us, is present in all instinctive acts. "In nature, creativity and instinct are inextricably entwined. They are in the act together, and play out together in the forward sweep of supernormal tendency carrying both to higher powers" (91). As a gesture of living beyond the given, survival, too, is creative and expressive. Survival is the possibility, always present, that the animal continues to enact gestures with vitality despite the rigidity of human exceptionalism that reigns supreme in a space like the zoo. When humans recognize this vitality, they assume their animality. Animal politics is thus sympathetic; it emerges when humans willingly relinquish their sovereignty. "There was never a child that did not become-animal in play," Massumi reminds us. "The project of animal politics: to make it so that the same could be said of adults" (89).

If there is a question to be raised about Massumi's politics, it is that he is perhaps not prescriptive enough. How might humans sympathetically connect to their animality—enabling them to reimagine and thereby intervene differently in the anthropocene at large—when so many arenas of everyday life mimic the dynamics of the zoo? How can we (humans) recognize animal vitality in a way that does not simply anthropomorphize; in other words, how can we bring ourselves closer to, rather than further from ourselves, opening up new political horizons in the process? Massumi offers us a hopeful starting point—noncognitive animal gesture as a way to move continuously between the "is" and the "could be"—but not a roadmap, however tentative, to arrival. Perhaps a roadmap would be antithetical to animal politics itself, a denial of the creativity intrinsic to animal instinct, and the difference that it could thereby produce.

If there is a critique to be leveled on Massumi's text, however, it is not so much with its ideas as with the way they are expressed. On the one hand, new thoughts demand new language to make sense of them; Massumi produces both in spades. However, his linguistic play at times seems more of a stylistic exercise than a means to propel us beyond rigid structures of thought. Does not, after all, animal play reproduce the world at least as often as it reinvents it? How far must one travel down the rabbit hole of neologisms in order to write like a bunny wiggles its nose, or as he puts it, "like a rat flicks its tail" (55)? Thankfully, Massumi's metacommentary on language rarely detracts from his broader argument; more often than not it produces a rhythm that, fittingly, recalls animal gestures themselves: a wolf cub bumbling out of its den, a hummingbird fluttering in a strong gust of wind, a chick pecking assiduously at its mother's head.

Lisa Poggiali is an interdisciplinary scholar who combines the insights of science and technology studies with ethnographic methodologies to interrogate the sociopolitical dimensions of new technologies and infrastructures in urban Africa, in particular Kenya. She is currently a postdoctoral fellow in the Program on Democracy, Citizenship, and Constitutionalism at the University of Pennsylvania.

Notes

1. With the concept "parliament of things," Latour (1993) attempts to decenter the human and foreground the "quasi-object" or "hybrid"—which are ways of knowing that gather together nature, culture, science, and society in complex interrelation—as a way to move beyond the dualistic thinking foundational to modernity (nature/society; object/subject).

Works Cited

Latour, Bruno. 1993. *We Have Never Been Modern*. Translated by Catherine Porter. Cambridge, MA: Harvard University Press.

Aesthetics, Ethics, and Objects in the Anthropocene

Timothy Morton's *Hyperobjects: Philosophy and Ecology after the End of the World*, Minneapolis, MN: University of Minnesota Press, 2013

Bethany Doane

The era that has come after postmodernism seems to be seeking ground primarily in the nonhuman—in spite of, or perhaps because of, this thing called the "Anthropocene." Timothy Morton's *Hyperobjects* offers some of this nonhuman ground, building on his own work in ecophilosophy (such as his 2009 *Ecology without Nature* and 2010 *The Ecological Thought*), as well as the object-oriented philosophy of Graham Harman. Merging these two approaches, Morton offers us the concept of the hyperobject: an entity that is "massively distributed in time and space relative to humans," but that is nonetheless an object (1). The two clearest examples of hyperobjects that recur throughout the book are global warming and radiation, both of which profoundly impact humans without ever being fully graspable. For Morton, the hyperobject serves as a kind of key that opens the door to a better understanding of *all* objects in this object-oriented ontology (OOO), while also forcing humans to face the implications of the Anthropocene both ethically and aesthetically in a way that the ironic distance of modernity/postmodernity has failed to do. The book succeeds in these two respects: the concept of the hyperobject sticks in the mind in a way that will surely affect how we think about human-nonhuman relations alongside the current ecological crisis in the future.

In the first half of the book, Morton unpacks the qualities of the hyperobject itself: its *viscosity, nonlocality, temporal undulation, phasing,* and *interobjectivity*. Briefly, what these qualities mean is that hyperobjects are vastly distributed through both time and space, such that they are never fully accessible or conceivable in their entirety. Thus, we can feel wind and raindrops (local manifestations), but not "weather." Hyperobjects pass in

WSQ: Women's Studies Quarterly 44: 1 & 2 (Spring/Summer 2016) © 2016 by Bethany Doane.

and out of our experience and awareness through these local manifestations (phasing), but they never go away. There is no *away* place for them to
go; they stick to us and other objects inextricably (they are viscous). These
five properties help to reveal the nature of objects writ large in Morton's
OOO: objects interact aesthetically with other objects (including humans), but they are never fully exhaustible in their aesthetic relationality.
They reduce to neither some atomizing materialism, nor to a smooth underlying or overlying whole. Instead, "we will find that all entities whatso-
ever are interconnected in an interobjective system" that Morton calls *the
mesh* (83). Yet objects also withdraw and hide, forming gaps between their
appearance and essence such that the mesh is made of both connections
and holes: there is both *no* distance and *only* distance at the same time.
For some, this apparent contradiction may be unforgivable, dissolving into
meaninglessness. But confronting this contradiction, he argues, is what we
must do if we want to move beyond the endless rationalization and non-
action that has marked modernity's response to the ecological crisis, a task
that he tackles in part two.

After explicating the somewhat abstract properties of hyperobjects,
in his second section, "The Time of Hyperobjects," Morton discusses the
implications for human coexistence with these strange, withdrawn-yet-in-
escapable entities. Here, Morton explains "the end of the world" not as a
literal apocalypse of fire and brimstone, but as the death of the notion that
humans are encircled by a Heideggerian world, and thus at the center of
something, rather than enmeshed with objects on every imaginable scale.
"What remains without a world is intimacy," he explains (125). Ultimately, *Hyperobjects* amounts to a call for new object-oriented forms of both art
and ethics that echo or embody this intimacy, and that will bring humans
closer to caring for hyperobjects as such—as *objects* rather than as flows
or phenomena, which are so often "managed" and redirected on to others.
Here there is some faltering, an asymmetry between the attention paid
to the practicalities of this emerging ethics, which receives little attention,
and art, which receives quite a bit. Both, Morton suggests, should affectively move us to action without deliberation, to "stamp out the burning
cigarette" without asking why (141). These are not the kinds of directives
that lend themselves to political policy—and this is precisely the point—
but one does have to wonder if these affective commands shift the ethical
dilemma problematically back onto the individual in a way that other cri-

tiques of scalar derangements have already problematized (for example, Timothy Clark's essay on scale).

Yet if some are tempted to dismiss *Hyperobjects* because of its dangerous scalar jumps from the quantum to the hyper, because its representation of previous (eco)philosophical scholarship is too generalizing, or its prose is too loose (the language is often redundant in its illustrative metaphors and examples)—to do so may be missing the point, or at least missing an opportunity. A rigorous and meticulous philosophical exegesis *Hyperobjects* is not—again, precisely because meticulous debate is what Morton argues against. These potential problems amount to petty complaints alongside the forward theoretical motion that the concept of the hyperobject demands, which tells us not to analyze more piles of data, but to put out the fire as an instinctive reflex. We will never cross the gap between appearance and the essence of the thing we are attempting to analyze—we will never graph all of global warming—but neither should we (re)turn to cynicism. As we are pulled into the future by and with an awareness of the thing called the Anthropocene (a hyperobject, perhaps, in its refusal to go away), Morton's book offers a useful reconceptualization to work with. In particular, this project is enticing for those of us who have ever been tempted by the decentering lure of posthumanism, if not totally convinced by its theoretical manifestations. Morton's object-oriented approach to ecology espouses a flat ontology—a proclamation of a (finally) final death to hierarchical thinking—while avoiding both the deflating nihilism that might potentially accompany it, and the awkward equivocations in posthumanism that attempt to extend the ethical subject into the realm of the nonhuman. Under a flat ontology, there are no more ethical taxonomies to draw. *Hyperobjects*, like its eponymous subjects, will surely resonate across time and space in several disciplines. As a scalar tool, the concept of the hyperobject may aid us as we plunge into the uncanny valley between human and nonhuman—or at least help us to see that we are swimming in that valley already, glued to the nonhuman always, both inside and out.

Bethany Doane is a doctoral student in English and women's studies at Pennsylvania State University. Her research focus is on gender and horror in contemporary literature and film.

PART VIII. **ALERTS AND PROVOCATIONS**

The Queer Art of Survival

Lana Lin

When I received a letter from Memorial Sloan Kettering Cancer Center inviting me to participate in a study for "Breast Cancer Survivors," rather than ignoring it as I had other appeals of this sort, I hung on to the enclosed card, as I imagined it might speak to the notion of survival that I was pondering for this contribution. The follow-up call that came a few weeks later made clear why I disown the category of "survivor" and turn instead to fashioning my own queer art of survival. On the phone the investigator asked if I had a few moments for her to evaluate my eligibility. After having her repeat herself several times, during which I misheard her say "distrust" and "stress," I finally agreed to submit to a "*distress*" monitor. This would consist of thirty-four questions that began with ranking my level of distress in the past two weeks including that day on a scale from one to ten. I selected "four." Had I experienced distress in the past two weeks including that day in relation to child care, housing, insurance, transportation, work or school, children, partner, depression, fears, nervousness, sadness, worried (*sic*), spirituality and religion, loss of faith, relating to God, appearance, bathing and dressing? I was to respond only with a "yes" or "no." This caused me some distress. I found the questions conceptually suspect and grammatically problematic, causing me to skip at least one of them. She then went through a list of eighteen physical symptoms to which I was again afforded a monosyllabic response. At the end of this barrage, she inquired if for any of the questions to which I answered "yes" was my distress related to my breast cancer. I replied "no." She promptly informed me that I was not eligible for the study, explaining that it was intended to help breast cancer survivors and they were looking for women who were expe-

WSQ: Women's Studies Quarterly 44: 1 & 2 (Spring/Summer 2016)

riencing distress in relation to their breast cancer or survivorship issues. I noticed that the study presumed that "help" for a "breast cancer survivor" was only warranted if distress was directly related to breast cancer, and that "survivorship issues" were equated with distress in relation to breast cancer. I ended the call with the frustratingly familiar feeling of estrangement I continually experienced with the cancer establishment during my diagnosis and treatment. The exchange brought into relief my discomfort with the homogenized and naturalized conception of the term "cancer survivor" that pervades cancer discourse. I am, of course, not alone in my disdain (Ehrenreich 2009; Jain 2013; Sulik 2011).

To the extent that I associate neither my distress nor my well-being to cancer, I fail to qualify for the kind of help that those designated as "survivors" would require. That is, survivorship research is neither addressed to me nor gains from my input. But what exactly is a "survivor" and what qualifies as a "survivorship issue"? The National Cancer Institute has an Office of Cancer Survivorship which is dedicated to "the unique needs of the growing population of cancer survivors and to enhanc[ing] our ability to address those needs." Despite the tautology that tends to cloud so much cancer related discourse, it is all too clear that, in cancer world, there is a distinction between *survival* and *survivorship*. In cancer lingo, I seem to have no choice but to be labeled a cancer survivor because I have indeed survived my treatment and am now five years cancer free. I am hailed as a cancer survivor on every piece of correspondence I receive from the hospital, including the invitation to the study for which I was rejected. But survivorship is a different matter from survival. Survivorship, it would seem, is not something to which one defaults as a result of surviving treatment. Rather, survivorship is a particular stance vis-à-vis one's ongoing status as a survivor, for survivors do not merely survive, but take on, handle, negotiate, and manage their survivorship. Survivorship is a category of experience that has been instrumentalized and politicized. *Cure*, the free magazine distributed to cancer patients and "survivors" which litters the tables of cancer-clinic waiting rooms across the country, has a special section devoted to "navigating survivorship." Apparently food, physical appearance, mobility, pain, sleep, and psychological states are survivorship issues, although, as the study for which I was ineligible attests, only to the extent that cancer is held responsible for such distressors.

What if those of us who have experienced or are experiencing cancer adopt a different relationship toward that which has been deemed "survi-

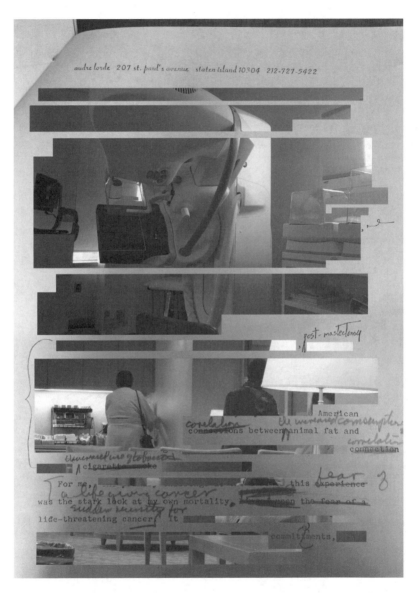

The Cancer Journals Revisited (work-in-progress, 2016), digital collage by Lin + Lam.

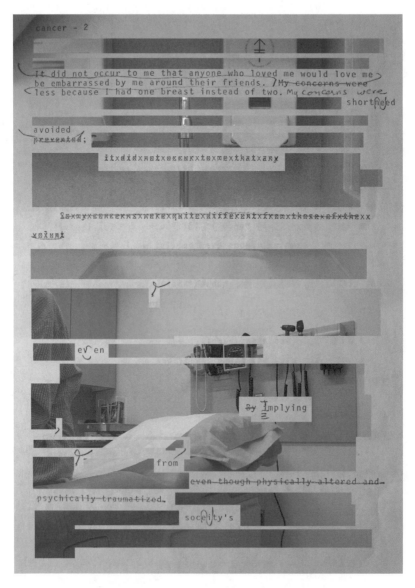

The Cancer Journals Revisited (work-in-progress, 2016), digital collage by Lin + Lam.

vorship"? Is there a way to "queer" survivorship, and to turn it into what I am somewhat playfully calling a "queer art of survival"? With this phrase, I borrow Judith Halberstam's "queer art of failure," which "dismantles the logics of success and failure with which we currently live" (2011, 2). Perhaps this impulse can be imported into the cancer complex to dismantle the logics of success and failure with which we live and die; that is, perhaps it can be used to dismantle the logics of survivorship. That easy slippage between distress and distrust, a slippage that may turn upon the failure to maintain composure or the failure to secure trust, is, I venture, precisely the mode of inhabitance many occupy post–cancer diagnosis. "Survivors" can fail to beat their cancer, fail to maintain optimism, fail to find spiritual transformation in their reconfigured relation to mortality. But given that the language of oncology is constructed around failure—it is the patient who fails the treatment, and not the other way around—how can survivorship be rehabilitated to encompass a range of survivals that include pessimism, disinterest, cynicism, indifference, distraction, uncertainty, contradiction, crankiness, and complexity? Although by no means mutually exclusive, queers and those who have had cancer can learn from one another as vulnerable groups who face threats to the prospect of survival on a regular basis. For Eve Kosofsky Sedgwick, who lived with her cancer for eighteen years, queer survival is made up of an "irreducible multilayeredness and multiphasedness" that upends those neat categorizations seeking to bureaucratize and institutionalize "survivorship" (1993, 3). Speaking of violence against queers in all its forms, including external assaults and the AIDS crisis, Sedgwick understood the multidimensionality of survival as necessarily "complicated by how permeable the identity 'survivor' must be to the undiminishing currents of risk, illness, mourning, and defiance" (3). This definition of queer survival acknowledges the protective distrust that Audre Lorde found justified for those who "were never meant to survive" (1978, 32). This queer art of survival embraces the entanglements of distress in their very unaccountability.

Lana Lin is an artist whose work has been shown at the Museum of Modern Art and Whitney Museum, NY; the Taiwan International Documentary Film Festival; and the Oberhausen Short Film Festival. Her book on the psychic effects of cancer, *Freud's Jaw and Other Lost Objects*, is forthcoming from Fordham University Press. She is associate professor in media studies at the New School and has collaborated with Lam since 2001.

H. Lan Thao Lam is an artist whose work has been exhibited at the Stedelijk Museum, Amsterdam; Yerba Buena Center for the Arts, San Francisco; and the New Museum, New York. She has received fellowships from Canada Council for the Arts and Vera List Center for Art & Politics. She is assistant professor at Parsons Fine Arts and has collaborated with Lin since 2001.

Works Cited

Ehrenreich, Barbara. 2009. *Bright-sided: How the Relentless Promotion of Positive Thinking Has Undermined America*. New York: Metropolitan Books.

Halberstam, Judith. 2011. *The Queer Art of Failure*. Durham, NC: Duke University Press.

Jain, S. Lochlann. 2013. *Malignant: How Cancer Becomes Us*. Berkeley, CA: University of California Press.

Lorde, Audre. 1978. "A Litany for Survival." In *The Black Unicorn*. New York: W. W. Norton & Company.

Sedgwick, Eve Kosofsky. 1993. *Tendencies*. Durham, NC: Duke University Press.

Sulik, Gayle A. 2011. *Pink Ribbon Blues: How Breast Cancer Culture Undermines Women's Health*. New York: Oxford University Press.

Race Agency
Place Philosophy

Women Write Iran
*Nostalgia and Human Rights
from the Diaspora*
Nima Naghibi

$28.00 paper | 224 pages

Civil Racism
*The 1992 Los Angeles Rebellion
and the Crisis of Racial Burnout*
Lynn Mie Itagaki

$25.00 paper | 336 pages

Claiming Place
On the Agency of Hmong Women
Chia Youyee Vang, Faith Nibbs,
and Ma Vang, editors
Afterword by Cathy J. Schlund-Vials

$30.00 paper | 376 pages

So Much to Be Done
*The Writings of Breast Cancer Activist
Barbara Brenner*
Barbara Brenner
Edited by Barbara Sjoholm
Introduction by Rachel Morello-Frosch
Afterword by Anne Lamott

$22.95 paper | 296 pages

Manifestly Haraway
Donna J. Haraway
In conversation with Cary Wolfe

$19.95 paper | 360 pages

What Gender Is, What Gender Does
Judith Roof

$27.00 paper | 296 pages

University of Minnesota Press
800-621-2736 • www.upress.umn.edu

PEN AMERICA

A JOURNAL FOR WRITERS AND READERS

ISSUE #19: HAUNTINGS

Featuring Conversations, Essays,
Fiction, Poetry & Art by
Tom Stoppard
Yusef Komunyakaa
Joyce Carol Oates
Mona Eltahawy
Laura Esquivel
Edward Snowden
Kimiko Hahn
& many others

www.PEN.org/journal